Mass Historia

Mass Historia

365 DAYS OF HISTORICAL FACTS AND (MOSTLY) FICTIONS

Chris Regan

Illustrations by Kathryn Rathke

Andrews McMeel
Publishing, LLC

Kansas City

ISBN-13: 978-0-7407-6869-9
ISBN-10: 0-7407-6869-7

Library of Congress Control Number: 2007038005

08 09 10 11 12 WKT 10 9 8 7 6 5 4 3 2 1

www.andrewsmcmeel.com

A Quirk Packaging Book
Design by Stislow Design + Illustration
Illustrations by Kathryn Rathke

ATTENTION: SCHOOLS AND BUSINESSES
Andrews McMeel books are available at quantity discounts with bulk purchase for
educational, business, or sales promotional use. For information, please write to:
Special Sales Department, Andrews McMeel Publishing, LLC, 1130 Walnut Street,
Kansas City, Missouri 64106.

For Susannah

Clio, the muse of history, is as thoroughly infected with lies as a street whore with syphilis.

—Arthur Schopenhauer

(sigh)

—Anyone Stuck in Conversation with Schopenhauer

Contents

Every day, History has a story to tell, and not just because History is old and lonely and desperate for some companionship. It is August 28, 2008, as I write this, and I have been bored most of the day. Yet History is quick to clear its throat, lean forward in its chair, and remind me that on August 28, riots started at the 1968 Democratic Convention, Woodrow Wilson saw suffragettes picket the White House in 1917, Union forces captured Cape Hatteras in 1861, and in 1879 King Cetshwayo, the last great ruler of Zululand, was captured by the British.

It's around 10:00 p.m. and, despite my best efforts, I doubt I will do anything important or interesting enough to overshadow the previous highlights of August 28—although I have crowned myself the new king of Zululand just for safe measure.

On every day of the calendar year, an anniversary of something historic is celebrated. So I have taken it upon myself with

Mass Historia to pass along, celebrate—but mostly mock—History's more interesting events and anecdotes. Since I've been the one doing all the writing while History just rambles on, I've added certain "embellishments" along the way for kicks. Enjoy this book, learn something from it, but do not reference it in any scholarly paper. Except the William Howard Taft fat jokes. That guy has had a free ride for far too long. (*Yes, History, I know he's dead. Go to sleep.*)

I have to put History to bed right now. He's starting in on August 29. Apparently Hubert Humphrey accepted his party's nomination on this day, and then slammed into the Gulf Coast with 125 mph winds. History is very old, he gets confused sometimes, but he does have a lot of funny stories.

Chris Regan
The New King of Zululand
Los Angeles, California
8/28/08

January

THE THONG HAD NOT YET BEEN INVENTED.

Julius Caesar Invents New Year's Day.

IT WAS ON THIS DAY IN 45 BC that Julius Caesar introduced the Julian calendar, named after himself, which created a 365-day yearly cycle. And like most celebrity calendars, a "portion" of the proceeds went to some silly animal rescue charity no one's ever heard of.

By doing this, he ditched the Roman calendar, which was based on a lunar cycle, and introduced the Egyptian concept of the solar calendar. (Conservatives in Rome, like Conservatives in America today, balked at the logic of anything solar-powered because too many sandal-wearing hippies supported it. Although in Rome, even the Conservatives were sandal-wearers.)

Caesar never stopped tinkering with his calendar. Before his death in 44 BC, he modified it by changing the name of the month Quintilis to Julius, again after himself. He later attempted to retroactively erase March 15 from the calendar, but all his senators kept stabbing the pen out of his hand.

HISTO-POURRI: Gloom and Doom Edition.

IT SEEMS AS THOUGH THE NEW YEAR'S DAY HANGOVER morphs into a general sense of grouchiness on January 2, because the second day of the year is the first name in suck.

JANUARY 2, 1882 America first experiences gas pains as billionaire **JOHN D. ROCKEFELLER** ← unites all of his holdings in Standard Oil, creating the first-ever oil monopoly. Drivers of gas-free Stanley Steamers use the opportunity to become a little too sanctimonious.

JANUARY 2, 1935 Bruno Hauptmann goes on trial for the kidnapping and murder of the Lindbergh baby. Like O. J. Simpson, Hauptmann's trial is called "The Trial of the Century." Unlike O. J., however, Hauptmann was probably innocent.

JANUARY 2, 1938 British serial killer Ian Brady is born, kills four children in the 1960s. The Smiths later write a song about him that manages to out-gloom his actual crimes.

JANUARY 2, 1968 Supermodel Christy Turlington is born, in an attempt to remind the rest of the world of their own pathetic physical ordinariness.

JANUARY 2, 1974 U.S. President Richard Nixon lowers speed limit to 55 mph during gas shortage. Twenty-six-year-old Sammy Hagar, on verge of quitting showbiz, finds new creative muse. (Also, last surviving owner of a Stanley Steamer uses shortage to become sanctimonious.)

A PRUNE PACKED IN OIL.

JANUARY 3, 1882

Lord of the Rings Author J. R. R. Tolkien Passes Through a Birth Canal.

UNLIKE THE MAJORITY OF HIS FANS, it wasn't his last time inside one.

JANUARY 4, 1896

Welcome, Utah!

Brigham Young: as fun as his namesake university.

TOP FIVE MORMON FUN FACTS:

1. AT ONE TIME, YOU COULD HAVE HAD AS MANY WIVES AS YOU WANTED!

2. NOWADAYS, YOU MIGHT BE ABLE TO SNEAK AN EXTRA WIFE OR TWO.

3. THERE IS NOTHING ELSE FUN ABOUT MORMONISM.

4. SEE NUMBER THREE.

5. SEE NUMBERS THREE AND FOUR.

ON THIS DAY IN HISTORY IN 1896, Utah became state number forty-five, which was also the average number of wives enjoyed by most Utah men at the time.

Utah was settled in 1847 by Mormons seeking religious freedom. Leader Brigham Young arrived with a band of 148 pioneers at the Valley of the Great Salt Lake and declared, "This is the place." Most settlers then began setting up tents before he could finish his statement with ". . . for me to take a whiz," but Young didn't bother correcting anyone because the evening was just beginning and he had twenty wives who were expecting "vacation sex."

A few years later, Young was named governor of the state, but soon Washington, D.C., began to bristle at the flagrant Mormon violations of anti-polygamy laws. (Jealous.) In 1857, President James Buchanan (a lifelong bachelor—REALLY jealous) removed Young from his post and sent the army to the state to maintain order. (The only other time the army was sent to Utah to maintain order was in the 1970s, when a herd of perennially dieting Donnie Osmond groupies rioted in Salt Lake City over the scant availability of Tab soda.)

JANUARY 5, 1976

Cambodia Becomes Kampuchea. Americans Can't Find Either on a Map.

ON THIS DAY IN HISTORY, brutal Khmer Rouge leader Pol Pot decided the name Cambodia was so "2 million unmurdered people ago," and renamed it Kampuchea. And if anyone bitched about having to update their address book, they were promptly shipped off to that nation's killing fields, which were made "popular" in the movie *The Killing Fields*.

Oddly enough, despite the massive name change, Pol Pot himself decided to stick with "Pol Pot," a name that seems like either a typo or an item on a wedding registry that you will use once and then put away for good. It doesn't really pack the genocidal wallop of a "Hitler" or "Stalin" or "Ming the Merciless."*

*INSERT THE WORD "BUSH" HERE IF YOU ARE A DISAFFECTED YOUNG PERSON IN FILM SCHOOL AND HAVE RECENTLY RENAMED YOURSELF "RODERIKK NIGHTSHAYDE."

OTHER NAMES CONSIDERED BY POL POT:
1 POT POL
2 THE NOTORIOUS P.O.T.
3 HOT POCKET

JANUARY 6
President's Day.

TODAY IS A DAY on which many important events occurred relating to the United States presidency. Ideally, every day of a presidency is important, although William Howard Taft stressed that his "Luau Thursdays" were "to take a vacation from the important," although they really existed so that the president could eat an entire pig while others looked on in horror.

JANUARY 6, 1853 Train wreck of a drunk and president-elect **FRANKLIN PIERCE** is involved in a violent train wreck on the way to Washington. He was heading there to kick off his administration, which would be described by historians as a train wreck. (He probably should have seen this accident coming.)

JANUARY 6, 1893 **BENJAMIN HARRISON** signs the charter for the establishment of the National Cathedral in Washington. Congratulations. You now know one thing about President Benjamin Harrison.

← FACT 2: HE HAD A BEARD.

JANUARY 6, 1919 Theodore Roosevelt dies at age sixty—an event that is marked every year with a Broken Teddy Bear Ceremony by the Association of American Plushies. He authored thirty-five books, served as New York City police commissioner and assistant secretary of the navy, was the youngest man to ever become president, commanded a cavalry unit in the Spanish-American War, led expeditions

A PRESIDENT NAMED FRANKLIN.

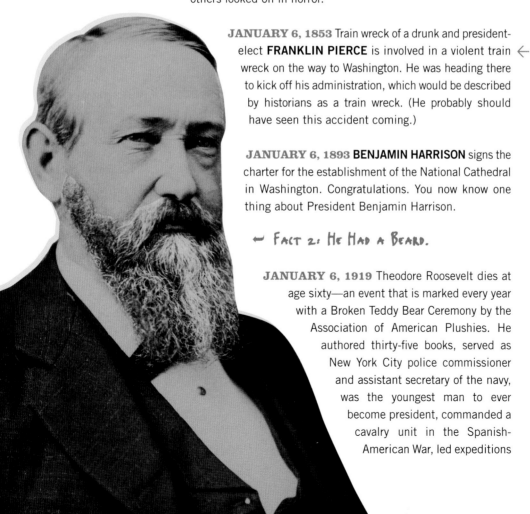

through Africa and South America, was the first president to ride in an airplane, won a Nobel Peace Prize, established 42 million acres of national forests and parklands, oversaw the construction of the Panama Canal, and is memorialized on the side of Mount Rushmore. Benjamin Harrison often sneered that TR was a show-off.

↤ **JANUARY 6, 1941 FRANKLIN DELANO ROOSEVELT** delivers his famous "Four Freedoms" speech during his State of the Union address. These "four essential human freedoms" included freedom of speech, freedom to worship, freedom from want, and freedom from fear. Norman Rockwell created four famous paintings based on these freedoms, which were slightly more reverent in tone than a 1981 study by Robert Mapplethorpe entitled "Four Freedoms (with Whip)."

ANOTHER PRESIDENT NAMED FRANKLIN.

LET FREEDOM STING.

CENSORED

JANERY 7
....

HISTO-POURRI: Science Fair.

TODAY IS A DAY THAT WITNESSED MANY IMPORTANT EVENTS in the world of science. Put on safety goggles and grab a partner before reading.

JANUARY 7, 1610 GALILEO discovers the four ← largest moons of Jupiter and names them Io, Europa, Ganymede, and Callisto. Drunken celebration that followed led to sighting of the "moon of Galileo."

ALSO DISCOVERED THE FIRST "TELESCOPE BLACK EYE" PRACTICAL JOKE.

JANUARY 7, 1785 Frenchman Jean-Pierre Blanchard and American John Jeffries cross the English Channel by hot air balloon and become the first humans to fly across the body of water. On the journey, they are forced to jettison extra weight from their gondola, including Blanchard's trousers—although many say that was a tribute to the 175th anniversary of Galileo's "moon."

JANUARY 7, 1893 Slovenian physicist Jozef Stefan dies. He was best known for his physical power law stating that the total radiation from a "black body" is proportional to the fourth power of its thermodynamic temperature—which is also the thesis of every Barry White song.

JANUARY 7, 1953 President Harry Truman announces that the United States has developed a hydrogen bomb. This is also the last day in history that a U.S. president displayed some knowledge of the proper pronunciation of "nuclear."

Despite developing the hydrogen bomb, the United States has yet to use one in a war. Talk about government waste!

JANUARY 8, 1905
Evelyn Wood, Inventor of Speed Reading, Born.

AND IF YOU HAVE STUDIED SPEED READING, by now you are done with this book, and it is already next to your toilet, beneath a stack of old *New Yorkers*. We hope you liked it and do not consider reselling it without providing the author his royalty.

JANUARY 9, 1894
Lights. Camera. Snot.

ON THIS DAY IN HISTORY, Thomas Edison released his film, *Edison Kinetoscopic Record of a Sneeze*, showing that while Edison held the patents on many different items, he somehow couldn't figure out how to manufacture an effective "spoiler alert."

The film, which is only a few seconds long, featured Edison's assistant, Fred Ott, taking a pinch of snuff and then sneezing, making this primitive film a million times more thrilling than *The English Patient*.

Ott starred in one other Edison film, called *Fred Ott Holding a Bird*, where we saw the star holding a bird. This proved less captivating than the Sneeze picture, and the much-spicier follow-up *Fred Ott Holding His Bird* saw limited release outside the sleazier nickelodeons.

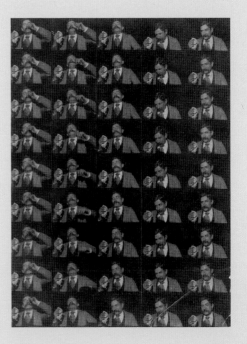

KLEENEX PRODUCT PLACEMENT.

Thomas's English Huffin.

ON THIS DAY IN 1776, Thomas Paine published *Common Sense*, a treatise much-despised by the colonies' Anglophiles, who instead preferred to read installments of their beloved serial *Art Thou Being Most Served? Or the Prissy Shoppe Clerk*. *Common Sense* was a pamphlet (an old-timey 'zine or blog, except that it wasn't about the Pixies or filled with snark, respectively) that made the case for America's independence from Great Britain. Over a half million were printed, which made it the best-selling work in eighteenth-century America, although Paine never saw a dime for it. (Needless to say, "securing copyright" was not one of the tenets of *Common Sense*.)

PAINE IN
ENGLAND'S ASS.

AMONG SOME OF PAINE'S POINTS:

• "A long habit of not thinking a thing WRONG, gives it a superficial appearance of being RIGHT." (Paine published *Common Sense* anonymously, but this passage made some think he was a very high college sophomore.)

• "Every thing that is right or natural pleads for separation." (This statement was also used whenever Paine wanted to break up with a girlfriend.)

• "But where says some is the King of America? I'll tell you friend, he reigns above, and doth not make havoc of mankind like the royal brute of Britain." (Note use of "friend." For radical pamphleteers like Paine, this concept usually exists in the abstract.)

• "O ye that love mankind! Ye that dare oppose, not only the tyranny, but the tyrant, stand forth!" (This was "colonial" for "Represent, yo.")

One of the work's biggest fans was George Washington, who supposedly had all his troops read it before they crossed the Delaware. Of course, soldiers being soldiers, they just pretended to read it while using the pamphlet to cover a smaller book of erotic cheesecake woodcuts.

HISTO-POURRI.

ALL SORTS OF INTERESTING STUFF HAPPENED TODAY. Browse this sweet-smelling assortment of events.

JANUARY 11, 1569 The first recorded lottery in England is drawn at St. Paul's Cathedral. It's much like American lotteries, except that the participants were referred to as "White Rubbish."

JANUARY 11, 1755 American politician, statesman, and second-rate duelist **ALEXANDER HAMILTON** born in the West Indies. He is on ← the ten dollar bill, which is how everyone knows he was president once.

JANUARY 11, 1807 Confederate General Alfred "Mudwall" Jackson is born. Called "Mudwall" because he was the cousin of "Stonewall" Jackson. Both were called "Brickwall" by their nagging wives for their poor communication skills.

JANUARY 11, 1892 Forty-four-year-old postimpressionist artist Paul Gauguin marries a thirteen-year-old Tahitian girl. And while his contributions to the art world are greater than those of fellow sex tourist Gary Glitter, his *Still Life with Mandolin* doesn't get you as pumped before a basketball game.

JANUARY 11, 1973 G. Gordon Liddy and cohorts go on trial for their part in the break-in at the Watergate Hotel. Historians are always grateful that the Democratic National Committee splurged on a suite at the Watergate, because the Ramada Inn Scandal would have been a silly name for something that would topple a presidency.

JANUARY 11, 1992 Paul Simon becomes the first major artist to tour South Africa after the cultural boycott is lifted. And the tour was successful because South Africa had previously lifted its own Yuppie Concert-Goer Embargo.

Psst—I Wasn't President.

JANUARY 12, 1737
Founding Father John Hancock Founded.

THE MAN WITH THE MOST FAMOUS AND IMPORTANT SIGNATURE in the world (sorry to disappoint readers who shelled out a ton of money for a track suit emblazoned with a "Sean John" signature across the back) was born on this day in Quincy, Massachusetts, where such grandiose personal flourishes are considered signs of being a "wicked queehah showoff."

A great deal of myth exists around Hancock's signature, the largest on the Declaration of Independence (after Ben Franklin agreed to erase his giant "Dick Hertz" contribution at the bottom). Hancock was believed to have exclaimed after signing, "There. John Bull can read my name without spectacles." (John Bull, of course, represented the Mad King George, who ironically had stopped wearing his spectacles because they would fog up every time he'd put a chamber pot on his head and declare himself "the High King of Night Soil.")

While this is an inspiring story of American colonial bravery, it's probably not true. Records show that Hancock was alone when signing the document, that he placed his name front and center because he was the president of the Continental Congress, and that he always signed his name in a large fashion, which probably suggests that Mrs. Hancock needed spectacles to find her husband's "Southern Colonies."

SIGNER OF HIS TIMES.

Mass Historia Mortality In and Out List.

PLENTY OF FAMOUS FOLK either entered the world today, or left it. See who shares your birthday. Or death day.

IN:

JANUARY 13, 1931 Flamboyant 1970s game show regular Charles Nelson Reilly is born.

JANUARY 13, 1934 Flamboyant 1970s game show regular Rip Taylor is born. (Note: Children born on this day who show early indications of flamboyance should be entered into any Game Show Head Start Program.)

JANUARY 13, 1966 Actor Patrick Dempsey is born. One-time teen star in a bunch of unforgettable movies later morphs into your wife's boyfriend, Dr. McDreamy. Jealously, you suggest to your wife that you heard he is "flamboyant."

JANUARY 13, 1977 Sword-and-bow-wielding actor Orlando Bloom born. C'mon—there's no way this dude isn't "flamboyant."

OUT:

JANUARY 13, 1864 Songwriter Stephen Foster dies very unflamboyantly in a New York flophouse at age thirty-seven, with 38 cents to his name. Wrote such enduring classics as "Oh Susannah," "Camptown Races," and "Suwannee River," although if one attempts to perform them today in their original minstrel style, they might meet an end more depressing than Foster's.

JANUARY 13, 1929 Western icon and OK Corral shoot-out veteran Wyatt Earp dies after having spent several years in Hollywood as a technical adviser on westerns. Died years before his bushy mustache made the leap from "rugged" to "flamboyant."

This Be Offensive.

JANUARY 14, 1963
Southern Man, All Talk.

MR. WIZARD.

IN ANOTHER GREAT MILESTONE IN SOUTHERN RACISM (sorry—"heritage"), George Wallace was sworn in as the governor of Alabama on this day in 1963.

During his inaugural address, he declared that the good people of his state would enjoy "Segregation Now, Segregation Tomorrow, Segregation Forever." So not only was George Wallace a racist, but an utter failure who couldn't keep his promises.

The speech was written for him by Ku Klux Klan leader Asa Carter, who later went on to write the novel *Gone to Texas: The Rebel Outlaw Josey Wales*, which was later made into a movie starring Clint Eastwood, which is shown and reshown on cable now, tomorrow, and forever.

JANUARY 15
Follow the Leaders.

ONCE AGAIN, prominent leaders hog all the history today.

CELIBATE GOOD TIMES—C'MON.

JANUARY 15, 1559 Elizabeth I, the pasty, red-headed virgin queen, is crowned in Westminster Abbey. Unfortunately, unlike at most parties for a virgin, no one tries to get the guest of honor laid. (While the theater flourished under Elizabeth's rule, the invention of the teen sex comedy was still many years away.)

JANUARY 15, 1929 Civil rights leader Dr. Martin Luther King Jr. is born. His birthday is a national holiday in the United States, except in the parts that are still holding out for George Wallace's "Segregation Forever" promise (see yesterday).

JANUARY 15, 1970 Mu'ammar al-Gadhafi, after deposing King Idris, becomes the premier of Libya. A complex character, Qaddafi later nationalized foreign-owned oil fields, and advanced the rights of women. Yet Khaddafi also came under fire for funding terrorist groups in the 1980s. Worse, Gaddafi never got around to finalizing the spelling of his last name, which strikes people as grammatically lazy.

HELLO my name is Gaddafi?

Hitler—Movin' On Down.

SORRY TO WAIT SIXTEEN WHOLE DAYS without a word on the star of the History Channel, German leader Adolph Hitler.

What would any book on world history be without Hitler? (Besides a happier one?) Indeed, Hitler's power to terrify and charm (at least on a few "White Heritage" Web sites) is the stuff of legend, and the subject of millions of written pages, hours of film, and assorted chapters of fan fiction (see "White Heritage" Web sites).

And this day in history marks the beginning of the end of Adolph Hitler, who moved into his bunker in Berlin on January 16, as Soviet forces were rapidly approaching the city.

Of course, like anyone who is down on his luck, Hitler had a little trouble finding people to help him move into the bunker. As the city was being bombarded with artillery, it wasn't wise to run around looking for man-with-a-van flyers, and a lot of his old friends had plenty of excuses ("death," "capture," "suicide") to avoid all the heavy lifting. It was not until the Nazi leader promised free beer and pizza that he got help from Hermann "Fatty" Goering.

Minister of Propaganda Josef Goebbels also helped with the move, and brought his six kids with him. While it must have been hell with six kids running wild around a bunker, their father would find a rather unique way to quiet them down about four months later.

DESTROYED NATIONS AND THE NAME "ADOLPH."

Hitler's Cutest Creation Arrives in the United States.

(SEE? IN HISTORY, ONCE YOU GET STARTED ON HITLER, IT'S VERY HARD TO STOP.)

ON THIS DAY IN HISTORY, Americans got a chance to drive four cylinders of pure fascism, as Adolph Hitler's beloved "People's Car," or "Volkswagen," went on sale for the first time in the United States.

Designed by Ferdinand Porsche, the VW had a low pricetag of $800, but only two wound up being sold to American consumers in 1949—about half the number of consumers who enjoyed and appreciated VW's Fahrvergnügen campaign in the 1990s.

As years passed, over 21 million VW Bugs rolled off the assembly line—most sold to high school art teachers—before Volkswagen ceased production of the car in 2003, around the same time that undersized, attention-starved cheapos began flocking to the new MINI Coopers.

FÜHRERGNÜGEN

The origins of the car date back to 1933, when Hitler (whose politics were slightly to the left of Henry Ford's) met with Porsche to see about creating a car for the common German, one that could carry two adults and three children. (Children of the Master Race had blond hair, blue eyes, and—apparently—no need for legroom.)

Hitler was supposedly the one responsible for the car's rounded design, which was inspired by the supple curves of Hermann Goering's abundant and aerodynamic muffin-top.

JANUARY 18

Europeans Discover Previously Discovered Non-European Places.

MANY BRAVE MEN AND WOMEN (WELL, ONLY MEN, ACTUALLY) made bold discoveries across the globe on this day in history, and in the process helped us understand a little bit more about this great big world. (Indigenous peoples, please keep your comments to yourself. This one is for the Anglos. They have so little to hold onto these days.)

JANUARY 18, 1778 Captain James Cook discovers the Hawaiian Islands. Originally, he called them the Sandwich Islands. (While many think this was in honor of Cook's superior, John Montagu, the fourth Earl of Sandwich, the islands were actually named for the activity those long at-sea crewmen were hoping to enjoy with some of the island women.) As thanks for the discovery, natives stab him to death.

JANUARY 18, 1788 The first-ever Australian penal colony is founded as 736 English convicts arrive in Botany Bay. Captain Cook discovered this bay only a few years before, and the prisoners probably received an even less humane reception in Botany Bay than Cook did in Hawaii.

JANUARY 18, 1912 British explorer Robert Scott discovers the magnetic South Pole. Unfortunately, he got there a month after Norwegian Roald Amundsen had discovered it, as evidenced by a **DELIGHTFUL TROLL DOLL** left behind. Scott and four of his expedition then subsequently died in an attempt to return to their base. But they did not die in vain, because in the years since, the discovery of the South Pole has been important to . . . well, um . . . Robert Scott died in vain.

FOUND IT.

What? Another "Discovery" Story About Antarctica?

APPARENTLY SO, because on this day in 1840, Captain Charles Wilkes caught sight of the eastern coast of the continent, and claimed it in the name of the United States.

The United States, while grateful, realized they were suddenly stuck with a lot of barren, useless real estate, and have spent the last 168 years trying to melt the damn thing.

Icy SOMETHING THAT STARTS WITH "A."

LOSER.

World Gets "Buzz."

ON THIS DAY, ASTRONAUT EDWIN EUGENE "BUZZ" ALDRIN WAS BORN. He, of course, was the *second* man on the moon.

Second.

Why the hell are we even talking about this loser?

Next.

Pinko, Commie Day.

A DAY OF PARTICULAR INTEREST to people who hate America and Freedom. Read on, comrade!

JANUARY 21, 1924 Vladimir Ilyich Lenin, the first leader of the Soviet Union, dies at age fifty-three after a series of strokes. You can still visit his embalmed corpse on display in Red Square, which shows that the former Soviet Union is still lagging behind the West in the Destination Tourist Attractions Race.

JANUARY 21, 1950 *Animal Farm* and *1984* author George Orwell dies. A Socialist who fought on the side of the Communists during the Spanish Civil War, Orwell later became a staunch anti-Stalinist and worked as a propagandist during the Second World War. While he died at age forty-seven, he had racked up enough "-ist" suffix credits for a man twice his age.

JANUARY 21, 1977 President Jimmy Carter pardons American draft dodgers, allowing them to return from their own war against blandness in Canada. Right Wingers are outraged, but to this day President Carter always gets appreciative high fives from both President Bush and **VICE PRESIDENT CHENEY**. ←

MY NAME IS DEFERRAL

Supreme Court Legalizes Abortion/Baby Killing.

ON THIS TRIUMPHANT/DARK DAY in history/the history of lesbian radicalism, the Supreme Court/Coven of Demonic Manbeasts legalized abortion/baby killing with their ruling/activist blasphemy in *Roe v. Wade*, which led to the long-running American battle of *Religious Kooks Who Hate Women v. Gleeful Baby Killers*.

Here's hoping this entry has satisfied all readers on both sides of this passionate debate. President Bush usually made some speech about "respecting all life" on this day, in an effort to provide more able bodies for "the great troop surge of 2028" during President Jenna Bush's disastrous second term.

WHATEVER BECAME OF . . . ?

"Jane Roe": **Norma Jean McCorvey, who never had an abortion due to the time it took the case to get through the courts, eventually became a lesbian, then a born-again Christian, then a Roman Catholic (she obviously has trouble carrying things out to full term). She is now past the age of having children, and therefore an abortion opponent.**

Henry Wade: **The Texas lawyer died in 2001, and it should be noted that *Roe v. Wade* was the first case he ever lost. It should also be noted that one of the cases he won was his prosecution of Jack Ruby, who murdered a man in front of millions of people on television. Lionel Hutz could have closed the deal on that one.**

Charles A. Lindbergh:
The "A" Stands for "Adolph-lover."

THE NAZIS SUCKED. Although you might not have been so quick to agree if you were an aviation pioneer who really wanted to convince people, once and for all, that Lindbergh was not a Jewish name.

And it was on this day in 1941 that Lucky Lindy hopped his way to the front of the House Foreign Affairs Commission (a commission not nearly as sexy as it sounds) to call for the United States to sign a neutrality pact with Hitler. Some think it was revenge on Paris for the shoddy presentation of cheeses and wine pairings offered when he landed there in 1927.

Lindbergh had spent a great deal of time in Europe in the 1930s, and became an admirer of Germany's mighty air power. Goering even presented Lindbergh with the Service Cross of the German Eagle in 1938, something he refused to return because it would be "an undue insult to the German people." But actually he just wanted to avoid another trip to the portly Nazi's home, for fear of Goering's "mighty wind power."

Lindbergh claimed the United States was being dragged into the war by "the British, the Jews, and the Roosevelt administration," thus dissipating the last ounce of good will he had over that whole kidnapped kid thing.

Roosevelt declared Lindbergh pro-Nazi and later barred him from serving in the Air Force Reserves after the attack on Pearl Harbor, showing that he was not a president who would take such actions, despite appearances, sitting down.

The First Man to Cross the Atlantic with a Depeche Mode Haircut.

<table>
<tr><td>

JANUARY 24
A Good Day to Rough It.

</td></tr>
</table>

TODAY IS A DAY that celebrates "Roughing It" in the great outdoors.

⬆ **JANUARY 24, 1908** The **BOY SCOUTS** officially began on this day in history, with the British publication of Robert Baden-Powell's book *Scouting for Boys*, a title that is also the main pastime of most men who become scout leaders. The book instructed all Boy Scouts about camping, deduction, patriotism, woodcraft, lifesaving, and how to keep your scouting activities secret from your friends once you entered high school.

Nerds.

ALWAYS BE PREPARED TO BE SUCKERED.

JANUARY 24, 1972 A Japanese soldier named Shoichi Yokoi is discovered living in a cave in a remote part of Guam, not having realized World War II had ended. After living in a cave for nearly thirty years, Shoichi's last act of war was a brutal Kamikaze attack on the nostrils of his finders.

JANUARY 24, 1986 Science-fiction writer and Scientology founder L. Ron Hubbard dies. In his bio, he claimed to have been the youngest person in history to have ever been made an Eagle Scout, and was later awarded merit badges in Metalwork, Wood Carving, and Scam Religion Founding.

<table>
<tr><td>

JANUARY 25, 1919
The League of Nations Founded.

</td></tr>
</table>

ON THIS DAY, the League of Nations, the forerunner to the United Nations, was proposed and accepted during the Paris Peace Conference following the end of World War I. Its mission? To stop all war.

At right is the unofficial symbol of the League of Nations, two five-pointed stars within a blue pentagon. Proposals for adopting an "official" symbol were bandied about for twenty years, but no one could reach an agreement.

So one can probably guess how well they did on the whole "stop all war" thing.

LEAGUE OF NATIONS

SOCIETE DES NATIONS

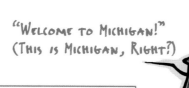

JANUARY 26
A Bad Day for Mapmakers.

IT APPEARS AS THOUGH mapmakers and cartographers should plan on working late today, because January 26 is a popular day for territorial makeovers.

JANUARY 26, 1837 Michigan is admitted as the twenty-sixth U.S. state. Its state motto was *Si quaeris peninsulam amoenam, circumspice* (Latin for "If you seek a pleasant peninsula, look about you"), which was later replaced with the more colloquial, "Once you get outside Detroit, it's really nice."

JANUARY 26, 1861 Louisiana becomes the sixth state to secede from the Union as the Civil War begins. Apparently, the only thing they wanted emancipated were the bosoms of young Mardi Gras revelers.

JANUARY 26, 1918 Ukraine declared its independence on this day, taking advantage of Russian disarray after the Bolshevik Revolution. Six weeks later, the region is annexed by Germany and Austria. Six months after that, it falls under the control of Poland, until it once again returns to Soviet control in 1922, the same year the Ukraine declared "What part of 'We've declared our independence' do you not understand?"

JANUARY 26, 1950 The most crowded democracy on Earth is born when the Republic of India approves its constitution. If you'd like to know more about the birth of this great nation, ask the sort of Midwestern-sounding guy who calls you during dinner tonight to get you to sign up for your credit card's Business Traveler Plan.

JANUARY 27, 1927
Video Begins Plotting Death of Radio Star.

THIS DAY IN HISTORY marks the first-ever television broadcast, as Scottish engineer John Logie Baird showed off his electromechanical television system, the Televisor. He broadcast two wooden ventriloquist dummies to an audience in London, and in the process also invented the Local Morning News Team.

To see how far television has come, walk into the other room and turn it on. (Warning: Chances are a woman in a bikini will be eating a length of pig ass for money. Steel yourself.) But you have to promise to shut it off after a few minutes, and resume reading this book. OK? It'll be easy. Go watch, and then re-embark on the glorious imagination adventure of reading.

Are you back?

Damn.

HISTO-POURRI.

JANUARY 28, 1521 The **DIET OF WORMS** begins in Worms, Germany. Had ← there been more hotel rooms in nearby Rüdesheim, this assembly of the twenty-four estates of the Holy Roman Empire might not have had such a repulsive name.

JANUARY 28, 1813 Jane Austen's *Pride and Prejudice* is first published in England. People who have not read it yet can relax, there will be another four or five movie adaptations made in the next week.

JANUARY 28, 1873 Smutty writer Colette born in Burgundy, France. If you have never attended or are not yet in college, you have not read her. If you are done with college, you will never read her again.

JANUARY 28, 1916 Louis D. Brandeis becomes the first Jew appointed to the Supreme Court. He was also "Hottest Jew on the Supreme Court" until the appointment of Ruth Bader Ginsburg in 1993.

JANUARY 28, 1956 Elvis Presley makes his first television appearance, singing "Heartbreak Hotel" on a program called *Stage Show*. Teenage girls everywhere thank their lucky stars for the birth of John Logie Baird. (See yesterday.)

JANUARY 28, 1978 *Fantasy Island* debuts on television. The anthology program follows characters in search of their lifelong fantasies, as long as said fantasies somehow involve a shouting French dwarf. The show made many TV critics imagine a fantasy where they go back in time and murder the infant John Logie Baird.

MANY YOUNG LADIES "ATTENDED BRANDEIS."

Poe's Stark "Raven."

ON THIS DAY IN 1845, the *New York Evening Mirror* ran "The Raven," Edgar Allan Poe's 1,126-word arabesque poem about a scary, talking bird. (Note: The *New York Evening Mirror*'s slogan was "All the scary, talking bird news that's fit to print.")

Poe's most famous work chronicles a narrator longing for a woman named "Lenore," who is haunted by a raven who only utters "Nevermore." The original version of the poem, in which the woman's name was "Helen" and the Raven utters "She's a dead 'un," lacked the same wallop.

"Lenore" was most likely Virginia Eliza "Sissy" Clemm Poe, the poet's thirteen-year-old cousin and wife, who died from tuberculosis. His loss also figures prominently in "Annabel Lee" and several less morose limericks that began with the line "There once was a gal in high school. . . . "

A FEW OTHER MILESTONES FROM THE WORLD OF POETRY ALSO OCCURRED ON THIS DAY IN HISTORY:

JANUARY 29, 1933 American lyric poet Sara Teasdale dies from complications related to being a poet (suicide). She is later inducted into the St. Louis Walk of Fame, along with that city's other famous poets, Maya Angelou, T. S. Eliot, and Yogi Berra.

JANUARY 29, 1963 Four-time Pulitzer Prize–winning poet Robert Frost dies at age 89. "The Road Not Taken" has led scores of artistic people to follow Frost's example and carve out their own unique paths in life, albeit without all the financial rewards, critical and popular acceptance, and four Pulitzer Prizes.

A Cake Less Eaten.

Jackson Action.

TODAY MARKS THE ANNIVERSARY of the first-ever attempt on the life of a president. Celebrate it with cake, a few glasses of wine, but do NOT attempt a reenactment.

In the House chamber, President Andrew Jackson was attending a funeral service honoring the late Representative Warren R. Davis of South Carolina (funerals were sad events for Jackson, especially if the deceased was not Native American), when a disturbed man named Richard Lawrence tried to kill him.

Lawrence had two pistols on him, but both jammed (readers who are NRA members can now snort loudly about the necessity of the so-called "Brady Bill"). He was then tackled by Davy Crockett and Jackson himself, and was later prosecuted by National Anthem composer Francis Scott Key—all of which makes Lawrence our most "Forrest Gumpy" failed presidential assassin.

Lawrence believed he was Richard III, and the jury only took five minutes to find him "not guilty by reason of insanity." Although he was found guilty of "excessive hamminess" when he took the stand and launched into the "Make My Heaven in a Lady's Lap" soliloquy from *Henry VI*.

Social Security System Begins Road to Bankruptcy.

IDA MAY FULLER, a spinster (old-timey word for "career woman") of Ludlow, Vermont, became the first person to receive a Social Security check on this day in 1940. The check was for $22.55, or twice the average payment of a Social Security check in 2008.

When the Social Security Act was passed into law in 1935, benefits were paid out in lump sums, but too many old people began to be victimized with the 1936 invention of the "Bus Trip to Atlantic City."

Fuller died in 1975 at one hundred years old, and had received payments totaling $22,000, although she herself had only contributed $24 into the system, showing that the term "spinster" can sometimes also mean "cunningly astute businesswoman."

February

FEBRUARY 1, 1960

I'll Have a Black-and-White Shake-up.

ON THIS DAY IN HISTORY, four African-American college students in Greensboro, North Carolina (can you see where this is going?), staged a sit-in at a segregated Woolworth's lunch counter, where the only thing that was allowed to be black was the decades-old grease in the fryer.

The four young men, Ezell Blair Jr., David Richmond, Joseph McNeil, and Franklin McCain, were students at nearby North Carolina Agricultural and Technical State University, which counts among its alumni the Reverend Jesse Jackson and 9/11 conspirator Khalid Shaikh Mohammed, the latter being an admissions office attempt to diversify the campus's overwhelmingly moral and noble student body.

The men were allowed to sit at the lunch counter but were not served. And they sat at the counter, not eating, nearly every day until Woolworth's integrated their counters in July of 1960, which was also when the now-emaciated Greensboro Four integrated the word "manorexia" into their list of other obstacles to overcome.

WOOLWORTH OFFERED LOW, LOW PRICES ON PROTEST PLACARDS.

THIS IS A COLOR PICTURE, COVERED IN SOOT!

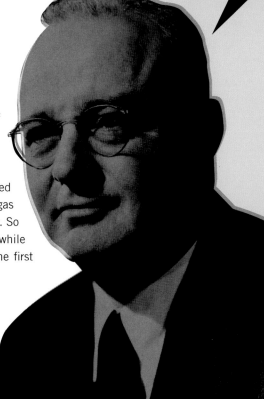

FEBRUARY 2, 1923

Gentlemen, Start Your Coughing.

TODAY WAS A BAD DAY for knocks and pings in the motors of American cars, and a good day for fans of pollution and watery eyes, as leaded gasoline went on sale for the very first time at a filling station in Dayton, Ohio.

While working for General Motors, inventor Thomas Midgley discovered that adding lead to gasoline prevented engine knocking and increased gas mileage. Midgley later discovered Freon, another enemy of the ozone layer. So thank Thomas Midgley next time you get a sunburn in the dead of winter, while swimming at your oceanfront property near Dayton, Ohio—the site of the first filling station to sell leaded gasoline.

The Day the Music Died . . . Born.

YES, TODAY MARKS THAT EVENT THAT DRUNK PEOPLE SING ABOUT when someone puts "American Pie" by Don McLean on the jukebox at the bar, which normally comes on the heels of a sorority sister bartop pantomime to "Paradise by the Dashboard Light."

Anyhoo, it was on this day that a single-engine plane crash took the life of music legend Buddy Holly and two other guys who subsequently became legends because they went down in a plane with a legend. The three men were touring together and crashed while en route to a show in Fargo, North Dakota, which at least freed the men from having to visit Fargo, North Dakota.

Fellow tour mates Dion DiMucci, of Dion and the Belmonts, and Waylon Jennings wound up traveling in the tour bus instead of by plane. Jennings later admitted to feeling tremendous guilt for many years because of an exchange he had with Holly right before the crash, when Holly jokingly said, "I hope your bus freezes up," to which Jennings replied "Well, I hope your plane crashes."

(His eerie sense of prophecy came true again in the 1970s, when he said to his frequent collaborator Willie Nelson, "Well, I hope you stay stoned out of your mind on pot forever.")

Mr. Washington Goes to Washington.

ACTUALLY, IT WAS NEW YORK, because "Washington" had yet to be founded and then named after our first president of the United States, who was elected to the position on this day in 1788. (Elections now take place in November, but results in 1789 were delayed because the young nation had not produced enough extremely elderly and feeble citizens to man the polling stations.)

The runner-up in the election, John Adams, was named vice president of the United States. His chief duties were feeling sorry for himself, rolling his eyes, and making passive-aggressive remarks about how the presidency was just a "popularity contest."

Washington was a reluctant president, although after a while the joy of rubbing it in Adams's face warmed him to the position. When the Senate proposed that he be addressed as "His Highness the President of the United States of America and the Protector of Their Liberties," Washington insisted on "Mr. President." Yet he also insisted that the Senate title Adams with the rather royal "Lady Penelope Bitchenmoan."

BELOVED BY ALL,
EXCEPT JOHN ADAMS.

On a side note, Vice President Dan Quayle was born on this day in 1947. (See tomorrow.)

34

FEBRUARY 5, 1947

J. Danforth Quayle Turns One-Day Old.

BABY CELEBRATES by halting any further cognitive development. ←

FEBRUARY 6

HISTO-POURRI.

ALL SORTS OF INTERESTING STUFF HAPPENED TODAY. Browse this sweet-smelling assortment of events.

FEBRUARY 6, 1756 Easily offended American politician and Vice President Aaron Burr is born. He demanded satisfaction from Alexander Hamilton and killed him in a duel on a New Jersey cliff—the same site where, as a horny teenager, he often demanded but rarely got satisfaction.

FEBRUARY 6, 1820 The first organized immigration of freed U.S. slaves kicked off from New York Harbor, after the former slaves naively took frequent shouts of "Go back to Africa!" as vacation suggestions.

FEBRUARY 6, 1840 The Treaty of Waitangi is signed, establishing New Zealand as a British colony, which is why locals still utter the Britishism "wanker" under their breath every time someone on a "*Lord of the Rings* vacation" asks for directions.

FEBRUARY 6, 1843 First minstrel show debuts in New York City. Slaves who left for Africa in 1820 surely kicking themselves for missing out.

FEBRUARY 6, 1911 Film star and U.S. President Ronald Regan born. People who have been campaigning to make this a national holiday are also the type who remember minstrel shows fondly.

FEBRUARY 6, 1971 Alan Shepard smuggles golf club on board Apollo capsule and becomes the first person to ever hit a golf ball on the moon. Gaudy plaid space suit probably a clue that something golf-related was going to happen.

FEBRUARY 6, 1985 Steve Wozniak leaves Apple Inc. People who celebrate this day also have a slide show of their *Lord of the Rings* New Zealand vacation that they should really stop showing to company.

Pope Not-So-Innocent.

ON THIS DAY IN 1550, sixty-three-year-old Cardinal Giovanni Maria Ciocchi del Monte was elevated to Pope Julius III. While Julius III was only pope for five years, his reign is notable for one particularly progressive appointment to the College of Cardinals, the nature of which would later become commonplace in the modern Catholic Church.

He elevated to "cardinal" a seventeen-year-old boy he had met on the streets of Parma some years previously. This encounter and later appointment is basically the reason why every year on Julius's birthday, the Church ceremonially pardons his remains and shifts them to a different parish.

The boy, Innocenzo Ciocchi del Monte, was illegitimate and illiterate, but still became the official "Cardinal Nephew" (seriously), which meant he was supposed to handle all of the pontiff's correspondence. Since he couldn't read, however, he had to settle for just making sure his quill was always at the ready for dipping into Julius's inkwell.

The office of Cardinal Nephew was abolished in 1692 and now the pope's correspondence is aided by someone holding the title of "Cardinal Microsoft Paper Clip."

CARDINAL NEPHEWS-IN-TRAINING.

Salem Tourist Board Gets a Big Break.

INNOCENT VICTIMS OF THE SALEM WITCH TRIALS: REBECCA NURSE, SUSANNAH MARTIN, ELIZABETH HOWE, SARAH GOOD, SARAH WILDES, GEORGE JACOBS SR., MARTHA CARRIER, GEORGE BURROUGHS, JOHN PROCTOR, JOHN WILLARD, MARTHA COREY, MARGARET SCOTT, MARY EASTY, ALICE PARKER, ANN PUDEATOR, WILMOTT REDD, SAMUEL WARDWELL, MARY PARKER, GILES COREY, BROOM-HILDAWARTS MCPOINTYHAT *

*PROBABLY GUILTY

TODAY IS A DAY OF SOME INTEREST TO OUR WICCAN READERS, the type who wear little pouches around their necks filled with various "healing crystals." (Sadly, for most Wiccans it appears there has yet to be unearthed a crystal with healing powers toward obesity.)

On this day in history, two girls in Salem, Massachusetts, were declared to be "under an evil hand," and consequently kicked off the hysteria that led to the hangings of nineteen people. (Note: No witches were burned in Salem. Although, they were "burned" metaphorically—but that still doesn't suck as much as being burned literally.)

Witnesses saw the two teenage girls, Abigail Williams and Betty Parris, experiencing demonic "fits and convulsions" (this was many years before scientists had isolated and identified the "hot slumber party pillow fight"). The girls claimed that a West Indian woman named Tituba had "bewitched" them (this was many years before scientists had isolated and identified "bicuriosity").

Eventually, arrest warrants were issued for whomever the teenagers declared to be a witch—predominantly people who were among the less popular within the devout community. Later, such hostilities would have a slightly less violent outlet when Salem established its first-ever "high school."

Nineteen innocent victims were sent to Gallows Hill, and one resident succumbed after having heavy stones pressed on his body over the course of two days. Actually, he hadn't been accused of witchcraft, but was deemed by some to be "pro-busing." That was never very popular in the greater Boston area, even in the years before scientists isolated and identified "buses."

FEBRUARY 9, 1950

Joseph McCarthy Launches Metaphorical Witch Hunt.

THREE HUNDRED FIFTY-EIGHT YEARS AND ONE DAY after the folks in Salem, Massachusetts, kicked off their honest-to-goodness REAL witch hunt, Republican Senator Joseph McCarthy announced that he had a list of over two hundred members of the Department of State who were "known Communists." He dropped this bombshell in Wheeling, West Virginia, at something called "the Ohio County Women's Republican Club," probably the only time the description "bombshell" has ever been associated with anything or anyone in the Ohio County Women's Republican Club.

The speech cast a spotlight on the previously obscure senator, whose hunt for Communists then preoccupied Washington for nearly three years before he was finally censured by the Senate and humiliated on national television during the Army-McCarthy Hearings. (Note: Before it became a network strategy, humiliating real people on television was once a novelty.)

Although McCarthy's reputation has been mud for decades, Ann Coulter praised him in a recent book and even posed for photos by his tombstone. To be fair, she likes to pose with props that diminish the size of her giant man hands.

(If you'd like to learn more about the McCarthy Witch Hunt, turn on PBS on any given day and watch one of the hundred earnest documentaries about the era, usually narrated by Lee Grant. Be patient. You might have to sit through either something about Irish people in America or something involving a combination of bellowing "tenors.")

TAKEN SERIOUSLY, DESPITE NICKNAME "TAILGUNNER."

TOM THUMB
(SECOND FROM RIGHT).

General Tom Thumb Ties Tiny Knot.

PT. BARNUM'S fame and fortune relied on the moment-by-moment birth of suckers, but the occasional birth defect was where he really made his money. On this day in history, America's love affair with pituitary disorders manifested itself in the excitement surrounding the marriage of General Tom Thumb, who, at two feet eleven inches, was a big star for the famous sideshow showman.

On February 10, Thumb was married in front of 2,000 guests at New York's Grace Episcopal Church to the equally diminutive Lavina Warren, who was therein known as the "Little Woman."

Afterward, guests attended a $75-a-head reception (See? Suckers.), where one unlucky man sustained a groin injury during the tossing of the bouquet. For their honeymoon, the couple went to Washington, D.C., where they were greeted by President Abraham Lincoln, who might—might—have had more important things to attend to in 1863.

Thumb, whose real name was Charles Sherwood Stratton, was a very wealthy man due to his association with Barnum, and eventually retired to a specially made home on one of Connecticut's Thimble Islands. Certainly an appropriate name, and slightly less insulting than a habitation on nearby Dicklevel Sandbar.

It Could Have Been Worse.

PEACE, BREAD, AND
HANDSOMENESS.

ON THIS DAY, we'll look at some sucky events that could have been way suckier.

FEBRUARY 11, 1916 Noted Communist agitator **EMMA GOLDMAN** arrested in New York for lecturing on birth control. **It Could Have Been Worse:** The stout, bespectacled forty-seven-year-old was arrested before she could *demonstrate* birth control.

FEBRUARY 11, 1945 The **YALTA CONFERENCE** ends with a large chunk of Europe handed over to Stalin, because he was running out of people to kill within his own country. **It Could Have Been Worse:** Roosevelt's Yalta Conference lady-cape does not catch on as a fashion accessory. ←

STILL, IT WASN'T THE
WORST FASHION CHOICE
MADE THAT DAY.

FEBRUARY 11, 1960 Funny yet tantrum-prone *Tonight Show* host Jack Paar walks off the program in tears, upset that censors had cut a sketch featuring the term "water closet." Cohost Hugh Downs was left to finish the monologue, which meant hope for laughter was flushed down the (redacted). **It Could Have Been Worse:** See any moment of *The Chevy Chase Show*.

FEBRUARY 11, 1979 The Ayatollah Khomeini seizes power in Iran, which kicks off a wistful international retro-trend celebrating glory days of brutal, U.S.-backed dictators. **It Could Have Been Worse:** If he'd answered to the title Imam, your hilarious "Assahola Khomeini" T-shirt would have been useless.

FEBRUARY 11, 2006 Vice President Dick Cheney shoots a friend in the face with a shotgun while hunting. Lack of functioning heart means Cheney doesn't go on television sobbing like Jack Paar. **It Could Have Been Worse:** He could have killed him, in which case it wouldn't have been so hilarious.

KHOMEINI IS FULL OF SHIITE.

MORE LIKE KHO-ZANY.

THE AYATOLLAH SUCKS, AND PERHAPS HAD THE UNITED STATES NOT WORKED SO HARD TO KEEP THE BRUTAL SHAH IN POWER, KHOMEINI'S FORM OF RADICAL ISLAMIC EXTREMISM MIGHT NOT HAVE SEEMED LIKE A BETTER ALTERNATIVE.

FEBRUARY 12, 1809
Abraham Lincoln Birthday Quiz.

OL' ENGRAVING POSER.

ABRAHAM LINCOLN was born on this day in 1809 outside of Hogdenville, Kentucky. (Although those manipulative, flashy attention-whores in Springfield, Illinois, would like you to forget that.) While Lincoln had no middle name, he was graced with scores of nicknames over the years. Which of the following monikers were bestowed upon our sixteenth president during his lifetime?

(a) Honest Abe
(b) The Railsplitter
(c) The Liberator
(d) The Great Emancipator
(e) The Ancient One
(f) The Martyr
(g) Penny

ANSWER: Trick Question. All were nicknames for Abe Lincoln, who was seemingly given a nickname for every little personality trait or action. (Note: The name "Penny" does not relate to his likeness on the penny, because that didn't occur until after he died. Penny was the result of our sixteenth president's beloved drag persona "Penny Farthing," a factoid that those manipulative, flashy attention-whores in Springfield, Illinois, would rather you forgot.)

FEBRUARY 13, 1945
Allies Launch Operation Overkill.

ON THIS DAY IN 1945, Allied air forces laid waste to the historic, art-filled German city of Dresden. Many say it was a fitting end to a war—that had kind of already ended—and totally made up for the lame-ass closing night festivities at the Yalta Conference, which had wrapped up two days earlier.

Some estimates say that nearly 50,000 people died in the firebombing of a city that was an art and architecture capital and of little strategic importance. Although it did fulfill Winston Churchill's promise that "we shall fight on the beaches, we shall fight on the landing grounds, we shall fight in the fields and in the streets, and we shall fight them if they are hiding under Gustave Courbet's painting, *The Stonebreakers*."

Members of the far-right National Democratic Party of Germany often speak of the Dresden bombing as the "Holocaust of Bombs," but they should probably just shut the hell up.

FEBRUARY 14
Happy Stupid Hallmark Holiday. Stupid.

HISTORY'S GREATEST LOVERS:
- ANTONY AND CLEOPATRA
- JULIUS CAESAR AND CLEOPATRA
- CLEOPATRA AND APPARENTLY ANY DUDE IN "MANDALS"
- ROBERT AND ELIZABETH BROWNING
- NAPOLEON AND JOSEPHINE
- QUEEN VICTORIA AND PRINCE ALBERT
- GEORGE AND MARTHA WASHINGTON
- JOHN ADAMS AND MARTHA WASHINGTON (REVENGE FOR THE WHOLE LADY PENELOPE BITCHEN-MOAN THING—SEE FEBRUARY 4)

YEP, IF THAT IS YOUR VIEW OF VALENTINE'S DAY, then you are a lonely and single sourpuss. Here are some crappy events that took place on this day that might make it seem less crappy.

FEBRUARY 14, 1556 Archbishop of Canterbury Thomas Cranmer is declared a heretic and later burned to death. You can relate, right? You're always the one who gets burned in a relationship. You're just like the archbishop, but without all the agonizing death and the Anglican martyr thing.

FEBRUARY 14, 1929 Seven gangsters are gunned down in Chicago. Well, at least they had a good excuse for not having a date.

FEBRUARY 14, 1945 The bombing of Prague takes place, as Allied pilots mistakenly hit the city during the Dresden campaign. You're the only person who ever spent a semester in Prague and didn't get laid. Who cares? Being single means freedom. That's the truth, but when you say that, people look at you as some kind of heretic, like Archbishop Thomas Cranmer.

FEBRUARY 14, 1945 FDR meets with King Ibn Saud on board the USS *Quincy*, kicking off U.S.–Saudi Arabian relations. Great, even FDR had a date on this day. And he was some kind of cripple.

FEBRUARY 14, 1961 Element 103, Lawrencium, is first synthesized. You're going to die alone.

FEBRUARY 14, 1989 A fatwa is issued against *The Satanic Verses* author Salman Rushdie. Have you seen Padma Lakshmi? That dude's ex-wife? Gimme a break. How come no Islamists want to martyr you? You're a bigger loser than Archbishop Thomas Cranmer.

FEBRUARY 15, 1898
Memorable Event Concerning the USS *Maine* That Makes You Remember the *Maine*.

REMEMBER TO CALL THE INSURANCE COMPANY.

ON THIS DAY IN HISTORY, the USS *Maine* sunk off the coast of Havana after a massive explosion, which the United States blamed on a Spanish mine and used as an excuse to launch the Spanish-American War. This was probably the most exciting and dramatic event ever to be associated with the state of Maine that was not "lobster-related."

In 1976, however, investigators concluded that the explosion probably resulted from a fire in the ammunition hold. At that point, the Spanish answered "Remember the *Maine*" with "Remember the Apology You Owe Us, Amigos?"

One might say the sinking of the *Maine* was to the Spanish-American War what the attack on the World Trade Center was to Iraq, although Saddam Hussein probably had more of a hand in the sinking of the battleship than he did with 9/11.

FEBRUARY 16, 1945
Venezuela Experiments with Post-Emptive Warfare.

AFTER SIX YEARS OF WORLD WAR II (the one that Tom Brokaw likes so much), and a couple days after the firebombing of Dresden, Nazi Germany lay in ruins, weeks away from total defeat. And what little nuts they had left were going to feel the mighty boot of Venezuela.

That's because on this day in 1945, Venezuela told the world that enough was enough, and they declared war on Nazi Germany. This announcement came just days after Paraguay declared war, and a couple days before Argentina, who had been too busy to enter the conflict because they were building tiny cities of Nazi retirement bungalow colonies.

Venezuela also never even got around to declaring war on Japan, and this traditional failure to declare war in a timely manner is probably why current Venezuelan President Hugo Chavez overcompensates. He declared war three times in 2007—once on the United States, once on the capitalist system, and a third time on Cindy Sheehan, for failing to put her wet towels back on the rack during one of her frequent visits.

FEBRUARY 17, 1982
Bebop Legend Thelonious Monk Dies.

MARK THE OCCASION by not clicking past "Mysterioso" on your iPod, which you have done every day since you downloaded it from the iTunes John Cale Celebrity Playlist.

OTHER FAMOUS PEOPLE
NAMED THELONIOUS:

• THELONIOUS BERNARD: FRENCH CHILD ACTOR IN THE FILM *A LITTLE ROMANCE*.

• SORRY, IF THE SECOND-MOST FAMOUS "THELONIOUS" IS A FRENCH KID WHO WAS IN TWO MOVIES, IT MIGHT BE TIME TO WRAP UP THE LIST.

FEBRUARY 18, 1930
How Now, Flown Cow?

ON THIS DAY IN HISTORY, a Guernsey named Elm Farm Ollie became the first cow to ever ride in an airplane. (Amelia Earhart was called the first cow to fly in a plane in 1926, but that was just by an airport baggage handler who thought her tip landed a little short of Runway Generosity.)

Ollie took her flight from Bismark, Missouri, to St. Louis, where even she was depressed by the St. Louis airport's sparse food court offerings. She also became the first cow to be milked on a flight, and supposedly a glass of her milk was later given to Charles Lindbergh who, in typical Nazi-friendly fashion, praised the beverage's "pure, clean whiteness."

Demanded the Vegetarian Meal.

This experiment was performed to examine the possibilities of transporting animals by air, a field of exploration still studied by the occasional brave soul on a cross-country flight who thinks it's perfectly appropriate to stuff a dachshund in a man-purse under the seat in front of him.

FDR Kisses Japanese-American Vote Good-bye.

FRANKLIN DELANO ROOSEVELT signed Executive Order 9066 on this day in history, which soon saw the civil rights of Japanese-Americans becoming history.

The order called for the removal of suspect people from military areas "as deemed necessary or desirable." The entire West Coast was considered a military zone after the Pearl Harbor attack (Oakland has yet to free itself from that designation), and 100,000 folks of Japanese ancestry in the region were soon relocated to internment camps across the country—while their businesses were taken over by branches of the oddly free-from-government-scrutiny franchise "Messerschmidt's German-American Listening Devices and Microfilm Outlet."

In 1988, President Ronald Reagan signed a bill that provided internment camp survivors with a check for $20,000, which in 1942 dollars was . . . still pretty insulting.

Sadly, Detainees Were Denied Snowboarding Privileges.

HISTO-POURRI: Space Blastoff Roundup.

FEBRUARY 20 is a good day to reach for the stars, and reach for a bunch of events that might make up something called a "Space Blastoff Roundup."

FEBRUARY 20, 1902 Photographer Ansel Adams born. Took lots of pictures of the moon floating over Yosemite, all of which are way too expensive to be reprinted in this book.

FEBRUARY 20, 1921 Test pilot Joseph Albert Walker born. In 1963, he made two X-15 flights to the edge of space, which qualified him as an astronaut under American air force rules. Qualifications later relaxed to "Completion of Weekend Space Fantasy Camp."

FEBRUARY, 20, 1943 Russian cosmonaut Aleksandr Pavlovich Aleksandrov is born. By his retirement in 1993, he had logged over three hundred days in space, which also marks the "Longest Stint of Sobriety by Any Russian."

FEBRUARY 20, 1962 Astronaut John Glenn becomes the first American to orbit the earth on board a capsule called *Friendship 7*. Later, he's badly injured by a fall in a bathtub called *Irony 1*.

FEBRUARY 20, 1965 *Ranger 8* space probe crashes on the moon after sending back over 7,000 photos of the lunar surface. Provided nice documentation for movie set re-creation of moon for "landing" three years later.

HISTO-POURRI: Commie, Pinko Edition.

YET ANOTHER DAY OF INTEREST to Lefties, February 21 marks many important events in the history of people who hate America and Freedom.

FEBRUARY 21, 1848 **KARL MARX** publishes the *Communist Manifesto*. He wrote the blueprint for Socialism when he was thirty years old and supported financially by someone else, thus creating the "lifestyle blueprint" for later self-proclaimed Socialists.

FEBRUARY 21, 1960 Fidel Castro nationalizes all the businesses in Cuba. Decreases the power of Big American Interests, increases the power of Big Rusting Studebaker.

BEARDED SHAM.

FEBRUARY 21, 1965 Malcolm X is assassinated at the Audubon Ballroom in Harlem, in an example of chickens ironically coming home to roost after "chickens coming home to roost" comment.

FEBRUARY 21, 1972 President Richard M. Nixon visits Communist China and meets with Chairman Mao, opening up the Bamboo Curtain. Resulting slow strangulation of American economy over the next thirty years ensures that bamboo curtains, bought at Wal-Mart, become inexpensive privacy shade for family of six living in two-room home.

FEBRUARY 22, 1732
Father of Country Makes Debut As Baby of Country.

ON THIS DAY IN 1732, George Washington was born, and given a teething ring that probably did more harm than good.

Of course, everyone knows that the father of our country was toothless, but some stories, like the one about the truth-telling cherry tree, are probably lies. Here are a few select truths about our first president.

• Washington was the only president to be elected unanimously, something that would have occurred again if the planned McGovern–Mondale Democratic ticket had ever taken off in the late 1980s.

• Washington had to borrow money to attend his inauguration in New York City. And like most people who visit New York from out of town, he kept all that money either in his front pocket, or in a conspicuous money belt.

• His wife Martha brought two children to the marriage who refused to call him anything but the Stepfather of Our Country.

• His presidential salary was $25,000— which he refused, much to the chagrin of the people who lent him money to get to his inaugural.

• His face was scarred from smallpox, and he had no teeth and giant size thirteen feet.

• He had two ice cream freezers at his Mount Vernon estate, probably to cope with the body issues listed above.

WASHINGTON, AGE TWO MONTHS.

"I CANNOT TELL A LIE— I HATE MYSELF."

Mass Historia Mortality In and Out List.

A WHO'S WHO OF WHO was born and who died on this day in history.

IN:

FEBRUARY 23, 1633 Samuel Pepys, famous diarist, born. Entry on day of birth mostly concerned with mother's bosoms. Kind of creepy.

FEBRUARY 23, 1868 **W. E. B. DUBOIS** born. Early founder of NAACP and BPFEUOI (Black People for Excessive Use of Initials).

FEBRUARY 23, 1918 Neo-Nazi Aryan Nations founder Richard G. Butler born. Probably thrilled that he shared a birthday with W. E. B. DuBois.

FEBRUARY 23, 1940 Peter Fonda born, an event he would sometimes relive after consuming pieces of mescaline birthday cake.

FEBRUARY 23, 1994 Dakota Fanning born. Probably screamed and cried a lot on this day, although not as loud and as shrilly as she did in the movie *War of the Worlds*.

OUT:

FEBRUARY 23, 1730 Pope Benedict XIII dies. Although he initially called himself Benedict XIV because he thought thirteen was unlucky, he went back to using XIII. And died. Idiot.

FEBRUARY 23, 1930 Nazi songwriter Horst Wessel, lyricist of Nazi Party anthem "The Flag on High," dies after being shot in the face. News probably made Richard G. Butler cry like Dakota Fanning.

FEBRUARY 23, 1969 King Saud of Saudi Arabia, "friend" of the United States, dies. The anniversary is marked by Dick Cheney and George W. Bush crying like Dakota Fanning.

FEBRUARY 23, 1995 British author and veterinarian James Herriot dies. Family told he was taken away to a farm in the country.

CALL ME "WEB."

FEBRUARY 24, 1868

An Errant Johnson Becomes the Subject of an Impeachment Trial.

ON THIS DAY IN HISTORY, the U.S. House of Representatives, considering him too soft on the South after the Civil War, voted eleven articles of impeachment against President Andrew Johnson, nine of which cited Johnson's removal of Secretary of War Edwin M. Stanton as a violation of their newly passed Tenure of Office Act, an act that was later ruled unconstitutional by the Supreme Court. The impeachment was motivated purely by political reasons, having very little to do with wrongdoings on the part of the president.

Whew. Never happened again.

THE MOST JOHNSONIAN JACKSONIAN DEMOCRAT.

FEBRUARY 25, 1956

Sylvia Plath Meets Ted Hughes.

AND IF THE NEWS OF THIS causes your eyes to fill with angry tears about what that "monster" did to her, you should probably put this book down. Chances are, you're not much of a "laugher."

"A LAUGH RIOT!"
—*Sarcastic Publisher's Weekly*

A Masters
in Breakfast.

FEBRUARY 26, 1852

Flakey Kellogg Born.

HEALTH NUT, cereal inventor, enema perv, and anti-masturbation zealot John Harvey Kellogg was born on February 26, 1852, and if you carry around that many titles, you should start every day with a good breakfast.

Kellogg ran the Battle Creek Sanitarium in Michigan, where he personally oversaw patient treatment, which mostly consisted of yogurt enemas and stool study. So in addition to inventing breakfast, Kellogg was also good at holding his down.

He claimed that 90 percent of all illness began in the bowels. And since he was also an advocate of radium cures, one assumes the other 10 percent began in giant, misshapen, and glowing thyroid glands. Kellogg was also antisex, and he particularly despised the sin of onanism. He suggested the cure to stop boys from masturbating was to have them circumcised without anesthesia, which today is still the traditional way to cure a boy suffering from Acute Gentilism.

Both he and his brother, Will Kellogg, developed various high-fiber cereals, but it was Will who founded the company that would eventually become Kellogg's. He cut John out of the business after the commercial failure of his distasteful colonic cereal called "Enem-Os."

Hermann Loved
To Camp It Up.

FEBRUARY 27, 1933

Reichstag Party!

WHILE MANY WORDS HAVE BEEN WRITTEN describing Adolph Hitler as evil, not many have discussed how lucky he was, at least outside the pages of Eva Braun erotic fan fiction.

But February 27, 1933, was a very lucky day for the chancellor of Germany, because the Reichstag caught on fire and enabled Hitler to seize power, freeze all the civil liberties people enjoyed within the nation, and arrest and try to kill off every known Communist. Also, it finally gave him an excuse to change the wallpaper in the Reichstag entry foyer. A thousand-year-empire does not do floral.

A Dutch arsonist-Communist-bricklayer (even then, employment opportunities abounded for the "hyphenate") named Marinus van der Lubbe was discovered staggering away from the fire, and confessed to setting it, although many think that he was tricked into it by undercover Nazis who had conspired with him. (Arsonist-Fascist-pseudo-Communists. The Nazis also appreciated hyphenates.)

During his trial at Nuremberg, pudge Hermann Goering was cross-examined about his possible role in setting the fire. He denied it, and said that he never lit a fire in his life that didn't end in an unholy carnival of s'mores consumption.

FEBRUARY 28, 1844
Tyler Turns Tragedy Into Tail.

Note: This is part eight of our series, *More Than You Ever Wanted to Know About President John Tyler's Virility.*

FIFTY-FOUR-YEAR-OLD PRESIDENT JOHN TYLER was on the Potomac River on board the USS *Princeton*, with dignitaries, cabinet members, his friend David Gardiner, and Gardiner's twenty-year-old daughter Julia, to whom Tyler had just proposed—emboldened by his recent purchase of Doctor Fenton's Tincture of Wormwood and Viagra Spirits (98 percent opium).

She had not given him an answer, probably because she thought his nickname "His Accidency" (he became president after the death of William Henry Harrison) may have had something to do with his advanced age and likely incontinence.

The ship's captain decided to test out a 30,000-pound cannon as the craft cruised toward George Washington's Mount Vernon home. (The science of creating loud disturbances on river cruises was in its infancy. It would be years before the pastime would be perfected with the invention of "Morning Zoo Blues Cruise.")

The cannon wound up exploding, killing many, including Tyler's secretary of the navy and secretary of state. (Ironically, his Secretary of Yacht Safety also perished, and the position was never re-filled). Also among the dead was David Gardiner, and when his daughter heard the news, she fainted into Tyler's arms, which were already extended because the president had been attempting his patented first-date move, "the Tyler Stretch."

The two grew closer after that day, and she eventually accepted his hand. Tyler became the first president to marry in office, and the two were together until his death, probably because he often "spiced things up" on their anniversary with flowers, sweet talk, and by blowing up a male member of her family.

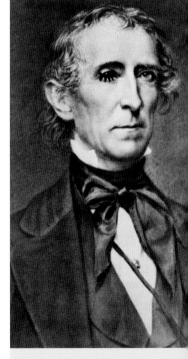

SMOOTH.

FEBRUARY 29, 1468
Pope Paul III Born.

AND SINCE HE WAS BORN IN A LEAP YEAR that means he's only 135 years old. Ha.

March

MARCH 1

A Bad Day to Be the Capitol Building.

IF YOU'RE A DUAL-WINGED, ROTUNDA-ED CENTER of the United States government, designed in the neoclassical style, you might want to keep your dome down today, because the first of March has twice been witness to violent events in the U.S. Capitol Building in Washington, D.C.

MARCH 1, 1954 Four Puerto Rican nationalists, standing in the Ladies Gallery, engage in some rather unladylike behavior by opening fire on the floor of the House of Representatives, wounding five congressmen in the process. (Three Democrats and two Republicans in a bipartisan effort to make themselves shoo-ins for "sympathy reelection.") The four shooters, three men and one woman, were imprisoned until 1979, when they were pardoned by Jimmy Carter, a radical always looking to free himself from the oppressive yoke of popularity.

MARCH 1, 1971 Radical left-wing organization the Weather Underground sets off a bomb in a men's room in the Capitol, to (officially) protest the invasion of Laos, and to (unofficially) protest the lack of toilet paper in the stall closest to the wall. Afterward, Richard Nixon declared it a "shocking act of violence that will outrage all Americans." This then led to another bombing by the radical organization known as the People for the Correct Usage of Past and Present Tense.

Bills Are Often Violently Watered Down Here.

MARCH 2, 1917
Welcome-o Puerto Rico.

ON THIS DAY IN HISTORY, a month or so after the United States entered into the First World War, President Woodrow Wilson signed the Jones-Shafroth Act, which granted U.S. citizenship to the inhabitants of Puerto Rico. It meant that residents of that island were protected by a Bill of Rights, and even, you know, allowed to join the U.S. Army.

Very few decided to take Wilson up on that last part, so a few weeks later the president decided to sign a compulsory military service act, and eventually over 20,000 Puerto Ricans were sent off to fight.

But hey? Who cares? Puerto Ricans don't mind. We've always had a great relationship. (See yesterday.)

Four Presidents Get Rock Hard.

ON THIS DAY IN HISTORY, the United States Congress authorized the Mount Rushmore National Memorial Commission to start work on the carving of four very white men on one of the Black Hills of South Dakota.

President Calvin Coolidge was the man who signed the commission into being. And despite a lot of "Aheming" on his part, and comments like "I've been told my chin is very statuesque," they wound up going with Washington, Jefferson, Lincoln, and Teddy Roosevelt.

The sculptor was an American named Gutzon Borglum, a renowned artist of his time who was born into a polygamist family and is thought by some to have been a member of the Ku Klux Klan, which is why the original model for the Lincoln relief featured a black eye and the word "Bitch" carved into the forehead.

Work went slowly. Washington's face was completed in 1934, Jefferson's in 1936, Lincoln's in 1937, and, two years after that, Roosevelt's visage was dedicated. There was a movement in Washington, D.C., to get Susan B. Anthony's face added to the memorial, but it was scrapped due to granite's inability to properly convey severe, female "handsomeness."

Borglum died in 1941, and his son Lincoln took over, but eventually the project was halted due to lack of funds. Mount Rushmore is actually an unfinished work. Borglum's original plans depicted Washington carved to the waist, Jefferson holding a quill, and Lincoln with his hand resting on his lapel.

Roosevelt? Well, let's just say that the original design gave viewers an eyeful of that big stick he spoke so softly about.

BULLY MAMMOTH.

MARCH 4, 1829
Old Hickory Splinters Executive Mansion.

ANDREW JACKSON celebrated his inauguration on this day with the brilliant idea of holding an open house at the White House, which soon became known as "the Soiled, Off–White House Reeking of Booze and Smokes."

Over 20,000 people showed up, and proceeded to trash the place. Furniture and dishes were destroyed, and Jackson wound up having to leave the party through a window. (The same window President Clinton would later escape through when he needed to leave for his own late-night parties with "supporters.")

Eventually, servants tried to get people to leave the building by placing tubs of wine and whiskey out on the front lawn, which is the same method George W. Bush would later use when he wanted his daughters to return to the White House.

"Louie, Louie" was playing on a nearby banjo.

Jackson ended up spending the night in a nearby hotel. Yet, for the remainder of his term he continued to hold such public events at the White House, at which the game "Pin the Tail on the Dirty, Live Redskin" was a perennial favorite.

The public continued to get invited to inaugural parties until 1885, when Grover Cleveland instead decided to hold the first-ever inaugural parade. This has been the tradition ever since, although it skipped the William Howard Taft inaugural, when no one was able to find a float that would sufficiently support the president-elect's weight.

This was also blamed on Bucky Dent.

MARCH 5, 1770
The Boston Massacre!!!

ON THIS DAY, the redcoats massacred five people, in the first recorded instance in which the Bostonian's sense of perspective, when it comes to tragedy, seems terribly askew.

For more, see the history of the Boston Red Sox up until 2004.

A Rotten Day to Be a Slave
(Number One in a Series of 365).

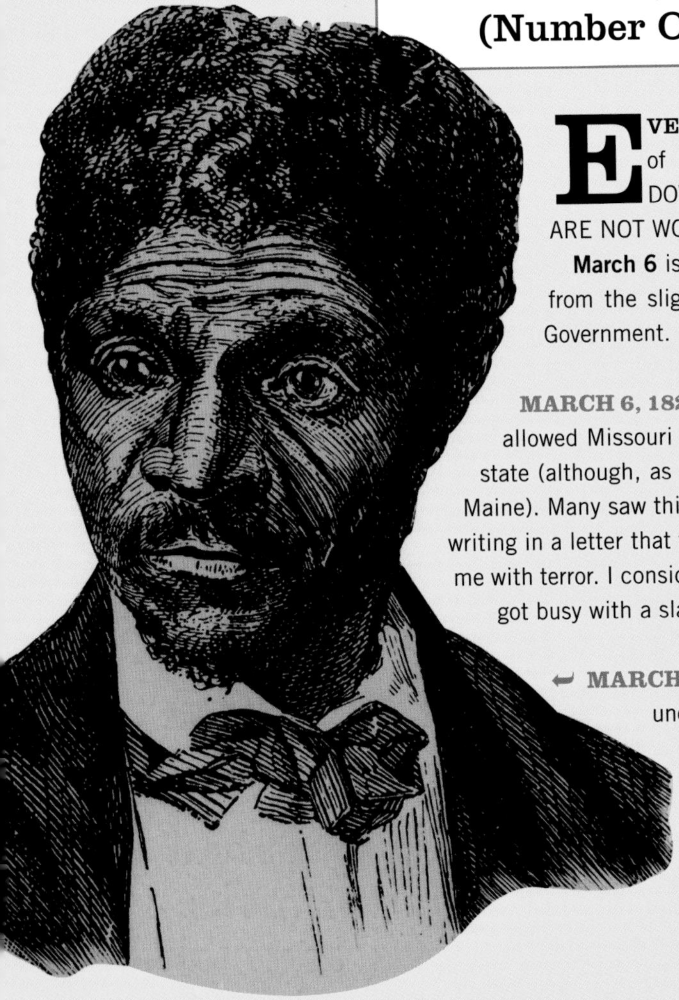

EVERY DAY IS A PRETTY ROTTEN DAY to be a slave. Unless, of course, you consider yourself a "slave," in which case PUT DOWN THIS BOOK, YOU MEALY MOUTHED LITTLE WORM. YOU ARE NOT WORTHY.

March 6 is a day in which our nation's "Peculiar Institution" got a little help from the slightly more Peculiar Institutions known as the Three Branches of Government.

MARCH 6, 1820 President James Monroe signs the Missouri Compromise, which allowed Missouri to enter the Union as a slave state, and Maine to enter as a free state (although, as of this printing, no black person has ever set foot in the state of Maine). Many saw this as the first step on the path to Civil War, with Thomas Jefferson writing in a letter that the Compromise "like a fire bell in the night, awakened and filled me with terror. I considered it at once as the knell of the Union." He then rolled over and got busy with a slave.

MARCH 6, 1857 The Supreme Court rules that the Missouri Compromise is unconstitutional in the case of **SANFORD V. DRED SCOTT**. It also ruled that slaves are not citizens, therefore rejecting Mr. Scott's claims that he deserved his freedom after having lived in several free states before living in Missouri. This marked the last time in history that the Supreme Court handed down a ruling that was not derided in the South as the work of "activist judges."

JUDGED DRED.

Aristotle Dies,
a Sad Day for the Friggin' Obvious.

All men are mortal.
Aristotle was a man.
Aristotle was mortal.

SEE? That is an example of one of Aristotle's "syllogisms," a kind of logical argument in which one proposition (the conclusion) is inferred from two others (the premise/argument) of a certain form, or some shit. Let's use syllogisms to examine other facts about this famous Greek philosopher.

Aristotle was Plato's student.
Plato was a pederast.
Aristotle was kept after class by Plato.

Computers back up data.
Aristotle did not own a computer.
Aristotle did not back up his data, therefore only about one-fifth of his writings survive.

Aristotle's writings on science are largely qualitative, not quantitative.
Mass Historia *author went to an American high school.*
Mass Historia *author does not know the difference between "qualitative" and "quantitative," nor is this an effective syllogism, because* Mass Historia *author attended an American high school.*

MARCH 8
HISTO-POURRI: Imperialist Pigs Edition.

IF YOU ARE AN AGGRESSOR or a victim of foreign aggression, today is a day of some note on your blood-soaked daily calendar. (We're talking metaphorically. Although the One-a-Day Blood-Soaked Cat Calendar is actually pretty blood-soaked.)

MARCH 8, 1906 The Moro Crater Massacre occurs when American troops kill over six hundred men, women, and children—all Muslim Filipinos, or Moros—during the Philippine-American War. Nowadays, depending on the blog, it is either held up as an example of "Why they hate us" or "What we should still be doing to those who hate us."

MARCH 8, 1966 An IRA bomb destroys Nelson's Pillar, the 130-foot stone monument to British Admiral Horatio Lord Nelson, which stood in the middle of O'Connell Street in Dublin. While a symbolic strike against British colonialism, it was also a strike against nearby Dublin residents who relied on it as a "leaning stop" after a long night in the pubs.

MARCH 8, 1983 President Ronald Reagan calls the Soviet Union the "Evil Empire" in a speech to the National Association of Evangelicals, who, for a second, thought the president was referring to them. The phrase was unique in that it pushed political polar opposites Yakov Smirnoff and Rage Against the Machine to greater artistic heights.

Today is also the birthday of teen stars James Van Der Beek and Freddie Prinze Jr. They both rule with an iron hand—over the Kingdom of Dreamy.

Alf Bicknell, the Fifth Beatle, Dies.

ON THIS DAY IN HISTORY, Alf Bicknell, the Beatles' chauffeur for two years in the mid-1960s, dies at age seventy-five. He claims he was the inspiration for "Drive My Car," and the little-known outtake "Pull Over. Ringo's Gonna Puke." He was often called the Fifth Beatle.

And here is a partial list of other people who have been called, or—as in Alf's case—have called themselves, the Fifth Beatle.

- Stu Sutcliffe
- Pete Best
- Brian Epstein
- Sir George Martin
- Billy Preston
- Tony Sheridan
- Jimmy Nichol
- Neil Aspinall
- Mal Evans
- Eric Clapton
- Klaus Vorman
- Yoko Ono
- Jeff Lynne
- Phil Spector
- Wilfrid Brambell
- Murray the K
- Charles Manson
- Maharishi Mahesh Yogi

Note: Please use blank space above to write your own name. Might as well. The qualifications don't seem strict.

Muthas of Inventions: The Telephone.

TWO SIGNIFICANT EVENTS occurred on this day relating to the development of the telephone, which, before the invention of the cell phone, was considered a good thing.

HELLO? TELEPHONE STOCK PHOTOGRAPH COMPANY?

MARCH 10, 1876 Alexander Graham Bell makes the first successful **TELEPHONE CALL**, ←
as he speaks through the device to his assistant in the next room, saying "Mr. Watson, come
here. I want to see you." The assistant, Thomas A. Watson, ran into the room, but was
disappointed to learn that Bell had not been trying to invent the Booty Call.

MARCH 10, 1891 A Topeka, Kansas, undertaker named Almon Strowger patents an early
rotary dial phone device called the Strowger Switch, which lets users dial numbers instead
of going through an operator. Telephone operators immediately get grumpy and uncooperative,
a condition that exists to this day.

MARCH 11, 1931
Happy Birthday, Mr. Murdoch!

ON THIS DAY IN HISTORY, the famous publisher Rupert Murdoch was born
in Australia, peeked into his diaper, and figured there might be some money in
publishing that stuff.

MARCH 12, 1933
Roosevelt's First Fiery Speech.

RADIO FANS GOT A RUSTIC EARFUL on this day in 1933,
when brand-new President Franklin Roosevelt gave his first-
ever fireside chat to the American public, eight days after his
inauguration (which apparently was such a fun party, they let him throw
three more after that).

A journalist dubbed FDR's frequent speeches "fireside chats" because
of their down-to-earth informality. He would start them off with the saluta-
tion "My friends," which was an improvement over his predecessor Herbert
Hoover's radio greeting of "Hello, poor people. Let me guess—you're pissed
off about something?" The listener felt as though he or she were sitting with
FDR in his living room, and if you closed your eyes, you could picture it. Just
down the hall from the president and the First Lady's separate bedrooms.

The subject of his first fireside chat was the planned reopening of the nation's banks
after their forced closure due to massive withdrawals. ("Folksy" on the radio, of course,
doesn't always mean "entertaining." See *A Prairie Home Companion*.)

Roosevelt later branched out into something called the "campfire-side chat," which
covered the story about the murderer on the loose with a hook for a hand, who was last seen
in this area!!!

Also came up with the Fireside Morning Zoo.

William Hershel Discovers Uranus.

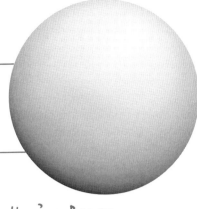

HA!

Did he at least introduce himself first!?

Here's a picture of . . . (snicker).

Albert Einstein Born, Starts Acting Like He's Some Kind of Einstein.

ALBERT EINSTEIN, *Time* magazine's Person of the Century (suck on that, Oprah), was born on this day in Germany. And yes, we all know that he didn't speak until he was three and wasn't much of a reader, but that doesn't mean your kid isn't a dimwit.

Einstein formulated the theories of relativity, and made inestimable contributions to statistical mechanics and quantum theory, and forever changed the way in which mankind views his universe. And by "mankind," we mean "people who know what the hell Einstein was talking about." The rest of us would have preferred he channeled his great intellect into something practical, like a good hangover cure or a jetpack or something.

After his death, large chunks of his brain were divvied up and placed in jars for further study. It was eventually concluded that Einstein's inferior parietal lobe, which is responsible for mathematical thought and visuospatial cognition, was 15 percent wider than normal. The part of the brain that tells you to write a will, requesting that people don't chop up your brain and put it in jars, was a little smaller than it ought to have been.

IN CASE OF

Mass-Energy Equivalence Emergency,

BREAK GLASS

Einstein

MARCH 15, 44 BC
The Ultimate Caesar Cut.

ON THIS DAY IN HISTORY, Julius Caesar, autocrat of Rome (that's *autocrat*—not the place where your grandfather met and seduced your grandmother), was called to hear a petition asking that he hand over power back to the Roman Senate. What he got was a vote of "No Confidence," and he was stabbed by approximately sixty or so men (still fewer than were shooting at JFK in Dealey Plaza), creating a scene slightly less disturbing than the thought of your grandparents doing it in an Automat.

Among the conspirators was Caesar's friend Senator Marcus Junius Brutus. Shakespeare theorized that Caesar's last words might have been "And you Brutus? Then fall Caesar." Although use of the third person may have been the playwright's device to make the title character seem like a pompous dick.

After the assassination, Brutus supposedly ran out onto the street and shouted "People of Rome. We are once again free." At that point, his enemy Marc Antony became the first-ever Italian to mutter "Fuggedaboutit."

The Roman people were outraged and Brutus later committed suicide by running upon his own sword, which was held by a second, although the second's giggling convulsions at the sexual connotations of "running upon a sword" meant that Brutus did not die quickly.

MARCH 16, 1751
James Madison Born!

OUR FOURTH PRESIDENT of the United States, James Madison, was born on this day in Virginia. Let's look at some fun facts about this long-moldering chief executive.

- **Madison was our smallest president, weighing 100 pounds and standing just 5 feet 4 inches tall, meaning he could fit easily into the colon of later president, William Howard Taft.**

- **During the War of 1812, when the British attacked Washington, D.C., MADISON was the first sitting president to find himself under enemy fire. He escaped by hiding inside an early prototype of WILLIAM HOWARD TAFT'S COLON.**

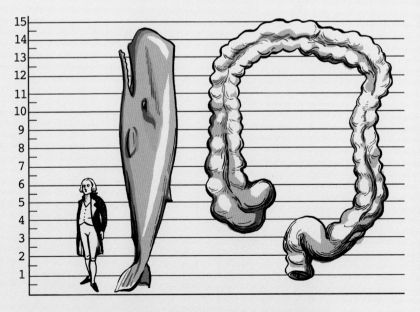

COMPARATIVE SIZES OF PRESIDENT JAMES MADISON AND WILLIAM HOWARD TAFT'S COLON.

ACTUAL SIZE.

More Fun Facts About James Madison:

• His wife, Dolley Madison, was the most gracious and popular hostess the White House had known, especially after her invention of the Saddle-and-Crop-Swap Tea, an early version of the Car Key Party.

• James Madison and George Washington were the only presidents to sign the Constitution. Washington was only allowed to sign because he was kind enough to give Madison a boost up to the signing table, and help him maneuver his Big Boy's Quill.

• Madison was sickly, frail, and our only epileptic president, although William Howard Taft did suffer a seizure after consuming an entire marzipan scale likeness of Madison.

• Madison's face appears on the $200 Series EE Savings Bond. Don't bother checking, yours hasn't matured yet.

• Madison wore a jacket to his inauguration that was woven from the wool of sheep raised at his Virginia plantation. This was disdained by the tastemakers known as *Ye Olde Us Weekly's* Fashion Constables.

LATER, GREEN BEER WAS INVENTED.

MARCH 17, 1762
Erin Go Back to Wherever You Came From, You Loud Bunch of Drunks!

ON THIS DAY IN HISTORY, we remember the first-ever Saint Patrick's Day parade, held in New York City. The parade consisted mostly of Irish soldiers serving in the British Army, who got together for a march that culminated at the Old Saint Patrick's Cathedral on Prince Street—way back before the neighborhood got overrun with wops. (Note: This last sentiment, while harsh, is still a kinder one than most Irish-Americans usually express toward their Italian-American neighbors, and vice versa.)

NOTE: THEY ARE ALL GAY!

The parade has been held in New York every year since then, although it has been marked in recent years by controversy over parade officials' refusal to allow Irish gay and lesbian groups to participate in the march. While this may seem discriminatory, they are mostly prohibited for fear that such celebrations will leave the city's churches dangerously undermanned.

On a related note, **March 17, 1992**, is the day we remember the last New York City Saint Patrick's Day the author of this book can clearly remember.

MARCH 18
HISTO-POURRI: Disaster Edition.

MANY DIFFERENT DEVASTATING EVENTS occurred on this day, perhaps inspired by the man-made carnage of yesterday's Saint Patrick's Day celebrations.

MARCH 18, 1241 The Mongols attack and destroy Krakow, which at the time was commanded by Prince Boleslaw the Shy. The Mongols had an even easier time sacking Warsaw, which was under the rule of King Vladisluw, the One Who Cries After Being Hit in the Nose.

MARCH 18, 1925 The Tri-State Tornado (not the defunct XFL expansion team) tears through Missouri, Illinois, and Indiana, killing seven hundred. At the time, it was considered a freak weather occurrence, although decades later the effects of global warming would make it seem like "sweater weather."

MARCH 18, 1937 The New London School explosion occurs in Texas, killing over three hundred students and teachers. While a gas leak eventually proved to be the culprit, that didn't stop pundits at the time from blaming heavy metal and video games, even though neither had yet been invented.

MARCH 18, 2003 The United States, England, and the rest of the Coalition of the Willing (Tonga) launch the war in Iraq. If you are listening to the book-on-tape version of this tome while flying around in your tornado-proof jetpack in the year 2030, we hope the war is still going well.

MARCH 19, 1928
Broadcasting in Colored!

ON THIS DAY IN 1928, *Amos 'n' Andy* debuted on a radio station in Chicago (and if you already knew this, you are currently watching many bids on eBay to make sure no one snatches away one of your coveted "ironic" Mammy saltshakers). The show was about the exploits of two bumbling, semiliterate black men, who were both portrayed by white comedians (due to a Wayans shortage at the time).

Since the comedy was chock-full of racial stereotypes, it was tremendously successful and ran for over thirty years.

In the late 1930s, the character of Amos retreated into the background somewhat, and more of the story lines revolved around a lodge leader named "Kingfish." The sitting governor of Louisiana, Huey Long, took his nickname from this character, after his other radio-inspired nickname, Fibber McGee, proved to be a liability for a politician—even in Louisiana.

(Note: *Amos 'n' Andy* is not to be confused with the Nicolas Cage/Samuel L. Jackson comedy *Amos 'n' Andrew*, which had nothing to do with the famed radio show, although there are probably more cheap VHS versions of it on eBay than there are Mammy saltshakers.)

ALSO ON THIS DAY:

MARCH 19, 1979 C-SPAN debuts, featuring characters significantly whiter than either Amos or Andy, but just as slow-witted and bumbling.

MARCH 20, 1854
Happy Birthday, GOP!

THE REPUBLICAN PARTY, or Grand Old Party, or Those Fascist Old White Guys (a moniker favored by either kids wearing Anarchy T-shirts, or adult males carrying "murses"), was founded on this day in 1854 in Ripon, Wisconsin. It was launched by former members of the Whigs who wanted to establish a party dedicated to ending the spread of slavery, and because they were tired of people snickering every time they identified themselves as "Whigs."

Chances are, Republicans everywhere will celebrate this momentous event from 1854 by enacting retro legislation that's nostalgic for 1854. (That heavy-handed joke was for the Men with Murses.)

ALSO ON THIS DAY:

MARCH 20, 1852 Harriet Beecher Stowe's abolitionist novel ***UNCLE TOM'S CABIN*** is published. Ironically, "Uncle Tom" is what most people nowadays call blacks who celebrate the birth of the Republican Party. ←

COLLECT ALL TEN UNCLE TOM TRADING CARDS!

LAWYER MARKS.
UNCLE TOM'S CABIN

REJECTED ACRONYMS FOR THE REPUBLICAN PARTY

❶ THE MOP:
(MOSTLY OLD PARTY)
REASON REJECTED:
"MOP" HAD UNPLEASANT, UN-REPUBLICAN OVERTONES OF MANUAL LABOR.

❷ THE FOP:
(FABULOUS OLD PARTY)
REASON REJECTED:
MEMBERS WHO PUSHED FOR IT ALSO SEEMED "SOFT" ON SAME-SEX MARRIAGE

❸ THE GOP
REASON REJECTED:
ACTUALLY, THIS ONE STOOD FOR "GROSS OLD PARTY," DUE TO ABUNDANCE OF WHOOPEE CUSHIONS AT INITIAL ORGANIZING CONVENTION.

62

Kevin Federline
(and Johann Sebastian Bach) born.

BOTH FAMOUS MUSICIANS share a birthday today. Bach was born in 1685, while Federline began to kick it, mortal style, in 1978. This puts "K-Fed" at thirty, so he should probably get serious about career goals and retirement plans, or maybe marry Jessica Simpson or something.

Trying to find some commonality between the two is not easy, although Bach's twenty children seems to be a "spawning benchmark" for the rapper-model-dancer-actor and future star of *I Pass for a Celebrity, Get Me Out of Here*. Also, Bach never had the vision to name one of his twenty kids "Preston Federline," which sounds like the name of a supporting character in *The Music Man*. Let's look at the two side by side.

NEVER DANCED WITH A PIMP

BACH: Held the position as organist in Arnstadt, Germany, from 1703 to 1707.
FEDERLINE: First held his organ while dancing on LFO tour in 1999.

B: Over a nine-year period (1711–1720), he composed the Brandenburg Concertos.
F: Between two cigarette breaks, he composed and recorded "Dance with a Pimp."

B: Imprisoned for a month in 1717 by Duke Wilhelm, who wanted to prevent him from accepting a position at Prince Leopold's court in Anhalt-Köthen.
F: Surprisingly, the self-styled "Pimp" of "Dancing with a Pimp" and third-person balladeer of "America's Most Hated" has yet to do jail time. In this case, Bach is significantly more "hard-core."

B: Was vision-impaired in later life.
F: Fondness for shark-skin jackets coupled with sweatpants suggests some sort of impairment, vision or otherwise.

First Motion Picture Shown, First Time Word "Focus" Shouted at Hapless Projectionist.

ON THIS DAY IN HISTORY, two French brothers named Louis and Auguste Lumière give the first public demonstration of the motion picture. They seemed destined to work in film—since their last names mean "light" in French—although not as destined as their contemporaries Jean Paul and Louis Odeur de Maîs Eclaté, whose last name means "Popcorn Smell."

The brothers' invention, the cinematograph, was a device that would shoot, process, and project a film. (A soup-to-nuts filmmaking device, the cinematograph was like the Apple Computer, except people using it didn't feel the need to lay down a Smashmouth tune under every birthday party scene.)

The film they showed, at Paris's Salon Indien du Grand Café (which was later carved up into a dozen smaller, less charming Indien du Grand Cafés), was a forty-six-second-long shot of workers leaving their factory. It was called *La Sortie de l'Usine Lumière à Lyon,* or *Workers Leaving the Lumière Factory.* Exciting. Apparently "Lights" and "Camera" were within the reach of the brothers, while "Action" proved a tougher nut to crack.

The brothers eventually moved onto color film processing, not believing that there was much future in their invention. Although the cool reaction to their film's sequel, *Workers Leaving the Lumière Factory II: Electric Boogaloo,* probably had some hand in their decision.

OK DOB.

"**OK.**" It's a term we use to express that we are . . . OK with something. No other abbreviation so thrillingly paints a picture of at least minimal agreement. And on this day in 1839 a newspaper editor in Boston decided that it was "OK" to run "OK," marking the first recorded appearance of the word.

It appeared in the *Boston Morning Post* in this passage: "The Chairman of the Committee on Charity Lecture Bells, is one of the deputation, and perhaps if he should return to Boston, via Providence, he of the *Journal*, and his train-band, would have his 'contribution box,' et ceteras, o.k.—oll korrect—and cause the corks to fly, like sparks, upward." Seriously, the paper actually had an editor.

VAN BUREN: NOT "OK" WITH HAIR PRODUCT.

The word's origin is still somewhat mysterious. Some say that "oll korrect" was a nod to Andrew Jackson, who once mortally wounded a library copy of a *Merriam-Webster Dictionary* in a duel. The Whigs, desperate to tie their unthrilling candidate Martin Van Buren to the more exciting Jackson, equated "OK" with Van Buren's nickname "Old Kinderhook." A more successful strategy than the one employed four years later, which tried to convince voters that Van Buren's nickname actually stood for "Omnipotent Kocksman."

Note: Some believe that OK is derived from the Choctaw word "okeh." Jackson probably heard "It is not okeh that you are killing us and relocating us, White Man" on numerous occasions.

MARCH 24, 1603
The Death of Elizabeth I.

ON THIS DAY IN 1603, Queen Elizabeth I died at age sixty-nine, after a forty-four-year rule in which she heightened England's power and influence across the globe, oversaw and encouraged a renaissance in the arts, and united warring religious factions within the country. All in all, she is considered to have been one of the most powerful and effective monarchs in world history.

Yet somehow, the pasty virgin queen wasn't able to turn all that power into a little "action." Her descendants would not make the same mistake.

MARCH 25
Flaming Heap of HISTO-POURRI.

ON THIS DAY IN HISTORY, tragic and not-so-tragic things happened with fire, explosions, and poetic descents into hell. Keep an extinguisher or bucket of sand at the ready.

MARCH 25, 1300 This is the day that Dante descended into hell in his poem, the *Inferno*. (Note: Please go look up the meaning of hendecasyllable while the author finishes reading *The Divine Comedy* so that he can write a proper joke about it.)

MARCH 25, 1865 The Claywater Meteorite explodes before hitting the earth just above Vernon County, Wisconsin. The meteorite was mostly rock, containing olivine, enstatite, and a variety of Fe-Ni alloys. Anyone who already knows these facts lives in their own personal inferno that is less poetic but more *Star Trek-y*.

THE MINE ISN'T THAT TINY, HE'S THIRTY FEET TALL!

MARCH 25, 1911 A fire breaks out in New York's Triangle Shirtwaist Factory, killing 145 immigrant girls who had been locked inside. The tragedy helped solidify the labor movement in America, which is right now in worse shape than the Triangle Shirtwaist Factory was on March 26, 1911.

MARCH 25, 1947 A **COAL MINE EXPLODES** in Centralia, Illinois, killing 111 miners. Afterward, the surviving miners got six days off. Again—thank you, American Labor Movement.

MARCH 25, 1990 On the seventy-ninth anniversary of New York's Triangle Shirtwaist fire, the Happy Land Social Club fire occurs in the Bronx, as a jilted boyfriend sets the only staircase at the after-hours club ablaze, killing eighty-seven people, mostly immigrants. Seriously, any and all immigrants in crowded places in New York on this day need to make note of the nearest possible exit.

MARCH 26, 1920
Paradise Found at Your Local Bookstore.

ON THIS DAY IN HISTORY, F. Scott Fitzgerald's first novel *This Side of Paradise* was published. It proves to be a huge success. To celebrate, someone suggests that Fitzgerald and his wife have a couple drinks. Probably not the best idea.

MARCH 27
HISTO-POURRI: Inventions Edition.

TODAY IS A GOOD DAY for inventors, patenters, and wine snobs who won't drink anything with a screw cap and who like peeing standing up. Read on.

MARCH 27, 1848 John Parker Paynard received a patent for medicated adhesive plaster, used to treat corns, bunions, and sores. John Parker Paynard was a man who aimed high.

MARCH 27, 1849 Joseph Couch patents a steam-powered percussion rock drill, which is a mining tool, not an instrument used by progressive rock drummers to create "rhythm pulses."

MARCH 27, 1855 Canadian Abraham Gesner patents coal oil, or kerosene. Kerosene can now be found in a dusty plastic bottle usually stored under most kitchen sinks, left over from the time someone gave the homeowner a rustic hurricane lamp that stopped being used when the wick ran down.

MARCH 27, 1860 New Yorker M. L. Byrn patents what his paperwork described as a "covered gimlet screw with a 'T' handle," later known as a corkscrew. Nowadays, these are often lost, and never where one needs it. (Look behind the plastic bottle of kerosene!)

MARCH 27, 1866 Andrew Rankin patents his designs for the **URINAL**. Pervs across the world are grateful his designs offered no indication in regards to proper distance *between* urinals.

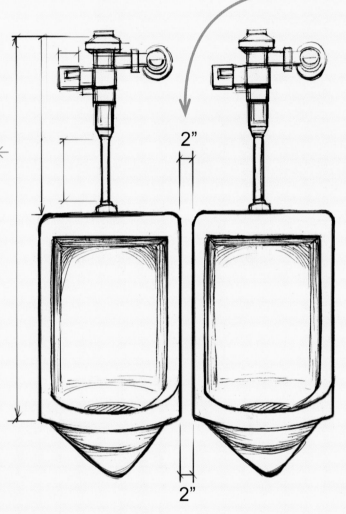

THIS WAS SUPPOSED TO BE TWO FEET!

2"

2"

MARCH 28, 1979
Three Mile Island Goes Completely Chernobyl.

ON THIS DAY IN HISTORY, everybody stopped snickering at the "No Nukes" hippies when the Three Mile Island nuclear generating station in Harrisburg, Pennsylvania, suffered a partial-core meltdown. It is still the largest nuclear power plant accident in U.S. history, unless by the time of this printing some terrorist finally did something devious to the Indian Point power plant, wisely situated right outside the desolate wilderness of New York City.

There is some debate about adverse health effects on the nearly 30,000 people within the five-mile radius of the accident. But scientists did discover elevated levels of radioactive iodine in the thyroid glands of nearby meadow voles. It was easy to study these thyroids since they were located on the outside of the voles' bodies. And it should also be noted that some of these voles previously had been human.

The accident occurred just a few days before the release of the Jane Fonda film *The China Syndrome*, about the dangers of nuclear power. It gained the movie more attention than the other toxic publicity stunt, in which costar Wilford Brimley participated in an all-you-can-eat atomic wings competition in Fresno, California. (Although that event was much more dangerous to the 30,000 people living within a five-mile radius after Brimley's core began to melt.)

DuH DuH DuH
DeeeAD!

MARCH 29

Beethoven Debuts, Gives Farewell Performance.

TODAY IS A DAY OF SOME SIGNIFICANCE to fans of the music of Ludwig van Beethoven, who perhaps would not be as well known today if Charles Schulz had decided that "Haydn" had a funnier ring to it. March 29 was the date when the famed pianist/composer made his first public appearance and his last public appearance. Although during his final appearance he did not hear the applause, and it wasn't because of his deafness.

MARCH 29, 1795 The twenty-four-year-old Beethoven made his debut as a pianist on this day in Vienna. Since he was not well known as a composer, the performance was mostly covers, which was fine because it would be 180 years before "Piano Man" or "Music Box Dancer" would totally ruin such recitals.

MARCH 29, 1827 Nearly 20,000 people attended the great composer's burial, also in Vienna. One person in the crowd may have cracked a joke about Beethoven "de-composing." And that was the first and only time the joke would ever merit a laugh, or be told by someone who was not a high school band teacher.

MARCH 30

HISTO-POURRI: Mapmaking Edition.

TODAY IS ANOTHER DAY that saw some border shifts in the map of the world, or in this case, the United States, which—as we all know—is the world. Got a problem with that? Then go get a map, find Russia, and go back to it.

⬅ **MARCH 30, 1822** The areas known as east Florida and west Florida are merged and become the geographic double-wide known as the **FLORIDA TERRITORY**, because "Whitetrashinsula" was deemed too hard to pronounce. The following year, most of Florida's current residents were born.

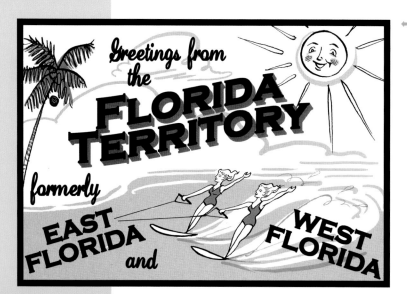

Greetings from the **FLORIDA TERRITORY** formerly **EAST FLORIDA** and **WEST FLORIDA**

MARCH 30, 1870 Texas is readmitted to the Union after having seceded during the Civil War. Their happiness to be rejoined with the United States lasts for about two hours, before the first dumbass with a ten-gallon hat attaches a "Don't Mess with Texas" sign to the back of a horse.

MARCH 30, 1870 Secretary of State William Seward agrees to purchase Alaska for $7.2 million from Russia. Critics attack the vast amount of money spent on the frozen tundra as "Seward's Folly," although many close to the sixty-nine-year-old man knew the real Seward's Folly was a young woman named Suki who made him feel young again, damnit. The following year, current Alaskan Senator Ted Stevens was born.

MARCH 31, 1889
Eiffel Offers Up Eyeful.

ON THIS DAY IN HISTORY, the French obtained a spectacular new way to look down on everyone, as the Eiffel Tower opened to the public in 1889. It was constructed to celebrate the Centennial of the French Revolution, and is more romantic than the other revolution-themed tourist trap, the Marie Antoinette Blood Flume.

When it opened, it replaced the Washington Monument as the world's tallest structure, although the Washington Monument still holds the title of Tallest Structure in Dullest City. The tower was supposed to be temporary, and was to be dismantled in 1909, but the French decided that removing such a notable beacon might make the city harder to find when neighboring countries wanted to easily invade them.

Made from over 18,000 separate pieces held together by 2.5 million rivets, Gustave Eiffel's masterpiece was loathed by writer Guy de Maupassant, who often ate at a restaurant at the tower because it was the one place in Paris that didn't have a view of the structure.

(Note: *Mass Historia* author would have gladly enjoyed a seat somewhere in his seventh-grade English class where he did not have to cast his gaze upon de Maupassant's "The Necklace." No such luck.)

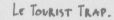

LE TOURIST TRAP.

April

APRIL 1

APRIL 1

April Fool's Day.

TODAY IS APRIL FOOL'S DAY, and by now, people across the country are breathless with laughter at the gag pulled by their favorite morning radio team, in which they announced the death of someone famous who had not died. Yet even before the invention of morning radio, plenty of unfunny stuff happened on April 1.

GAG
OVERBOARD!

APRIL 1, 1873 White Star steamer the RMS *Atlantic* sinks off the coast of Nova Scotia, killing 546. All the dead were fearful of sitting down in lifeboats, after a daylong shipboard scourge of April Fool's whoopee cushion pranks.

APRIL 1, 1970 Phil Spector finishes syrupy orchestral overdubs on Beatles album *Let It Be* as an April Fool's joke. Unfortunately, the record company didn't "get it" and released it as it was.

APRIL 1, 1976 Apple Computer is founded. Author currently writing this book on a $1,500 Apple MacBook, which keeps playing the hilarious joke of shutting off at random times before author hits "save."

APRIL 1, 1980 Actress, singer, and model Bijou Phillips is born. (Note: Author attempted to do search on Web to research her appearance in *Playboy* in April of 2000, but his computer shut off again for no reason. Very funny.)

APRIL 1, 2004 First same-sex marriage becomes official in Quebec. Thought to be an April Fool's joke, until Quebec natives remember that they have no sense of humor about anything.

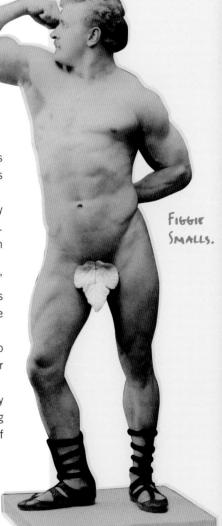

FIGGIE SMALLS.

APRIL 2, 1867

Eugen Sandow Born, Ushers in (Pumping) Iron Age.

YOU MIGHT BE OVERWEIGHT NOW, but at one time a physique like yours was considered robust. That all came to an end with the birth of Eugen Sandow, who is often referred to as the Father of Modern Bodybuilding.

As a boy, Sandow was a great admirer of Greek and Roman statuary, and he would literally measure marble statues in museums and try to get his physique to match the measurements. Sadly, he didn't need to work that hard to physically match the statues' traditionally smallish and hairless genitals.

Eventually, Sandow went to work doing something called "muscle display performances" for showman Florenz Ziegfeld, which would cool down audiences still reeling from Ziegfeld's other showstopper, *Women Walking Down Staircases*. (Let's all stop complaining about the garbage on television now.)

Sandow became Ziegfeld's first big star, and women would pay him for the opportunity to feel his muscles backstage after the show. (Women of limited means just had to settle for groping the veined and bulging snout of the other Ziegfeld headliner, W. C. Fields.)

Sandow eventually authored five books about bodybuilding (twice the number of books read by most future bodybuilders) and later organized the first-ever bodybuilding contest in 1901. Among the judges was Sir Arthur Conan Doyle, whose interest in "physical culture" later manifested itself in the curious Sherlock Holmes short story "The Adventure of the Dancing (and Oiled) Men."

APRIL 3

Western Roundup, Partner. Yeee-Hah!

EVERYONE LOVES THE MYSTIQUE AND MAGIC of the American West (and by "everyone," we mean Americans over sixty, foreigners, and 1950s schoolkids). So strap on your six-shooter and let's saddle up for an exploration of all the neat cowboy stuff that took place on this day in history.

APRIL 3, 1860 The first successful run of the Pony Express kicked off on this day, starting in dazzling St. Joseph, Missouri, and winding up in exciting Sacramento, California, which explained the Pony Express's initial slogan, "From ZZZ to Shining ZZZZZZZZZ."

APRIL 3, 1882 Again in St. Joseph, Missouri, the coward Robert Ford shot Jesse James, like a coward, in the back. In fairness to Ford, had he shot him in the front, the bullet could have ricocheted off one of James's many Medals of Valor awarded for killing unarmed bank cashiers.

APRIL 3, 1904 Famous actor and Western icon Iron Eyes Cody was born. He's now remembered as the "Crying Indian" from the popular Keep America Beautiful PSAs of the 1970s. Unfortunately, his real name was Espera DeCorti and his parents were Sicilian immigrants. This was obvious to anyone who saw the sequels to the Crying Indian commercials, in which Iron Eyes Cody submitted a sealed bid to have trash picked up by his cousin Iron Eyes Rocco's sanitation firm.

How Now, Exploited Cow?

APRIL 4, 1841

William Henry Harrison—Record Breaker!

ON THIS DAY IN 1841, President William Henry Harrison set out to break as many records as possible. Not content with holding the record for "Oldest Person Ever Elected to the Presidency," the overachieving Harrison then topped himself by dying in order to hold the record for "Shortest Time Spent in Office."

Just thirty days earlier, the man had delivered—in the pouring rain—the longest inaugural address in history. It was over 8,000 words and took over two hours to read. (Less time than it took the current president to famously read *My Pet Goat*.)

Also Our "Most Clefted -Chinned President."

Harrison later caught a cold, enabling himself to take the record for "Most Tissues Used in White House" (later broken by bachelor President James Buchanan), and was soon terribly ill. While trying to recover, he was overwhelmed by visits from people hoping to get themselves jobs within the administration—including several Japanese statesmen who challenged him to break their hot-dog eating record. He died at age 68.

Vice President John Tyler then became the "First Vice President to Take Over for a Dead President," although as a father of fifteen children, the most persistent "Broken Record" in his house was his wife's repeated cries of "C'mon. Tie a knot in it already, Tyler."

APRIL 5
HISTO-POURRI: Judgment Day!

NO, **NO,** calm down, Rapture fans. April 5 is not the day you will be judged by the Lord. Everyone knows that's November 2. (You didn't know? Then put down this book and drop to your knees, sinner.) **April 5**, however, is a day when many famous people throughout history wound up on the wrong side of the law.

APRIL 5, 1895 OSCAR WILDE loses libel suit against John Sholto Douglass, the Marquess of Queensberry, who had accused the Irish playwright of "posing as a sodomite." (Wilde found fault with the "posing" suggestion.) Unfortunately, the jury assumed that anyone with "Queensberry" and "Marquess" in his job description probably knew what he was talking about. ←

SODOMY FOR DUMMIES

POSING AS A RELAXED SODOMITE.

APRIL 5, 1951 American Communists Ethel and Julius Rosenberg are sentenced to death for handing over atomic secrets to the Soviets, who probably would have gotten them anyway. It later takes Ethel about three minutes to die in the electric chair, more time than it takes to find plans for an atomic bomb on Google.

APRIL 5, 1996 Pop culture train wreck John Wayne Bobbitt, whose penis was lopped off by wife Lorena in 1989 and then later reattached, is sentenced to 120 days of house arrest in Las Vegas for beating up his girlfriend. By this time, the mutilated Bobbitt has segued into a career in pornography, appealing to fans who felt Ron Jeremy was too easy on the eyes.

Napoleon Abdicates, Stepping Down Causes Him to Appear Shorter.

ON THIS DAY IN HISTORY, Napoleon Bonaparte, or Napoleon I, Emperor of France, King of Italy, Mediator of the Swiss Confederation, and Protector of the Confederation of the Rhine (he collected titles to later stack and stand upon), abdicated his throne amid mounting losses during the War of the Sixth Coalition. The sixth coalition included the United Kingdom, Russia, Sweden, Austria, Spain, and Prussia. (Sometimes called the Fifth Coalition because, even then, people thought "Prussia" was just a typo.)

At first, Napoleon abdicated and left the throne to his son, Napoleon II, who was only three years old but already considerably taller than his father. The Allies at first warmed to the idea, but the toddler's prompt Edict of Cooties issued against all of Spain proved untenable.

The ex-emperor was promptly banished to Elba, a small island off the coast of Italy, although "small" was always relative to the tiny general. He was made Emperor of Elba (to be able to keep his health insurance in the Emperors Union) and given a guard of six hundred men, which turned the island into a *Festival de Saucisson*.

He escaped a year later, hid himself in a lady's snuffbox, assembled an army, but was later defeated at Waterloo, which has come to be known as his "Waterloo."

A Day of Good News, Bad News.

APRIL 7, 1920 **The good news?** Ravi Shankar, the acclaimed Indian sitar player, is born. He is perhaps best known for his 1960s association with Beatle George Harrison, aka "the Quiet One Easily Suckered into All that Hippy Stuff." He is also the father of Norah Jones, whose first album people really need to stop playing at dinner parties. **The bad news?** During the height of his fame, hippy fans subsequently get stoned and then try to dance to his sitar playing. Not a pretty sight.

APRIL 7, 1927 **The good news?** The first-ever long-distance television broadcast occurs, as images of then–Commerce Secretary Herbert Hoover are beamed from Washington, D.C., to New York City. Dullness of broadcast heavily influences later C-SPAN coverage. **The bad news?** Since the camera always puts on ten pounds, Hoover is struck with manorexia, leaving him unable to feel empathy for people on bread lines during upcoming Depression.

APRIL 7, 1940 **The good news?** Author and educator Booker T. Washington—not the guy who played keyboards on that *Green Onions* song—becomes the first African-American to be depicted on a postage stamp. **The bad news?** Several Southern women seen licking the stamp are later tried for violating miscegenation laws.

SITAR FUN FACT:
PAUL YOUNG'S HIT SINGLE "EVERY TIME YOU GO AWAY" FEATURED AN ELECTRIC SITAR, IN WHAT MANY CLAIM WAS AN EFFORT TO CREATE A TUNE LESS FUNKY THAN ANYTHING BY RAVI SHANKAR.

APRIL 7, 1964 **The good news?** Australian actor Russell Crowe punches his way out of the womb, which was a less confining environment than his snug *Master and Commander* pirate outfit. **The bad news?** Baby must wait a full twelve months before he grows a functional set of "Barfight Biting Teeth."

APRIL 7, 1992 **The good news?** Republika Srpska announces its independence from, apparently, vowels. It has something or other to do with Bosnia. **The bad news?** As of 2008, Republika Srpska still unable to convince world that they aren't a fictional "gag" nation.

Handy Tip:
How to Avoid a Fight with Russell Crowe: Avoid Russell Crowe.

APRIL 8, 1986
Feeling Elected, Punk?

CALIFORNIANS LOVE ELECTING ACTORS (Ronald Reagan) and nonactors who've been in films (Arnold Schwarzenegger) to office. This fine tradition continued on April 8, 1986, when actor, director, and dried-applehead-doll Clint Eastwood was elected mayor of Carmel-by-the-Sea (a town that will change its name to Carmel-under-the-Sea when the long-awaited "Big One" hits).

SOME CLINT EASTWOOD FUN FACTS

- Clint is a descendant of Plymouth Colony governor William Bradford, whose threat "How many bullets did I shoot, punk?" was ineffective in the days of single-shot, front-loading muskets.

- Clint got his big break on the television series *Rawhide*. (There's a bar in New York's Chelsea neighborhood called Rawhide. If one goes in and declares to the other gentleman patrons that he is a big Clint Eastwood fan, he will be bought a drink.)

- Clint didn't become a movie star until he landed in Sergio Leone's spaghetti westerns. To learn more about these movies, go study the posters on the dorm-room wall of the film student who never gets any.

- Despite starring in so many westerns, Clint is allergic to horses.

- Despite starring in so many films with the actor, Clint is allergic to Morgan Freeman.

- In 1971, Clint played the title role in *Dirty Harry*. His costar was a giant .44 magnum. And yes, Mr. Film Student with the *Fistful of Dollars* Poster on His Wall, we all know what that's supposed to represent.

- One of Clint's biggest hits was the comedy *Every Which Way But Loose*. He costarred with an orangutan named Clyde, who died in the late 1990s (autoerotic asphyxiation).

- If you leave Clint in a glass of water overnight, he will grow to over fifteen times his normal size!

- The seventy-eight-year-old Clint can beat up the author of this book.

- Clint supports gay marriage and his name is an anagram for "Old West Action." (Bring up these factoids when at the bar Rawhide. The drinks will keep rollin', rollin', rollin' in.)

MILLION DOLLAR CRAGGY.

APRIL 9, 1939

APRIL 9, 1939

Marian Anderson Performs on Washington Mall, Nearby White House Feels Very "White."

THE CITY OF WASHINGTON, D.C., was the site of an important milestone in the destruction of our nation's racial barriers on this day in 1939. (And no, the event did not take place inside any of those Washington, D.C., buildings where they make anti-segregation laws and stuff. Don't be naive.) African-American contralto Marian Anderson performed a concert on the mall for 75,000 people.

Anderson had been banned from performing at Constitution Hall, which was owned by the Daughters of the American Revolution, whose collections of doilies, tea cozies, and floral throw pillows probably made for pretty crappy acoustics anyway.

Many were outraged, and First Lady Eleanor Roosevelt resigned from the DAR, which was planning to boot her anyway for not meeting the genetic requirements of a "daughter."

Eventually, Secretary of the Interior Harold Ickes gave the OK for a free concert on the steps of the Lincoln Memorial, a place where nowadays color-mixing is musically celebrated with Lee Greenwood's ugly concert wardrobe.

Anderson wowed the crowd with a stirring rendition of "America (My Country, 'Tis of Thee)," paving the way for Aretha Franklin to later do fifteen-minute versions of the song at every Republican fund-raising event providing carfare and lunch.

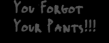

APRIL 10, 1877

First Human Cannonball Debuts in England. What a Blast!*

CANNONS were always serious business in England, unless you were strapping mutinous Indians to the front of them and blowing them to bits just for fun. But on this night in 1877, an acrobat at the Royal Aquarium amazed onlookers with the first-ever display of a human cannonball. It was such a magic moment that the next comedy act, "Mutinous Indian Tied to Front of Cannon and Blown to Pieces," fell a little flat.

*ACTUALLY, THE HUMAN CANNONBALL WAS PROPELLED BY ELASTIC STRAPS WITHOUT THE NOW-FAMILIAR USE OF FIRE-WORKS TO SIMULATE A BLAST. SO IT WAS A "BLAST" IN THAT IT WAS "FUN." WE WILL TRY TO MAKE UP FOR THE PUN-DEFICIT DISPLAYED HERE IN OTHER PORTIONS OF THIS BOOK.

The man who invented the human cannonball was a Canadian named William Hunt, who performed under the name the Great Farini. (He chose the Italian name because his original moniker, "The Magic Hunt," when said too quickly, made people think his act involved a woman shooting items from her privates.)

Farini's "cannonball" was a performer with the exotic name Zazel, and if you Google that name, you will get many hits for a 1997 pornographic film called *Zazel: the Scent of Love*. Hey, where are you going?

Zazel was fourteen-year-old acrobat Rosa Richter, and in the days of child labor, being shot from a cannon was a cushy gig. Even better, since she was performing at an aquarium, the young girl was rewarded with a large bucket of herring after performing her feat.

APRIL 11, 1979
Dada Says Bye-Bye!

AFTER EIGHT YEARS as dictator of Uganda, General Idi Amin Dada packed up a doggie bag of enemy flesh, and ran away from his ravaged nation on this day in 1979. His work was considered unfinished by many since there was a rumor that one or two Ugandans were still left breathing.

Amin was one of those colorful characters that the West liked to ridicule, until 2001 when such characters started plying their trade where Westerners live. In addition to all the genocide, Amin threw every Asian out of the country, which destroyed the financial sector and killed the nation's ability to compete on the global Spelling Bee scene.

After Tanzanian forces invaded Uganda, Amin fled to Libya, then Iraq, and finally settled in Saudi Arabia, doing a Goldilocks porridge-tasting tour of evil empires. He lived for another twenty-five years, courtesy of a stipend from the Saudi government that included a mansion, luxury cars, horses, and servants. To be fair, "one mansion" is Saudi Arabian for "brown-bagging it."

Some say the Saudis sheltered the Muslim tyrant because he was harming the world's image of Islam, which is, of course, the job of Saudi Arabia.

OK. ENOUGH OF CANNIBAL AFRICAN DICTATORS. LET'S CELEBRATE SOME NICER EVENTS ASSOCIATED WITH APRIL 11:

APRIL 11, 1905 Albert Einstein, not a cannibal, reveals theory of relativity.

APRIL 11, 1966 British pop star Lisa Stansfield is born. Known for big 1989 hit "All Around the World." Killed no Africans, not a cannibal (not intentionally).

APRIL 11, 1987 British pop star Joss Stone born. Like Stansfield, never killed an African. (Cannibal, though.)

Got Lazy When Writing April 12 Entry.

Mass Historia Author Born.

ON THIS DAY IN HISTORY in the city of New York, the author of *Mass Historia*, Chris Regan, was born to Michael and Rita Regan, parents who always dreamed their child would grow up and spend many, many months writing a comedy book about obscure events in history.

Regan later grew up and enjoyed a varied career as a writer for Nickelodeon game shows, a stand-up comedian, an actor in television commercials and Korean action TV miniseries, and a writer on *The Daily Show with Jon Stewart*, for which he won five Emmy Awards and two Peabodys over seven seasons. He was a coauthor of the best-selling *America: the Book*, and is currently a writer on Fox's *Talkshow with Spike Feresten*.

Regan is married to a wonderful woman named Susannah Keagle and is coguardian to a cat named Dash. He divides his time between New York City, Los Angeles, and a converted 1861 one-room schoolhouse in Sullivan County, New York, where one hopes that history was taught with a bit more respect and accuracy, and fewer jokes about Chester Alan Arthur's facial hair.

OTHER LESS NOTABLE EVENTS THAT OCCURED ON THIS GLORIOUS DAY:

APRIL 12, 467 AD Anthemius becomes emperor of the Western Roman Empire. Anthe-who? Whatever. He never wrote a book.

APRIL 12, 1945 President Franklin Delano Roosevelt dies. Lifted his nation out of the Great Depression and saw it through a terrible war. Only gaping hole on resume was lack of book-writing.

A Great Day for Massacres.

WHILE APRIL 12 WAS A TRIUMPH on all levels, April 13 is a multipronged hot fork in the ass of all that is good. Lots of people got killed today, and they got killed in bulk.

APRIL 13, 1873 The Colfax massacre occurs in Louisiana, as members of the White League (not a baseball team) clash with the state's nearly all-black militia (none of whom would have been allowed on a baseball league at the time), killing one hundred. Fortunately, shoddy treatment of blacks in the state ends shortly thereafter forever.

APRIL 13, 1919 The Amritsar massacre occurs in India, as British soldiers open fire on scores of unarmed men, women, and children, killing over 1,000. (Note: This massacre was not meant as an observance of the Colfax massacre—just a happy coincidence.)

APRIL 13, 1943 Germans discover a mass grave filled with Polish prisoners of war killed during the 1940 Soviet-led Katyn Forest massacre. The Soviets killed about 28,000. Germans realize they need to step up their A-game.

APRIL 13, 1945 With the war winding down, Nazi forces in the German town of Gardelegen try to keep the buzz going and massacre over 1,000 POWs, and any future chance of Gardelegen becoming a tourist hot spot.

APRIL 13, 1984 Baseball great Pete Rose brutally slammed his 4,000 hit, a continued massacre of the spirits of countless pitchers. Unfortunately, his later indiscretions mean that nowadays he can't even participate in games played by the White League.

APRIL 14, 1912
Most Romantic Loss of Life Ever!

O N THIS DAY IN HISTORY, on what has been called "A Night to Remember" (no, not your prom), the RMS *Titanic* smacked into an iceberg in the North Atlantic, and the giant ship dipped below the waves about three hours later, less time than it takes to watch the movie *Titanic*, but more time than it takes for you to realize that the movie *Titanic* is kind of sucky.

Since the ship had been considered "Unsinkable," the need for lifeboats was considered "Unnecessaryable," and more than 1,500 passengers soon found themselves "Unfloatable." Of the seven hundred people who survived, many were wealthy women and children and . . . wealthy men willing to dress themselves up as wealthy women and children.

One of the many dramatic memories of that evening was the sound of a string quartet onboard the ship as it was sinking, playing "Nearer My God to Thee" to keep the passengers calm. Unfortunately, the ship went down before they dusted off the other cruise ship favorite, "Hot Hot Hot," which was intended to get the doomed passengers pumped.

OTHER FAMOUSLY SUCKY THINGS THAT OCCURED ON APRIL 14 THAT HAVE YET TO BE MEMORIALIZED IN SONG BY CELINE DION:

APRIL 14, 1846 The Donner Party starts their voyage in Springfield, Illinois. Not enough lunches are packed.

APRIL 14, 1865 President Abraham Lincoln gets shot in the head by John Wilkes Booth while watching a play in Washington, D.C. Republicans from then on suspicious of the arts.

APRIL 15, 1865

President Abraham Lincoln's Dream Comes True.

ABE LINCOLN once described a dream in which he stood in a crowd of people as a funeral train went by. One of the weeping mourners turned to Lincoln and said, "The president has been shot, and he has died." Then the president found himself nude while addressing cabinet members Horatio King and William P. Fessenden. Only the first part of the dream came true, although some biographers suggest Lincoln might not have been opposed to the latter half of the dream/fantasy occurring.

Lincoln had been shot the evening before while watching the comic play, *Our American Cousin*. His assassin, John Wilkes Booth, was familiar with the play (like most struggling actors, he was a notorious "second-acter") and waited for an audience laugh that would cover the sound of his gunshot.

The punchline was "Well, I guess I know enough to turn you inside out, old gal—you sock-dologizing old man-trap..." The hilarity of this line soon led to the invention of the phrase "You had to be there."

Lincoln's body was carried across the street to a boarding house, and he was attended to by Dr. Charles Leale. Upon Lincoln's death, Leale said, "Now he belongs to the Ages," although some on hand claim he said, "Now he belongs to the angels." And by "some," we mean a middle-aged divorcee boarding house resident who wore "angel" pins on all her sweaters, had angel pictures all over her walls, and owned too many cats.

APRIL 16, 1943

LSD First Ingested, Word "Groovy" Invented Shortly Thereafter.

ON THIS DAY IN TRIPSTORY, Dr. Albert Hoffman, a Swiss chemist, accidentally consumed LSD-25, a synthetic drug he had invented a few years earlier while studying medically beneficial ergot alkaloid derivatives (as if that wasn't enough of a natural high).

Hoffman bicycled home and lay down, probably on an uncomfortable, Swiss sleek-looking bed and he recounted the experience in his journal:

At home I lay down and sank into a not unpleasant, intoxicated-like condition characterized by an extremely stimulated imagination. I perceived an uninterrupted stream of fantastic pictures. Holy Crap my hands are gigantic. why do they call it a pen anyway have you ever really felt paper I'm gonna put the pen down and feel the paper man I'm gonna lick it . . .

HOFFMAN'S BIKE "TRIP" WAS A PRETTY LONG ONE.

Hoffman felt the drug had promise as a psychotherapy tool, although he did cop to a down-side after giving a listen to the Bill Wyman tracks on *Their Satanic Majesties Request*.

April 16 is also the birthday of basketball great Kareem Abdul Jabbar, who wrote in his 1984 autobiography *Giant Steps* that he once experimented with acid. Unfortunately, the trip went bad when Jabbar became convinced he could fly and leapt off himself.

APRIL 17, 1964
The Mock Heard 'Round the World.

ON THIS DAY IN HISTORY, thirty-nine-year-old Jerrie Mock, wearing a skirt and high heels, became the first woman to fly solo around the world in a Cessna 180. It took her twenty-nine days with twenty-one stopovers (they ALWAYS ask for directions).

And why haven't you heard of her? Because unlike Amelia Earhart, Jerrie Mock actually did it right. Let that be a lesson to you, women. The only time a man will appreciate you—or name a line of luggage after you—is if you fail and have to come crawling back.

Mock's plane, the *Spirit of Columbus*, hangs in the Smithsonian Institution's National Air and Space Museum, not far from Charles Lindbergh's *Spirit of St. Louis*. Lindbergh didn't travel nearly as many miles as Mrs. Mock did, nor did he do it in a skirt and high heels, although such a scenario was frequently and gleefully envisioned by Lindbergh pal Hermann Goering.

The Midnight Ride of Paul Revere (and Some Other Men Who Were Ignored by Longfellow).

THE BRITISH ARE COMING, THE BRITISH ARE COMING.

THE MIDNIGHT SIDE VIEW OF PAUL REVERE.

EVERYONE KNOWS that Paul Revere galloped around the greater Boston area, shouting "The British are coming, the British are coming." (It was rumored that a smutty jokester yelled after him, "Perhaps it would serve them well to turn their thoughts to the starting lineup of the Boston Red Sox." A lie, since it would be one hundred years until Abner Doubleday invented baseball. Which is also a lie, although Doubleday is credited with being the first man to think of baseball during sex, usually repeating to himself the mantra: "How can I get people to think I invented baseball?")

Paul Revere was not the only patriot galloping around the greater Boston area that night, however. He was aided by a tanner named William Dawes and a Dr. Samuel Prescott. Dawes and Prescott didn't make it into Longfellow's poem, and therefore receded into history, but at least neither was tainted by the suckiness of the song "Indian Reservation" by Paul Revere and the Raiders.

Ironically, Prescott was the only one to complete the mission. Revere was captured and Dawes got lost, which was immortalized in the lesser-known Longfellow poem, "The Midnight Traffic Circle Nightmare of William Dawes."

HISTO-POURRI: Total Bastard Roundup.

TODAY IS AN IMPORTANT DAY in the history of metaphorical (and literal) bastards.

APRIL 19, 1618 A poet known for his epigrams (short poems with clever twists, popular in the days before "clever" was banished from poetry), the Reverend Thomas Bastard died on this day in 1618 at age fifty-three. One hopes all his works will one day be collected in something called *The Complete Bastard*.

APRIL 19, 1993 Bastard, Jesus, Rocker, Molester, and "Civil Liberties Martyr" David Koresh is killed inside his sex-and-gun compound in Waco, Texas. Please Note: Koresh is often called a "Civil Liberties Martyr" by people who don't traditionally like the idea of Civil Liberties.

APRIL 19, 1995 Oklahoma City bomber Timothy McVeigh becomes the "Oklahoma City Bomber," when he and a few other hillbillies explode a truck bomb in front of the Alfred P. Murrah Federal Building, in retaliation for the Koresh killing (man-crush). The truck was full of fertilizer, as was Timothy McVeigh.

APRIL 20, 1841
Edgar Allan Poe Invents the Detective Story, Celebrates with Prebreakfast Laudanum Binge.

WE ALL LOVE ANGELA LANSBURY and her feisty, crime-solving character Jessica Fletcher on *Murder, She Wrote*. But there would never have been a Jessica Fletcher had Edgar Allan Poe not invented the detective story with the April 20, 1841, publication of "Murders in the Rue Morgue," just six weeks after Ms. Lansbury was born.

"Rue Morgue" has been called the first detective story, but Poe called it "a tale of ratiocination," a word he loved to slur in an effort to dazzle easily amused bartenders during "buyback" time. The story contains many of the genre's prototypes: the locked-room crime, the sidekick-narrator, and the gentleman-amateur detective (a fancy way of saying "confirmed bachelor").

Poe published the story in Philadelphia's *Graham's* magazine, in what was the magazine's first—and last—"Apes with Knives" issue. (If that's a spoiler, then you never had a hip ninth-grade English teacher who introduced Poe to the class as "The Original Stephen King"!)

Success continued to elude Poe, and he abandoned the detective genre. His own personal demons took hold of his life and work, as evidenced by such masterpieces as "The Pit and the Pendulum," "The Masque of the Red Death," and "You Want Creepy? I Just Married My Thirteen-Year-Old Cousin!"

GOD FORBID HE INVENTS HIMSELF A SMILE!

Rome Gets Built on This Day.

THE CITY OF ROME will be adorned in festive "party soot" today because on April 21, 753 BC, Romulus and his twin brother Remus founded the city on the site where the orphaned infants were suckled by a she-wolf. Of course, this being Italy, the she-wolf forced the babies into this with repeated howls of "Eat! EAT!!!"

Romulus (the Cute One) and Remus (the Quiet One—traumatized by infant-suckling incident) were the sons of Rhea Silvia, the daughter of King Numitor of Alba Longa. Numitor was deposed by his younger brother Amulius, who forced Rhea to become a Vestal Virgin so that she would not give birth to heirs to the throne. (The high priestesses of the Vestal Virgins were kind of like the members of a campus abstinence organization, except one didn't get the sense they were all gay.)

However, Rhea gave birth to Romulus and Remus after being impregnated by the war god, Mars. Back then, "Mars" was often the excuse for twins, because even in 753 BC, some parents refused to come clean about their fertility treatments.

Amulius ordered the infants drowned, but they survived and washed ashore at the foot of the Palatine Hill, where they were suckled by the she-wolf until being found by the shepherd Faustulus, who has the distinction of being the only guardian in history who encouraged thumb-sucking as a way to break an even worse habit.

Reared by Faustulus, the twins became warriors, attacked Alba Longa, and restored their grandfather to the throne. Despite this victory, the brothers soon turned on each other, and Romulus killed Remus in an argument over whose turn it was to walk their mother.

MAMMA

Germans Try Yet Again to Make the Great War Less Great.

ON THIS DAY IN 1915, German forces during the Second Battle of Ypres in the First World War (that's the one that's two wars before the war with Hawkeye in it) fired nearly 175 tons of chlorine gas against two divisions of French and Algerian soldiers. It also marks the first and only time that Algerians found, in the Germans, a European more loathsome than the French.

The Germans had been dabbling in poison gases since the start of the war, and had fired shells loaded with xylyl bromide at Russian troops in 1914. This poison killed over 1,000 Russians, who sadly never got to die from the more fun alcohol poisoning.

Despite this attack, the Germans didn't advance very far. Some say the men were shocked by the gravity of their actions, despite encouragement from a young soldier named A. Hitler, who kept shouting, "What? Why the long faces?"

The French and British soon began developing their own chemical weapons and gas masks. The masks, like all fashions from these two nations, later proved to be too snug a fit for the American forces.

Mustard gas became the poison of choice for both sides, but protective technology kept pace and eventually negated the strategic power of chemical weapons. Despite the fact that during the Bush administration, the threat of chemical weapons proved effective in fatally bogging down American forces in otherwise harmless oil-rich nations.

Gases Used by the Germans in World War I: Chlorine, Mustard, Phosgene, Sauerkraut (Germans just used this on other Germans, usually after lunch.)

APRIL 23, 1564

William Shakespeare Born, Trippingly Mewls and Pukes.

WHILE NO ONE IS CERTAIN, many believe William Shakespeare, the man who gave the world Baz Luhrmann's *William Shakespeare's Romeo + Juliet*, was born on this day in Stratford-upon-Avon, England.

In 1582, he married Anne Hathaway (not the sonnet-worthy *Princess Diaries* actress), and by 1592, he was a well-established actor and playwright in London. The ten years in between are called the "Lost Years." Like most theatrical types, these years were probably spent either temping or waiting tables at Ye Olde Bennigan's.

To this day, historians debate whether or not Shakespeare actually wrote all the plays attributed to him, and the exact chronology of his plays (although *Othello II: Electric Boogaloo* is presumed to have come after *Othello*). Some even suggest that Shakespeare was a homosexual, an observation based on his 126 sonnets addressed to a "Fair Lord" and by the more damning evidence that he once wrote a play.

One thing for sure is that Shakespeare added more to the English language than any other writer, with the possible exception of the Sniglets guy.

MULLET.

EXAMPLES:

- "Something is rotten in the state of Denmark." (From *Hamlet*, and later a borrowed slogan for Fungakkin, a Danish athlete's foot powder.)

- "All the world's a stage, and all the men and women merely players." (From *As You Like It*, and the side of the tote bag that your ninth-grade art teacher used to carry.)

- "The first thing we do, let's kill all the lawyers." (From *King Henry VI, Part III*, and the front of a T-shirt your ninth-grade art teacher used to wear.)

- "If you prick us, do we not bleed?" (From *Merchant of Venice*, and the one play your ninth-grade art teacher considers problematic because of the Jew stuff.)

APRIL 24, 1961
Macanu-D'oh.

ON THIS DAY IN 1961, President John Fitzgerald Kennedy released a statement claiming sole responsibility for the failed Bay of Pigs invasion. It was this sort of honesty that all but assured that this rube was never going to see a second term.

PRESIDENT KENNEDY GIVES GO-AHEAD FOR ONE BRIEF SHINING STRATEGIC BLUNDER.

A week earlier, 1,500 Cuban exiles armed with U.S. weapons landed on the southern coast of Cuba at the Bay of Pigs, hoping to find support from the local population. Unfortunately, after years of living in a place known as the Bay of Pigs, the self-esteem of the locals was such that they felt they were ultimately too fat and unpopular to lend much support.

This lackluster landing led to Kennedy's decision to cancel several bombing raids on the Cuban Air Force, thus sparing their plane.

With the failure of this invasion, Cuba was able to continue on as a Communist island paradise, if you refuse to measure "paradise" on the international "Access to Medicine and Protein Paradise Scale." Her music was later heard around the world thanks to the album *The Buena Vista Social Club*. You may have heard that album if you attended any boring cocktail party over the last five years thrown by someone who had misplaced his or her Norah Jones album.

"HAPPY ANZAC DAY, SUGAR TITS!"

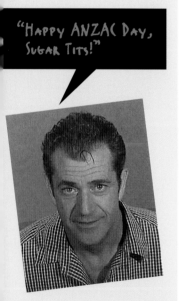

APRIL 25
Happy ANZAC Day!

IN AUSTRALIA AND NEW ZEALAND, ANZAC Day celebrates the bravery of the Australian and New Zealand Army Corps ("It's Australian for Cannon Fodder"), who landed in Gallipoli on this day in 1915. (Note: To learn more about the Gallipoli campaign, rent the movie *Gallipoli*, which stars Mel Gibson back before he became an auteur of movies in nonsense-speak.)

In addition to the two nations celebrated, ANZAC Day is also a national holiday in the Cook Islands, Niue, Samoa, and Tonga, where the eat-or-be-eaten hustlers on the Cocoanut Index are grateful for the day off.

In Australia, the holiday is marked with somber and solemn "Dawn Services," although with the amount of drinking one encounters in that nation, most events at dawn are marked with some solemnity.

IN ADDITION TO THE LANDING AT GALLIPOLI, APRIL 25 HAS SEEN MORE THAN ITS SHARE OF GLOOMY EVENTS:

APRIL 25, 1792 Nicolas J. Pelletier becomes the first person executed by guillotine. One might say he was "a head of his time," if that person were writing jokes for the side of a Dixie cup.

APRIL 25, 1878 Anna Sewell dies shortly after publication of her only novel, *Black Beauty*. On the plus side, she never lived to see her book title used as the URL for a variety of niche "ebony sex" Web sites.

APRIL 25, 1916 England declares martial law in Ireland after the Easter rebellion. By sundown, the Irish have written 113 plays and over five hundred songs about the day.

APRIL 26, 1937
The Pain in Spain Falls Mainly on the Village of Guernica.

ON THIS DAY IN HISTORY, the Nazis took the Luftwaffe out for a test drive and bombed the hell out of the Spanish town of Guernica. This was later turned into a powerful artistic statement by Pablo Picasso. Thomas Kinkade's take on the assault, entitled *Guernica Cabin at Twilight*, is less powerful, but makes a better jigsaw puzzle.

PICASSO'S LESSER-KNOWN PAINTINGS OF SPANISH TRAGEDIES:
DEATH IN VIGO, SLIGHT INCREASE IN HEART DISEASE IN GREATER PALMA

THE WEEPING WOMAN (WHO HAS JUST LEARNED SHE IS OUT OF SAFFRON)

APRIL 27, 1897
Tomb of the Well-Known Soldier Dedicated.

ON APRIL 27, 1897, over 1 million people attended the dedication ceremony of Grant's Tomb, on Manhattan's Riverside Drive and 122nd Street. The celebrants were entertained by Civil War reenactors, a parade, and nearby Columbia University students protesting the "Gross and inequitable use of marble and granite!"

Designed by architect John Duncan, the structure was completed after many years of planning and remains the largest mausoleum in North America (after Boca Raton).

The Grant Monument Association had been formed in the early 1880s to raise funds for constructing a monument in the general's name, and the organization had actually been formed *before* Grant died, which led to the then-popular trick question of "Who is not yet buried in Grant's Tomb?"

THANKFULLY, THIS AREA WAS LATER SPRUCED UP WITH THE WEST SIDE HIGHWAY.

Ultimately, 90,000 people donated $600,000 to the project. This aggressive fund-raising push inspired the former Confederate states to establish the first-ever Do Not Call Registry. (Although this didn't go into effect until 1971, when most Southern states finally got phone service.)

ASSORTED CORRECT ANSWERS TO "WHO IS BURIED IN GRANT'S TOMB?"
- "NO ONE! HE IS ACTUALLY ENTOMBED THERE!" (THEN BRACE YOURSELF—SUCH A SMARTYPANTS ANSWER ALWAYS WINDS UP WITH YOU GENTLY SWAYING FROM ATOP A URINAL BY YOUR UNDERWEAR.)
- "NOW, BY 'GRANT'S TOMB,' YOU'RE REFERRING TO THE 'GENERAL GRANT NATIONAL MEMORIAL,' RIGHT?" (THIS WILL ALSO EARN YOU A WEDGIE.)
- "WHAT? *MELROSE PLACE* HUNK GRANT SHOW IS DEAD?!"
- "GENERAL GRANT AND HIS WIFE, YOU SEXIST!"
- "GENERAL GRANT AND HER HUSBAND! YEAH!" (FOLLOW WITH HIGH FIVE.)

SHARP-DRESSED UOMO.

APRIL 28
When Bad Things Happen to Bad People.

IF YOU ARE EVIL, mark your spot in this book with a length of your enemy's intestines and go hide. April 28 is not your day.

APRIL 28, 1789 Captain William Bligh, of *Mutiny on the Bounty* fame, is (SPOILER ALERT) set adrift in an open boat as mutineers take over his ship and set sail for Tahiti. Once on Pitcairn Island, the sailors promptly mutinied against the concept that inbreeding was bad.

APRIL 28, 1937 Saddam Hussein born from a Mother of all Mothers. It was a difficult birth because, even then, Saddam never liked being rousted from his hiding holes.

APRIL 28, 1945 In a rare show of overheated emotion from the Italian people, fascist dictator **BENITO MUSSOLINI** and girlfriend are murdered and strung up by their ankles in public. Even more humiliating, Italian guys whistle and catcall at mistress's mangled corpse for days.

APRIL 28, 1994 CIA official Aldrich Ames is sentenced to life in prison for selling secrets to the Soviets and causing the execution of ten spies. Even more shocking, his bulky aviator specs and droopy mustache are not part of some agent disguise.

Adolph and Eva 4-Ever.

THERE PROBABLY WASN'T A DRY EYE in the bunker (and in the case of Herr Goering, there was certainly a lot of smeared eyeliner) when Adolph Hitler wed Eva Braun on this day in 1945. Now, before you feel too warm and fuzzy for the happy couple, keep in mind that because of the events of April 30, they should have returned all of their wedding gifts—but never did. Nazi lovebirds suck.

BREAKING NEWS

EVOLPHA SPOTTED CANOODLING!

NOT AS FUN AS
BRANGELINA.

APRIL 30, 1945

Adolph Hitler Commits Suicide.

May

No One Dared Mention His "Führer Breath."

MAY 1, 1945

After Hitler Commits Suicide, Josef Goebbels Commits Suicide.

MAY 2, 1945

Hermann Goering Finds Comfort in Food.

HITLER'S EIGHTEEN-ROOM BUNKER had gotten pretty crowded, especially since one of the occupants was Luftwaffe head Hermann Goering, a three-hundred-pound morphine addict fond of wearing makeup and silk kimonos in his downtime. Even under the best of circumstances, a giant, fascist drag queen can really fill a space.

So Adolf Hitler poisoned his wife and his dogs, took a cyanide capsule, and then shot himself in the head, escaping the many lawsuits that would be filed over reneged promises of a thousand-year Reich. And if you read the suicide note made out to Josef Goebbels (right), it becomes clear that the Minister of Propaganda would be faced with a huge task that would also leave him no choice but to take his own life.

Goebbels worked the phones and, like any good flack, tried several different approaches in his press release: "Hitler Executes Nazi Bigwig," "Hitler Treated for Exhaustion," "Blondi and Puppies Depressed for Days Beforehand: Lack of 'Walkies' Cited."

Nothing worked, a big comedown for the man who all but invented the "Big Lie" propaganda technique, or argumentum ad nauseam, a policy of repeating a point until it is taken to be the truth. It had always been a magic bullet for Goebbels, although no one bought his repeated claims in 1942 of having a girlfriend in Canada.

> DEAR JOSEF,
> I COMMITTED SUICIDE. SO DID EVA, AFTER WE BOTH POISONED MY DOG BLONDI AND HER PUPPIES. GET A HOLD OF THE PAPERS TOMORROW AND SPIN IT POSITIVE.
> ADOLPH
>
> PS: TOMORROW'S MAYPOLE DANCE SHOULD CONTINUE AS SCHEDULED. HERR GOERING'S HAD HIS HAIR IN PIGTAILS ALL WEEK IN ANTICIPATION. DON'T LET FATTY DOWN.

MAY 3, 2003

Old Man, Look at You Now!

ON THIS DAY IN 2003, New Hampshire's tourism department realized they'd have to rely a little bit more on the tax-free booze and fireworks sector, as their beloved rock formation known as the Old Man of the Mountain, which kind of looked like an old man—from certain angles—came crashing down after years of threatening to do so.

The Old Man was a series of five granite cliff ledges in the White Mountains, and it was first sighted in 1805 by a surveying team who had no doubt grown tired of lying on their backs while stoned, trying to see things in the passing clouds.

A TWO-BIT OLD MAN.

In 1900, experts began to realize that the Old Man was deteriorating, and they tried to maintain the aging face with all manner of cosmetic spikes and cables (the same has been attempted recently with the aging face of New Hampshire native and Aerosmith front man Steven Tyler).

Unfortunately, it collapsed sometime between midnight and 2:00 a.m. on May 3, 2003, just a few years after it had been selected to appear on the flipside of New Hampshire's state-hood quarter, which is notable because it is the only U.S. coin with a profile on both sides. (Keep in mind, it is easy to achieve "notable" in the fast-paced world of coin enthusiasts. It's also considered notable because it is shiny.)

MAY 4
HISTO-POURRI: Violent Struggle Edition.

STAY LOW, HIPPY. If you have a problem with the Man today, it might be a good idea to keep it to yourself and toe the line, because May 4 traditionally is a day when authorities clash with protestors—and by "clash" we mean "kill."

THE SLAY HAY KIDS.

← **MAY 4, 1886 THE HAYMARKET SQUARE RIOT** occurs in Chicago, as German radicals toss a bomb at police, the police start firing, lots of people die, and a bunch of innocent men are later executed. Thankfully, this sort of conflict now only occurs in Chicago when the Bulls win a championship.

MAY 4, 1970 The National Guard is called in to quell an antiwar demonstration at Kent State University in Ohio and promptly displays the reason why the National Guard is only trusted with weapons for two weeks out of the year. Sixty rounds were fired into a crowd of students, killing four and providing others with valuable credit hours toward a major in Disillusionment when the Guardsmen are later cleared of all wrongdoing.

MAY 4, 1975 Moe Howard, of the Three Stooges, dies at age seventy-seven. He is beloved by that guy at the office who rebels against conformity by wearing red high-tops and Hawaiian shirts. Everyone he works with secretly wants to go "Kent State" on his ass.

Erwin "Cannonball" Baker Gets His Motor Runnin'.

ON THIS DAY IN 1914, Erwin "Cannonball" Baker began a cross-continental trip that made him the first man to ride from the Pacific to the Atlantic on motorcycle.

Baker set off wearing leather riding trousers and carrying nothing but a one-gallon canteen, a Smith & Wesson .38, and a supply of cardboard and markers so he could fashion "Show Us Your Tits" signs in the event of a bike rally.

To fight thirst while driving through the desert, Cannonball employed the old Native-American method of carrying a small pebble under his tongue. Needless to say, this was the first of many Native-American traditions later copied by bikers . . .

His revolver came into use when he shot and killed a German shepherd that was chasing his bike in Ellsworth, Kansas. A violent act, but a kinder response than the one Paul Sr. displayed that time Mikey brought him the wrong wrench on *American Chopper*.

Cannonball eventually traveled 3,379 miles across the United States. His exploits later became the inspiration for the race known as the Cannonball Run, which itself became the inspiration for a series of films that are to "humor" what a cross-country motorcycle trip is to "testicles."

A VROOM OF THEIR OWN.

MAY 6

Big Feats in No Time.

THINGS SPED UP considerably on the planet in the twentieth century, and today is a day to commemorate our very fast modern world with a fairly brief entry that can be read and forgotten in no time.

MAY 6, 1937 The world's largest airship, the *Hindenburg*, incinerates entirely in under a minute. The bawling radio announcer who reported the events was probably embarrassed for years.

MAY 6, 1954 British athlete Roger Bannister runs a four-minute mile, enjoys fifteen minutes of fame.

MAY 6, 1994 The Channel Tunnel, or Chunnel, officially opens, which means that once you leave England, it takes only twenty minutes for you to realize that everything they say about the French is true.

MAY 7, 1915

The Thing with the Ship in World War I Happened.

ON THIS DAY IN HISTORY, the British ocean liner the *Lusitania* (not the "King of the World..." one) was torpedoed by a German U-boat and sank off the coast of Ireland. A total of 1,198 people drowned, or roughly half the number of people who died after drunkenly falling off their Carnival Cruise in the first quarter of last year.

"Tonight's Limbo Contest Has Been Canceled."

The death of many countrymen united Americans against the Germans, which led to the American entry into the global conflict . . . two years later. (Americans are beloved for their habit of arriving fashionably late for bloody world parties.)

Either way, the attack is one of two things people today know about the First World War, the other being that it started because some guy in a feathered hat got shot in a country that doesn't exist anymore—or something. (Although that last summation is slightly more succinct and clear than the ones usually floated to explain the United States' participation in the current Iraqi war.)

The Truman Shows Up.

ON THIS DAY IN 1884, Harry S. Truman was born in Lamar, Missouri. The "S" in his name didn't stand for anything, and his attempts later in life to convince people that it stood for "Studmuffin" were a bitter failure. Let's look at some fun facts about this fiery president.

- Truman was plagued by lousy approval ratings throughout his tenure, but nowadays often winds up on historians' lists of Top Ten Presidents. (Source: Fox News, every five minutes when topic of George W.'s miserable presidential approval ratings comes up.)

- He was our last president to not attend college, which is sometimes confused with G. W. Bush's distinction of "last president to attend yet not pay attention in college."

- Early political career spent as part of corrupt Missouri political machine, yet he proved to be an honest and effective politician once he arrived in Washington. (Source: *The Encyclopedia of Assbackward Politicians*.)

- Gained fame on a national level by heading up the Truman Committee in the early 1940s, which investigated wasteful spending in the military. Seriously—in those days the army would spend ten dollars on a toilet seat.

- Coined the sayings "The buck stops here," and "If you can't stand the heat, get out of the kitchen." (The last one rather cruelly used after Hiroshima and Nagasaki incidents.)

- His Marshall Plan helped rebuild Europe after the Second World War. Europeans seem to forget this when American tourists ask for directions to the museum in English.

- Truman eventually desegregated the armed forces, so that in 2008, we might have an "Armed Forces."

- Was such an underdog in the 1948 presidential race against Thomas Dewey that newspapers ran the headline "Dewey Defeats Truman." Although some papers played it safe by offering the subheadline "As Most Mustached Candidate."

- The only Missourian to ever become president, pending outcome of 2012 attempt to draft St. Louis native Kimora Lee Simmons for the Ghetto-fabulous ticket.

HE WAS DA BOMB(ER OF THOSE CITIES IN JAPAN).

Mother's Day!

WELL, MAYBE, depending upon the calendar year in which this is read, but May 9 has seen a few significant events in the history of being a mother—and in some cases, not wanting to be a mother.

MAY 9, 1914 President Woodrow Wilson declares the first-ever Mother's Day, after lobbying Congress to declare the second Sunday of every May as a day to honor our nation's mothers. He called it a chance to show "love and reverence for the mothers of our country." And added "Now maybe they'll shut their pieholes about wanting to vote."

MAY 9, 1946 Actress Candice Bergen is born. Her television character, Murphy Brown, became one of the first sitcom characters to have a child out of wedlock. Vice President Dan Quayle criticized the show, saying Brown was "mocking the importance of fathers by bearing a child alone and calling it just another lifestyle choice," displaying a prudishness that once again hammered home the point that he was no John Kennedy.

MAY 9, 1960 On this day, the Food and Drug Administration, realizing no one was impressed by the aged condom it was carrying around in its wallet, approved the first-ever birth control pill. Women who took the pill had new power over their choices and reproductive freedoms. And women who "forgot" to take the pill had new powers over the boyfriends who still hadn't popped the question after five years.

Rend Me a Tenor—
The Astor Place Opera House Riot.

READY TO KICK
SOME ASTOR.

THE ASTOR PLACE RIOT was a violent night of carnage that erupted due to a competition between two egotistical actors. (Note: Competitions between egotistical "has-been" actors eventually led to even more carnage with the invention of reality television.)

On the evening of May 10, 1849, there was to be a performance of *Macbeth* at New York City's Astor Place Opera House by a British actor known as Macready the Tragedian. Macready's great rival was an American actor named Edwin Forrest, a minstrel show favorite whose own 1843 performance of *Macbeth* was booed and hissed in London, most likely because he performed the play in blackface and had decided to rename the character Da Kingly Laz-E-Bones.

When Macready arrived in America, Forrest riled up violent, working-class gangs in the Astor Place area, convincing them that it was a terrible affront that a British actor would perform for the upper crust so close to a neighborhood of poor, "real" Americans. (SPOILER ALERT: If you walk around Astor Place and the surrounding neighborhood these days, you'll see that poor folk eventually won this battle. The area is an unholy carnival of poverty and despair.)

A crowd of 20,000 began to riot outside the opera house that evening, and the National Guard was deployed to subdue the crowd. The Guard would not be called up for another opera house–related emergency until 1989, when Luciano Pavarotti went on a rampage over a shortage of Double Stuf Oreos in his dressing room.

Eventually, thirty-one were killed and eighty-six rioters were tried and sent to prison. Macready was ushered away from the opera house dressed as a woman. Being an actor, he first demanded to know "Who is this woman? Why is she running away? Could she have a Creole accent?"

Macready never returned to New York because of this clash, and because his subsequent one-man show, "The Running Creole or the Manhattan Skedaddle," was a big hit on the dinner theater circuit.

OBVIOUSLY CHINESE.

MAY 11, 1811

Siamese Twins Chang and Eng Born, Siam Distances Self.

CHANG AND ENG BUNKER were creepy—even for twins. They were joined at the sternum by a five-inch-long, three-inch-wide band of flesh and cartilage, and they were born on this day in Siam in 1811. They lived in a village along the Mekong River (Siamese for "mercury-laden") and in a few short years everyone would know about the "Siamese Twins."

(Chang and Eng were actually three-quarters Chinese and, around their village, they were known as the "Chinese Twins." The fact that "Chinese Twins" never caught on as a term for conjoined twins was a burr in the saddle of the Siamese for many years.)

The King of Siam demanded that the two be put to death, no doubt worried that his tiny kingdom would forever be associated with conjoined twins, and not nice things like Margaret Landon's book *Anna and the King of Siam*, the Rodgers and Hammerstein musical *The King and I* (based on Margaret Landon's book,

Anna and the King of Siam), the Rex Harrison film *Anna and the King* (also based on Margaret Landon's book, *Anna and the King of Siam*), and the 1999 remake of *Anna and the King* starring Chow Yun-Fat (which was based on the Rex Harrison film *Anna and the King*, which was based on Margaret Landon's book *Anna and the King of Siam,* which became the basis for the Rodgers and Hammerstein musical *The King and I*).

The king relented after hearing there had been cases of conjoined twins in other countries (see?!). When the boys were teenagers, their mother sold them for $500 and soon they were touring the world as an attraction—a very bitter, mother-hating attraction.

The two dazzled audiences with gymnastics and feats of strength—dull by today's standards, but folks back then had never been dazzled by programs where Howie Mandel tries to get chubby women to open briefcases.

Eventually, both retired, settled in North Carolina, and took the last name "Bunker." The brothers married sisters and churned out twenty-one children between them. (Again, no Howie Mandel to pass the time.)

As they grew older, Chang became a heavy drinker and Eng fond of gambling (probably Fan-Tan, popular with the Chinese). Death came in 1874, first to Chang and then, a few hours later, to Eng. Eng used those few hours to make the moves on Chang's wife. She was at first receptive, but then they both realized that if they got down to it, it would spoil the mystery . . . of making love to a person who you always either saw or heard making love to your sibling while you pretended to be asleep or reading.

MAY 12
A Day of Good News, Bad News.

← **MAY 12, 1641** **The good news?** In England, **PRINCE WILLIAM II** (fourteen) marries Princess Henrietta Mary Stuart (nine). **The bad news?** Irreconcilable cooties still not grounds for divorce in most nations.

MAY 12, 1777 **The good news?** The first advertisement for ice cream in the United States appears in the *New York Gazette*. Merchant Philip Lenzi announces that the product is available "almost every day." **The bad news?** The following week, the *New York Gazette* runs first advertisements for "Relaxed-fit Britches" and obesity scooters called "Donkey Cartes for the Enlarged Persons."

MAY 12, 1908 **The good news?** Wireless radio broadcasting is patented by Nathan B. Stubblefield. **The bad news?** The word "Stubblefield" never catches on in place of "radio." The Buggles never able to explore creative possibilities of "Video Killed the Stubblefield Star."

WILLIAM II, LONG AFTER
CHILDHOOD MARRIAGE
LOST ITS SPARK

MAY 12, 1955 **The good news?** Country star Kix Brooks, of duo Brooks and Dunn, is born. **The bad news?** Fondness for overly snug dungarees makes Brooks a bad role model for male fans hoping to one day have little Kix of their own.

MAY 12, 1993 **The good news?** The classic sitcom *Cheers* ends on a high note after a triumphant eleven seasons on the air. **The bad news?** Drunken postshow partying on *Tonight Show* means America witnesses awkward "Ratzenberger Stretch" makeout moves on Jay Leno.

MAY 13
Birthday Roundup.

MAY 13, 1655 Pope Innocent XIII born. He was the last Pope named Innocent. And perhaps the last human named Innocent. (Although in the early 1920s, noted gangster Al Capone, unhappy with nickname "Scarface," tried to make the scene as Al "Innocent" Capone. He saw his trade slip somewhat.)

MAY 13, 1926 Bea Arthur born in New York City. Moments after doctor slapped her, she did her first "slow burn."

MAY 13, 1939 Harvey Keitel born in Brooklyn. Kind of a late bloomer, Keitel was thirty-four when he appeared in *Mean Streets*. He's made up for it by appearing in nearly every movie made since then.

MAY 13, 1939 Harvey Keitel's penis born in Brooklyn. Kind of a late bloomer, Keitel's penis was fifty-three when it appeared in *Bad Lieutenant*. It's made up for it by appearing in nearly every movie made since then.

MAY 13, 1947 David Hughes born. He plays (or played) **CRICKET**. We must apologize to our international readers: We don't know much about cricket here in the United States, except that it was invented in the 1400s when a patch of lawn dared to become too exciting.

MAY 13, 1950 Peter Gabriel experiences birth. He has been alive for fifty-eight years now, or about how long it takes for him to perform *Biko* live.

MAY 13, 1961 Former NBA forward Dennis Rodman emerges from womb in what was probably a showy display, and he may do something outrageous today to draw attention to himself. For our international readers: Basketball was invented in the 1850s when a patch of hardwood floor dared to become too exciting.

The State of Israel born.

WE WOULD MAKE SOME JOKES HERE, but since a large chunk of the world refuses to recognize the State of Israel, any jokes about something they don't recognize would go right over their heads. (Although the people who don't recognize Israel aren't traditionally the biggest laughers.) Too bad. There really are a lot of chuckles to be had about the State of Israel.

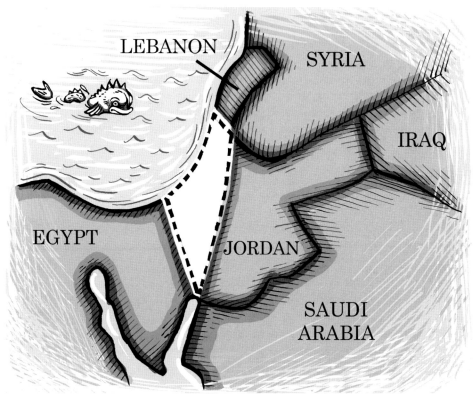

MAP: COURTESY TEHRAN CARTOGRAPHY LTD.

Feel Better.

YOUR OFFICE JOB SUCKS. Monday rolls around, kicking off the five-day count-down to Friday, which begins the two-day countdown to you returning to your job on Monday again. So examine what else has happened on this day in history, and maybe you'll feel a little better about your own miserable existence.

MAY 15, 1625 Sixteen rebellious farmers hanged in Vöcklamarkt, Austria, most likely strung up with own overalls, after revolting against counterreformation measures and Bavarian rule. **Why should this make you feel better?** Now you don't feel so bad that your brave, one-man/woman revolt against your company's "No Headphones" policy was totally ignored.

MAY 15, 1718 A London lawyer named James Puckle patents world's first machine gun, because lawyering was not doing enough to crush the soul of mankind. **Why should this make you feel better?** Tim, the weird quiet guy in ad sales who was fired last week, hasn't come back into work carrying one—yet.

MAY, 15, 1829 Mormon leader Joseph Smith claims he is ordained by John the Baptist, who also gave him a waiver to "Marry as many chicks as you want." **Why should this make you feel better?** Those anti-depressants you order on the Internet have kept you from becoming as nutty as Mormon leader Joseph Smith. Although now that Tim, the weird quiet guy in ad sales, is gone, you are the office's only weird quiet person.

MAY 15, 1941 Nazi occupiers in the Netherlands forbid all Jewish music, meaning local Jewish hipsters can stop pretending to like Klezmer. **Why should this make you feel better?** Hey man, you were right to fight the company's fascist "No Headphones" policy. That's how the Nazis started. "First they came for the ad sales department—and I did nothing."

MAY 16
HISTO-POURRI: Tragic Young Love.

HISTORICALLY, today is a good day for underage couples getting together and having sex. And please, Mr. Postmaster, read that last sentence in context, please.

MAY 16, 1770 "Let them eat cake, but not before they rub it on one another's faces to the delight of the crowd at the reception." Yes, on this day in history, in an effort to prove to the world how very "French" they could be, the fifteen-year-old dauphin Louis marries the fourteen-year old Marie Antoinette. They would be married for over twenty years, until they split. Into four parts.

MAY 16, 1836 Twenty-six-year-old Edgar Allan Poe takes a thirteen-year-old as his bride. But before you get creeped out by the age difference, make sure you are first creeped out by the fact she was his first cousin. Virginia Eliza "Sissy" Clemm Poe died from tuberculosis, long before she was old enough to be embarrassed by the nickname "Sissy."

MAY 17, 1961

Enya Swept Out of Womb on a Timeless Wave of Passion and Melody.

AS PEAT FIRES BURNED NEARBY on an emerald land once walked by Celtic kings, Enya, or Eithne Ní Bhraonáin, was born of woman on this day in a hospital (in the Druid Beehive Stone Hut Wing) in Gweedore, or Gaoth Dobhair, County Donegal, or Counghaintrity, Doooneghailbraignkennethbranagh.

Doctors report that the baby's cries were soothing at first, but at the same time unsettling and a little bit creepy, and that those in attendance felt a burning desire to run out of the delivery room to go buy candles and fancy kaleidoscopes that have their very own bronze stand.

MAY 18, 1830

Edwin Budding Manufactures First Lawn Mower.

EDWIN BUDDING was a man who made more money off grass than "Amalgamated Cheech: a Chong Company." On this date in 1830, he signed an agreement for the manufacture of his revolutionary invention, the lawn mower.

Budding was an engineer in Gloucestershire, and noticed that at a nearby mansion, fifty men were employed with scythes to cut the lawn. Scything was a time-consuming task that involved great labor—especially true in England where great labors can't be tackled until another team arrives and, by hand, inserts a "u" into every "labour."

In 1830, he had been working with nap-cutting machines, which trimmed nap on carpets, and even patented something called a "Rug Muncher," but saw no profits from it since he was subsequently jailed for "lewd patenting." His new idea was based on the nap cutter, and eventually he patented and started manufacturing his lawn mowers.

The lawn mower's blades were driven by a series of cogs that were driven by a large roller, making it very similar to many modern mowers, although it took two people to operate. The machine took off when it became a one-person operation, and served the dual purpose of cutting a lawn and allowing a man to step outside of the home he is now disenchanted with to work with a machine loud enough to drown out his tears.

Anne Boleyn Gets Royal Screwing.

ON THIS DAY IN 1536, Anne Boleyn, the Queen of England and the second of Henry VIII's six wives, had her head chopped off in a private execution on the Tower Green in London (the exact spot is currently marked by an American tourist in shorts and black socks, sorting and re-sorting his postcards of punk rockers).

The relationship between Anne and the King had started out promisingly with adultery and out-of-wedlock pregnancy. In 1532, Anne was pregnant, and to avoid any questions of the legitimacy of the child, she and Henry were secretly married. In fact, it was such a hush-hush affair that Henry disguised himself during the wedding with a thick layer of pork grease. (Or he had just had lunch.)

Anne had a daughter, and then a stillborn child. In 1535, she became pregnant again but miscarried. Unfortunately for Anne, Henry fell for one of Anne's ladies-in-waiting, so he had the Queen arrested and charged with a litany of crimes, including treason, adultery, and incest. (This was before incest had been made compulsory for royal wedding arrangements.)

The Queen was found guilty and condemned to death. A swordsman from Calais had been summoned, which meant she could look forward to a cleaner blow with a sharper sword than the more traditional ax. This was an unintentional act of kindness from the King, who, when initially demanding *A Swordsman from Calais*, was actually requesting a volume from his collection of "Ye Royal Stroke Books."

OFTEN HIDDEN UNDER YE OLDE PILLOW.

"Hey Buddy, Where's the Fire?" First Sarcastically Uttered.

ON THIS DAY IN HISTORY, a cabbie in New York City by the name of Jacob German was issued the world's first recorded speeding ticket. He worked for the Electric Vehicle Taxi Company ("We get you there cleanly and smugly"), and was stopped by a bike patrolman named Raymond Schuessler, who later changed his name to O'Schuessler in an attempt to get ahead in the force. (Note: Being a bicycle cop was a dignified and noble position in the New York City police force until the 1968 invention of "bicycle pants.")

The cab had been going down Lexington Avenue at approximately 12 mph, which is now the speed that most modern cabdrivers slow down to when you want to leap out.

THE ONLY OTHER EVENT OF SPEEDING IMPORTANCE TODAY IS:

MAY 20, 1971 Race car driver Anthony Wayne "Tony" Stewart born. He has gone by many nicknames, including "the Columbus Comet," "the Rushville Rocket," "Smoke," "Tony the Tiger," and "Tony 'for Chrissakes, can't someone just call me Tony?' Stewart."

It Could Have Been Worse.

LOUSY AND UNPLEASANT THINGS have happened with lousy and unpleasant frequency on this day. But still, it could have been worse.

MAY 21, 1758 Ten-year-old Mary Campbell is abducted from Penn's Creek, Pennsylvania, by a tribe of Lenape during the French-Indian War, as part of their protest over that conflict not being more correctly named the French–Native American War. She is held for seven years, and is at first reluctant to return home, a condition known as "Red Skin Syndrome" before it was stolen by the "Very White Man" and renamed "Stockholm Syndrome." **It could have been worse:** See abduction story below.

MAY 21, 1924 Nietzsche-misunderstanding rich kids Nathan Leopold and Richard Loeb invent the homosexual thrill killing when they kidnap and murder fourteen-year-old Robert Franks, a distant cousin of Loeb. In 1936, Loeb forced to reconsider his own "Superman" status when he is stabbed over seventy times in the prison shower at Joliet. **It could have been worse:** While the case later became the inspiration for the films *Rope* and *Compulsion*, it occurred too early to be properly "ripped from the headlines" for a *Law & Order* episode.

MAY 21, 1972 Michelangelo's *Pietà* is attacked and damaged by a sledgehammer-wielding vandal. **It could have been worse:** Vandalism didn't spread to all the *Pietà* copies adorning the front lawns of Italian-American homes throughout the nation.

MAY 21, 1998 After murdering his parents, fifteen-year-old Kipland Kinkel goes on a shooting spree at his school, killing two. **It could have been worse:** Name "Kipland Kinkel" at least offers easy answer to hand-wringing pundit question, "How could such a thing have happened?"

HISTO-POURRI.

MAY 22, 1939 Hitler and Mussolini sign Pact of Steel, an alliance promising immediate aid and military support in the event of war and collaboration in military policy. Their *Buns of Steel* Workout Pact was less successful physically but far less devastating globally.

MAY 22, 1967 *Mister Rogers' Neighborhood* debuts. Kids are in awe of Mr. Rogers and a selection of puppets, all of whom sound just like Mr. Rogers. Nerves of steel needed to tolerate overly caffeinated Mr. McFeely.

MAY 22, 1967 Langston Hughes dies at sixty-five. He lived long enough to see the reading of his poem "The Negro Speaks of Rivers" become a little uncomfortable.

MAY 22, 1970 Naomi Campbell born, hurls first rattle. Shows that possessing "Buns of Steel" could also lead to fascistic tendencies.

MAY 22, 1972 Ceylon becomes Republic of Sri Lanka as its constitution is ratified, adding eye-catching new name to nation most people can't find on a map. On the plus side, the words "Made in Sri Lanka" add an exotic zing to drab casual wear bought at Marshalls.

MAY 22, 1992 Johnny Carson hosts his last episode of *The Tonight Show*. TV critics who exclaim "For years, he was the last face we saw before we went to bed at night" reveal own personal lives to be infinitely sadder than Carson's death thirteen years later.

MAY 23
A Day of Good News, Bad News.

MAY 23, 1701 **The good news?** William Kidd, aka Captain Kidd, is hanged for piracy and murder. Did not live to see perversion of term "booty." **The bad news?** Kidd attempts to read a prepared statement, "Today, my yarn ends with the hangman's rope. To a forgiving Lord I offer my soul." Unfortunately, the hangman pulled the lever on "yarn," and created irritating pirate "Yarghh!" phrase.

KIDDING AROUND.

MAY 23, 1824 The good news? The birthday of **AMBROSE EVERETT** ←
BURNSIDE, the somewhat undercompetent Union Civil War general
whose eye-catching facial hair became known as "Burnsides," then
later "Sideburns." **The bad news?** The Union became so infatuated with
hipster grooming that it gave commissions to the even less competent
Admiral Eurastus Goatee and Colonel T. Willard Caesar-Cut. The South,
of course, awarded a commission to Corporal Dennis Mullet.

← **MAY 23, 1911 The good news? THE NEW YORK PUBLIC LIBRARY**
on Fifth Avenue is dedicated by President William Howard Taft.
Main reading room slightly smaller than Taft's White House
bathtub. **The bad news?** Several illuminated
manuscripts carelessly soiled by president's
cheesesteak drippings.

MAY 23, 1934 The good news? Robert Moog
born, develops early dislike for the rich tone of
the family piano and goes on to invent the
Moog synthesizer. **The bad news?** Sometime
in the mid-1960s, Mr. Emerson meets
Messrs. Lake and Palmer.

MAY 23, 1966 The good news? Helena Bonham Carter born,
approximately ninety years after every character she has ever played.
The bad news? She is born into a world bathed in sunlight. It seems
to disagree with her.

MAY 24, 1844

Samuel Morse Connects the Dots (and Dashes).

TODAY WAS THE DAY when **SAMUEL F. B. MORSE** (the F. B. stood for "Fullest ←
Beard") sent the first-ever telegraph message in what has now come to be known
as Morse code.

Morse enrolled at Yale when he was only fourteen and quickly began to work on a
method of telegraphing some signal to others that he was not a virgin.

While Morse did develop the code that carries his name, the telegraph was actually first patented by Joseph Henry at Princeton University. Since he had no code to speak of, he merely
used the beeping invention as an early prototype for what would later be called the "Remote-
Controlled Fart Machine." (Something that is much more practical today than Morse code.)

A scientist named Charles Jackson claimed that Morse stole the code from him, and in 1989, Little Richard declared that Morse's "invention" was, like everything under the sun, first invented by Little Richard.

After securing all his patents, Morse decided it was time to show off what this little invention could do. Morse sent out the signal "What hath God wrought" from the Supreme Court room in Washington, D.C., to Baltimore. Morse also tapped out "Dot Dot Dash Dash" (he also held a patent on Meta Humor which, even in the 1840s, was only funny to people with no senses of humor and is less practical than a remote-controlled fart machine).

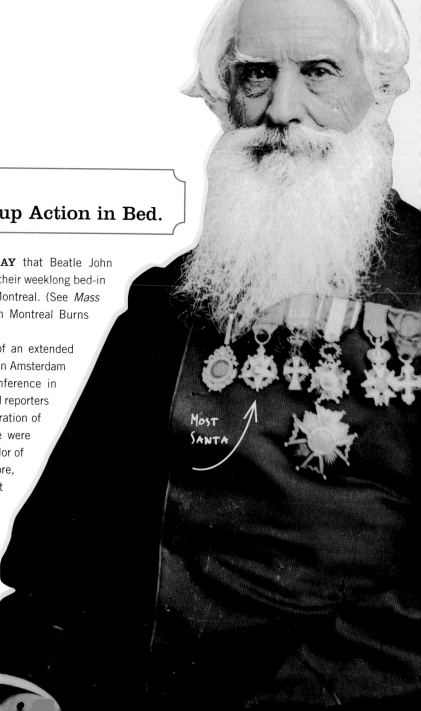

One of the medals is for "Most Santa."

Most Santa

MAY 25, 1939
Sir Ian McKellen Outed!

. . . from inside of a woman.

MAY 26, 1969
Hippies Have Nonsexy Group Action in Bed.

IT WAS THIRTY-NINE YEARS AGO TODAY that Beatle John Lennon and his "Teller," Yoko Ono, kicked off their weeklong bed-in for peace at the Queen Elizabeth Hotel in Montreal. (See *Mass Historia*, June 3, 1969: Queen Elizabeth Hotel in Montreal Burns Large Pile of Sheets.)

This was their second bed-in, which was part of an extended honeymoon for the newlyweds, the first having been in Amsterdam in March, followed by a peace-themed press conference in Vienna where they ate chocolate cake and addressed reporters from inside of a large, white bag. This was an illustration of the couple's "bagism" concept, which says if one were living in a bag, others could not judge you by the color of your skin, the length of your hair, the clothes you wore, or your age, and would only be able to go on the fact that you might be a bit of an idiot.

The couple could not enter the United States because of a previous pot bust of Lennon's, so they decided to head to Montreal, where pot possession is mandatory. During their seven-day stay, surrounded by cameras, the world media, and a room-service waiter named Pierre—who was getting sick and tired of hearing, "Sorry, I'm in me pj's, mate, I don't have me wallet on me"—the two were visited by Timothy Leary, Tommy Smothers, Dick Gregory, Petula Clark, and cartoonist Al Capp, which is a testament to the diverse nature of the peace movement and how hard it is to find a celebrity in Montreal at any given time.

Most of the celebrities sang on the anthem "Give Peace a Chance," which was recorded in the hotel room (if you listen carefully to the CD, you can hear a room-service waiter named Pierre angrily kicking over a wastepaper basket after being stiffed on his tip).

MAY 27
....
A Landmark Day for Landmarks.

TODAY IS A DAY TO SAY "HAPPY BIRTHDAY" to many a monumental engineering feat of stone and steel. Although if one attempts to enter any noted landmark with a birthday cake ablaze with candles, they will probably be treated as a terror threat and tackled by security.

MAY 27, 1849 London's grand Euston Station opens, and no, no "H" was dropped at the beginning of "Euston." Later torn down and replaced with 1960s modern eyesore, which connects to the Euston Tube Station in Travelcard Zone 1, right alongside the hopelessly lost American college student/tourist.

MAY 27, 1930 New York's striking art deco masterpiece the **CHRYSLER BUILDING** opened to the public on this day, and is still one of the most gorgeous structures in the world. Same design excellence can be enjoyed today with Chrysler's line of family minivans, provided you park somewhere that has a view of the Chrysler Building.

MAY 27, 1937 San Francisco's Golden Gate Bridge opens to pedestrian traffic, which today links rich hippies in the city with slightly richer hippies in Marin County. (BTW, the people jumping off the bridge today are not exactly in a celebratory mood.)

MUCH NICER THAN
THE YUGO TOWER.

MAY 28, 1934
Callander Girls.

FIVE FOR (LATER LITIGIOUS) FIGHTING.

ON THIS DAY IN HISTORY IN CALLANDER, ONTARIO, (NOW the title makes sense!) the famous Dionne Quintuplets were born and soon became the most heavily exploited Canadian tourist items after those little plastic Mountie statues.

The girls were the first identical quints to make it out of infancy. Although the five later regretted ever having done so, once the government took them from their parents and installed them in something called Quintland, where thousands of tourists got to watch them play behind glass in a controlled environment. (This was part of Canada's bold initiative to launch a vacation destination slightly duller than Niagara Falls.)

In the 1990s, the Canadian government finally paid the surviving quints a lump sum of $4 million in compensation for their years as prisoners of a tourist attraction. This precedent was reversed when *Underpaid Man in Goofy Suit v. Happiest Place on Earth* was thrown out in 1996.

Apparently, the chances of having identical quintuplets are one in 57 million. Although nowadays, if you are an older couple who decided to work on your career before having children, fertility drugs will insure that your chances of *not* having quintuplets are one in 57 million.

QUINTUPLET FUN FACT:
UM, THERE'S NOTHING FUN ABOUT QUINTUPLETS. UNLESS YOU FIND CHANGING DIAPERS OR WATCHING OTHER PEOPLE'S QUINTUPLETS ON THE DISCOVERY CHANNEL "FUN."

MAY 29
Mass Historia Mortality In and Out List.

IN:

MAY 29, 1265 Dante, author of *The Divine Comedy*, is born. He most likely did a lot of screaming and fussing on this day, just like every student in the world who has been forced to read his stuff and write a paper on it.

MAY 29, 1736 Patriot Patrick Henry born, promptly proclaims "Give me liberty or give me death. Or maybe I'll just take that boob there."

MAY 29, 1903 Comedian and camp follower Bob Hope born in England. Loud infant cries expertly read off nearby cue cards.

MAY 29, 1906 T. H. White born in India, later becomes acclaimed author of the series of King Arthur novels *The Once and Future King*. He was the last-known person whose interest in Arthurian legend provided a career outside the confines of a comics 'n collectibles shop.

MAY 29, 1955 Presidential wannabe-assassin John Hinckley Jr. born. Although he only became truly alive seven years later with the 1962 birth of hard-to-impress muse Jodie Foster.

OUT:

MAY 29, 1453 Constantine XI, last Byzantine emperor, dies at forty-nine. Explanation of fall of Byzantine Empire too Byzantine to fit into such a small space.

MAY 29, 1847 French general, Emmanuel, Marquis de Grouchy dies. He is only on this list because he was the Marquis of "Grouchy." One assumes death only worsened this state.

MAY 29, 1911 W. S. Gilbert, of famed Gilbert and Sullivan operetta team, becomes the very model of a rigor-mortis lyricist.

⬆ **MAY 29, 1942 DREW BARRYMORE'S GRANDFATHER JOHN** dies at age sixty, after drinking too many things that had been aged for twelve years or more.

MAY 29, 1979 The original "America's Sweetheart" (before Drew Barrymore), **MARY PICKFORD** dies, ushering in a ← whole new silent era for herself.

MARY PICKFORD IN A REVEALING OUTFIT.

PARTIED LESS THAN HIS GRANDDAUGHTER.

MAY 30, 1431
Joan of Arc Gets Totally Lit.

DOES THIS ARMOR MAKE ME LOOK SAINTLY?

TODAY IN 1431, in Rouen, France, Joan of Arc was burned at the stake for heresy. When she was sixteen, at the age when most French teenagers are making their third attempt to quit smoking, Joan began hearing the voices of saints. At first she ignored the saints because they tried to speak to her in English. But after a while, they at least made the effort, so Joan decided not to be too horribly rude to them.

These voices told her to assist the dauphin, the future Charles VII, in capturing British-held Reims and therefore the French throne. They also told her that the government was sending coded alien messages into her fillings and that a tin foil hat would repel them, but since neither fillings nor tin foil had been invented yet, she decided to take them up on the dauphin thing.

She went on to lead a series of stunning defeats against the British, and in a matter of weeks, Charles VII was crowned King of France. After more military triumphs, she was captured in a battle with the Burgundians, who were fuller-bodied fighters than the Merlotians and known for their triumphs in standing up to both duck and lamb. They handed her over to the British, who put her on trial for heresy.

She was found guilty, and the nineteen-year-old Joan was to be burned at the stake. Before the pyre was lit, she instructed a priest to hold a crucifix high enough into the sky for her to see and to shout out prayers loud enough to be heard above the roar of the flames.

Her third instruction, to keep a bucket of water handy, was sadly ignored.

MAY 31, 1860
Happy Birthday, Alleged Jack the Ripper.

ON THIS DAY IN 1860, noted English Impressionist painter Walter Sickert was born. Like most artists, Sickert had to hold down two jobs, one of which was butchering prostitutes in London's Whitechapel district.

This is according to the writer Patricia Cornwell, who fingered the painter in her book *Portrait of a Killer: Jack the Ripper—Case Closed*, in which the novelist closed the case without conclusive DNA proof and despite evidence that Sickert was in France at the time of the killings. (See Sickert's famed study, *Self-Portrait, Not Killing Anyone, Paris, August 31, 1888. What?*)

Either way, nowadays, he is the leading suspect for many people, which now narrows down the field to just him and Prince Albert Victor (Queen Victoria's grandson), author Lewis Carroll, a disturbed schoolteacher named Montague John Druitt, a serial poisoner named George Chapman, Polish butcher Aaron Kominski, bootmaker John Pizer, career criminal Michael Ostrog, Sir John Williams (Queen Victoria's doctor), James Kenneth Stephen (tutor to Prince Albert Victor, Queen Victoria's grandson), Queen Victoria (why not?), Francis Thompson, Alexander Pedachenko, James Maybrick, George Hutchinson, and your grandfather Eamon (your parents won't tell you, we will).

So . . . let's just say it's Sickert and be done with it. Case closed.

TRAITOR HATAH.

June

Benedict Arnold Starts Voyage Toward Becoming a Real "Benedict Arnold."

WAR HERO COLONEL BENEDICT ARNOLD was court-martialed on this day for malfeasance, misusing government wagons ("unseemly pimping"), illegally buying and selling goods, and favoritism to the British Loyalists (nowadays known as "Staying in on Friday nights to watch Britcoms on PBS").

Arnold had been badly injured in the thigh during the Saratoga campaign in 1777, and after several painful surgeries, one leg wound up two inches shorter than the other, which marked his first experience with being "crooked."

Congress refused to compensate him for some wartime expenses and as a result he got involved in shady financial dealings. (This was long before the era when colonels could make money by going on one of the twenty-four-hour news networks and opening their mouths so that words can come out.)

Eventually, he was cleared of the charges, but his former friend General George Washington publicly reprimanded him, which inspired Arnold to coin a new nickname for his commander: "The Mutha of Our Country."

Many believe it was the insult of this reprimand that led Arnold into his treason, when he was offered 20,000 pounds to help the British conquer West Point. Of course, this could have been easily achieved had they just swapped their redcoats for football uniforms with the word NAVY across the front.

Grover?
I Hardly Know Her!

JUNE 2, 1886
Cleveland Steamy!

PRESIDENT GROVER CLEVELAND had a saying, "I have only one thing to do, and that is to do right."

Unfortunately, on June 2, 1886, that one thing to do right was make guests in the Blue Room shift uncomfortably and clear their throats as the confirmed bachelor wed a beautiful young woman, after the minister asked her, "And do you, Frances, take your legal guardian to be your lawfully wedded husband?"

The forty-eight-year-old Cleveland had been twenty-one-year-old Frances Folsom's legal guardian since she was eleven, after the death of her father, Cleveland's law partner Oscar Folsom. As she reached her late teens, Cleveland fell in love with her, and she with him. (Before you judge, notice how today's teenage girls positively flip whenever Wilford Brimley comes on television to talk about his body's difficulties producing insulin.)

During the early years of their marriage, the press remained most interested in the lovely Mrs. Cleveland, particularly after she had given birth to little Ruth. Mrs. Cleveland would push the baby around the White House lawn, and the papers just loved it. (A recent sighting of the Bush daughters passed out in a shopping cart on the White House lawn did not have the same PR effect.)

JUNE 3, 1800
President Adams Is First President in Washington (Not the Former President).

JOHN ADAMS became the first president to ever reside within the brand-spanking-new city of Washington, D.C., on this day in 1800, and like most visitors to the town, by June 4, he had seen everything he wanted to see and was ready to go home.

The Executive mansion was not yet completed, so Adams had to take temporary digs in a watering hole called the Union Tavern in Georgetown, which at 5:30 p.m. every day would be packed with very attractive yet boring young people who worked for some congressman no one's ever heard of.

He eventually settled into the mansion (which was not yet nicknamed "the White House" by Teddy Roosevelt, nicknamed our "worst nicknamier president") the following November. He later wrote in a letter to his wife "I pray heaven to bestow the best of blessings on this house, and on all that shall hereafter inhabit it. May none but wise men ever rule under this roof."

At the very moment he was writing that letter, in upstate New York, a young boy named Obadiah Newcomb Bush dropped his schoolbooks down the privy and started referring to himself as a Texan, even though that territory wouldn't be annexed for another forty-five years.

Loved the Mansion's Powdered Wig Humidor.

JUNE 4, 1919

Congress Passes the Nineteenth Amendment in Effort to Get Someone to Vacuum the Voting Booth Curtains.

ON THIS DAY IN HISTORY, the United States Congress passed the Nineteenth Amendment to the United States Constitution, which granted women the right to vote. It stated that "the rights of citizens of the United States to vote shall not be denied or abridged by the United States or by any state on account of sex." Some swingers thought this meant "on account of (having) sex," which led to awkward "get a room" shouts at many a polling station.

It was ratified by the states in a matter of weeks, and soon women had the right to . . . help elect the handsome yet vapid and corrupt Warren G. Harding into office. (Note: Women soon realized the error of their ways, and many ugly-yet-competent presidents have been elected since. Although there was nearly a red-alert situation during the 2004 election thanks to an all-female write-in effort for dreamy-yet-unexperienced President Orlando Bloom.)

JUNE 5

A Boom in Boomer Milestone.

Baby boomers are now approaching retirement, after having worked so hard all their lives trying to convince the entire world that theirs was the most significant generation to have ever walked the earth in Birkenstock sandals. Here are some events of importance to them—so of course they are important to everyone.

JUNE 5, 1956 Elvis Presley performs "Hound Dog" on *The Milton Berle Show* and scandalizes the audience with his suggestive hip gyrations. To be fair, the audience was there to watch a man with a giant penis deliver jokes while wearing a dress—not to see something depraved.

JUNE 5, 1956 Saxophonist Kenny G., whose albums often play as accompaniment to boomer white-wine binges, is born on the same day people are shocked by Elvis Presley. There is some irony here, but irony is not allowed in the world of Kenny G.

JUNE 5, 1963 British Secretary of War John Profumo resigns after having lied to Parliament about his role in a sex scandal, which, in Britain, means "someone had sex."

JUNE 5, 1968 Senator Robert Kennedy is shot to death by a crazed gunman in the kitchen of the Ambassador Hotel in Los Angeles. While a tragic event in real life, recently it served as a merry signal of hope that the movie *Bobby* was coming to an end.

JUNE 5, 2004 President Ronald Reagan dies at age 209. He won in a landslide in his 1984 reelection bid, which showed that more than a few boomers had quickly forgotten about that whole "Don't trust anyone over thirty" business.

JUNE 6, 1933
First Drive-In Theater Opens After All Popcorn Sufficiently Staled.

ON THIS DAY IN 1932, a young inventor named Richard Hollingshead from New Jersey opened the first-ever drive-in theater—an attraction that combined his passion for movies, cars, and testicles aching with lust.

He experimented in his own driveway in the city of Camden, a place where driveways are now exclusively used to advance drive-by shooting technology. The inventor mounted an old projector on the hood of his car, nailed a screen to trees in his backyard, and used a radio placed behind the screen for sound. His groping of an underage neighbor girl on the front lawn completed the experience.

Hollingshead did all sorts of experimentation on this backyard drive-in and discovered that by spacing cars at various distances and placing ramps under the front wheels of cars farther away from the screen, everyone would have an ideal viewing experience, although not as ideal as the one enjoyed by a TV set in the living room, which would eventually kill the drive-in.

The first patent for the drive-in theater was issued on May 16, 1933, and after spending $30,000, Hollingshead opened his beloved invention to the public. The price of admission was 25 cents for the car and 25 cents per person. Although by its second day of operation, some elderly customers were trying to get a broad daylight, matinee discount.

Ford Begins Designing Their "Edsel," the Edsel.

EDSEL FORD was the mild-mannered son of auto pioneer Henry Ford, a man who came in any mood you liked, as long as you liked black. The elder Ford made his diffident young son president of the company in the 1930s, and undermined and verbally abused Edsel until he died of complications from bleeding ulcers at the ripe old age of forty-nine.

Considering all this to be "good luck," the Ford Motor Company on this day in 1954 began to design a car that would be called the Edsel.

Ford sunk a ton of money into the design of the vehicle, and after a while, someone suggested that the car be named after current president Henry Ford II's father, Edsel, the same "someone" who later revolutionized an assembly line method for bolting his lips onto Ford II's backside.

The Edsel project was launched with great fanfare and a huge advertising campaign ("This isn't your tyrant father's car."). But in the years between the car's conception and its release in 1957, the American economy took a downturn, as chronicled in that now-famous *Leave It to Beaver* episode "Wally Turns Out the Beav."

Public reaction to the car's over-the-top styling was tepid, and no one seemed to like the unique "horse collar" grill. (Experts say it was akin to strapping an ugly Pontiac Aztec to the front of an ugly Pontiac Aztec.) Sales for the car started slowly and then sank.

Robert McNamara, newly appointed Ford vice president and future secretary of defense, was charged with the task of saving the Edsel, but his suggestion of dropping the cars all over North Vietnam was met with puzzled stares.

Muhammed, Founder of Islam, Dies.

YEAH, RIGHT. We're gonna make a joke about this one. Although we have left a space below where you can draw your own cartoon of the Prophet. Enjoy.

Baby, You Can Drive Your Car.

WOMEN DRIVERS. There are plenty of jokes about how awful they are behind the wheel. (This, of course, is a ridiculous stereotype, especially since it is obvious that Asians are much more dangerous.) Alice Huyler Ramsey must have been quite the able motorist, however, because on this day in 1909, she started a journey that would see her become the first woman to drive a car across the United States.

She was twenty-one years old at the time and the president of the Women's Motoring Club in New Jersey (a place where, to this day, driving is still done without turn signals or regard for any other car on the road). She took off from New York City with three other female friends, none of whom could drive. Based on modern chick flick cinematic evidence, chances are this road trip between four young women was interrupted on several occasions so that they could all lip-synch to Motown music using hairbrushes as microphones.

Along the way they encountered washed-out bridges, Native-American tribes, and a sheriff's posse, and the car broke down several times. Thankfully, Ramsey was an able mechanic. And no, she was married.

In 2000, seventeen years after her death at age ninety-six, Ramsey became the first woman ever inducted into the Automotive Hall of Fame. The only others are National Hot Rod Association champ Shirley Muldowney and someone known as "Seminude Woman Atop Ferrari Hood in Dorm Room Poster." That poster is available at the Automotive Hall of Fame gift shop.

ALICE DOESN'T LIVE ANYMORE.

AA DOB.

ON THIS DAY IN 1935, two alcoholics founded Alcoholics Anonymous, an informal twelve-step-based organization helping problem-drinkers abstain from alcohol and problem-American-politicians abstain from taking responsibility for their sexual and/or financial improprieties.

AA was founded by a New York stock speculator named Bill Wilson and a surgeon named Dr. Bob Smith. They had their first meeting in Akron, Ohio, and then—as is the ritual following most AA meetings—they both drank an ungodly amount of coffee and smoked hundreds of cigarettes.

By the way, Wilson eventually became known as "Bill W.," in keeping with the anonymous nature of the organization's treatment. Although a "Bill W." sticker slapped on the bumper of a car usually transforms the owner of the vehicle from "Anonymous Driver" to "Anonymous Driver Who Will Be Randomly Pulled Over by a Cop Looking to Meet His Quota of DUI Arrests."

JUNE 11
A Good Day to Dive.

TODAY IS A DAY TO SLAP ON A SPEEDO and honor notable events in the world of swimming, diving, and getting wet.

JUNE 11, 1910 Famed underwater explorer Jacques Cousteau is born in France and later becomes famous for having invented the underwater breathing device known as the Aqualung. Jethro Tull's *Aqualung* later becomes famous with those who spend too much time breathing through the water-filled apparatus known as the bong.

No Animals Were Harmed . . . Only Embarrassed.

JUNE 11, 1936 The London International Surrealist Exhibition opens—or does it, rubber telephone? A highlight was a lecture given by Salvador Dalí while wearing a diving suit, in which he almost suffocated. The title of the lecture? "Let Them Know You're Quirky: Eight Surreal Steps to Trying Too Hard."

JUNE 11, 1962 Hardened criminals Frank Lee Morris and John and Clarence Anglin probably become softened corpses as they bust out of Alcatraz Federal Penitentiary and dive into the ice-cold San Francisco Bay. Some say theirs was the only successful escape from Alcatraz, which was dramatized in the film *Escape from Alcatraz*, the title of which was later incarcerated in Spoiler Jail.

JUNE 12
HISTO-POURRI.

Kingfisher, Seat-Saver.

JUNE 12, 1935 U.S. Senator **HUEY LONG** of Louisiana ← makes the longest speech on Senate record. The speech took fifteen-and-a-half hours to read and was 150,000 words. Dubbed "Huey Long-Winded" by then-three-year-old piano-playing political satirist Mark Russell.

JUNE 12, 1942 Anne Frank given a diary for her thirteenth birthday. Filled with frothy girl stuff, for about a month.

JUNE 12, 1963 Civil rights leader Medgar Evers fatally shot in front of his home in Jackson, Mississippi, by Klan member Byron De La Beckwith. Southern justice stereotypes shattered when he is convicted, forty years later.

JUNE 12, 1964 Nelson Mandela is sentenced to life in prison in South Africa. Upon release in 1997, he sadly tries to revive Dashiki craze missed while in jail.

JUNE 12, 1977 The Broadway musical *Pippin* closes at the Imperial Theater in New York City, after 1,944 performances. Such songs as "Magic to Do" and "Corner of the Sky" still strike a chord . . . with those who wear piano keyboard ties and who have seen *Wicked* sixteen times.

JUNE 12, 1978 Son of Sam serial killer David Berkowitz sentenced in New York Supreme Court to twenty-five years to life. Neighbor dog who instructed him to do killings cops plea.

JUNE 12, 1991 Russians go to the polls and elect Boris Yeltsin as the president of their republic. Yeltsin suggests a toast to democracy, wakes up shoeless on a bus eight years later.

JUNE 12, 1994 O. J. Simpson takes a knife and does some rhetorical research on the throats and torsos of his ex-wife and her boyfriend that will eventually take the shape of his book *If I Did It*.

THE GREAT'S PROFILE.

JUNE 13, 323 BC
Death Doesn't Think Alexander Is So "Great."

ON THIS DAY, ALEXANDER THE GREAT, the young Macedonian military genius who forged an empire stretching from the eastern Mediterranean to India, dies in Babylon, in present-day Iraq, at the age of thirty-three. And since he died in Iraq, the more conservative Macedonians observed this by affixing yellow stickers to their chariots.

At the age of sixteen, Alexander led his first troops into combat and two years later brought Greece under Macedonian rule—after the Macedonians threatened to withhold the Greeks' cigarettes (you don't want to do that to Greeks). When his father, Phillip II, was assassinated, Alexander ascended to the throne, settling on the title "Great" since the probably homosexual Alexander was unable to choose between "King" or "Queen."

By 330 BC, all of Persia and Asia Minor was under his control. Within his empire, he began to establish great cities, such as Alexandria in Egypt ("Greater Narcissist" was too long an address for the empire's primitive envelope technology), and by 327 BC, he had conquered central Asia, northern India, and Afghanistan. A triumph, because in 327 BC, "conquering Afghanistan" didn't just mean "force the Taliban to live out of a suitcase for a few months."

Alexander reached Babylon a few years later and fell sick after a prolonged drinking binge and died. (In addition to perfecting the base 60 math system, the Babylonians also pioneered a system of mixing alcohol with Jell-O in small but deceptively potent portions.)

Totally Flaggy.

TODAY IS FLAG DAY, which is maybe the most important day on the calendar for flags and flag-related products, and it is celebrated in an effort to keep American interests in flags from flagging. Below we unfurl a few important events that occurred on this day.

JUNE 14, 1777 Congress adopted the Stars and Stripes as the official flag of the United States. Philadelphia seamstress Betsy Ross supposedly designed the flag, although there is no historical data to back this up. (Although she is responsible for the first-ever American flag "Tryest Burneth This One, Thou Assholeth" T-shirt.)

JUNE 14, 1846 American settlers in California rebel against the Mexican government (in California, this animosity will spread to "all Mexicans everywhere"), and proclaim the California Republic under a makeshift flag featuring a grizzly bear. This was later adopted as the state flag. (Note: A "California Bear Flag" is also a colored handkerchief that when placed in the appropriate pocket, declares your allegiance to the company of robust and hairy homosexual men. This sometimes leads to confusion.)

JUNE 14, 1937 Pennsylvania becomes the first (and only) state in the United States to celebrate Flag Day officially as a state holiday. Some celebrate by visiting Philadelphia's Betsy Ross house, where history apparently was not made or even sewn.

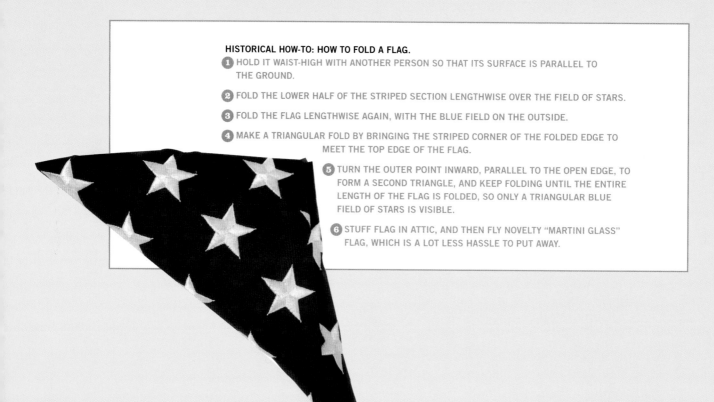

HISTORICAL HOW-TO: HOW TO FOLD A FLAG.

1 HOLD IT WAIST-HIGH WITH ANOTHER PERSON SO THAT ITS SURFACE IS PARALLEL TO THE GROUND.

2 FOLD THE LOWER HALF OF THE STRIPED SECTION LENGTHWISE OVER THE FIELD OF STARS.

3 FOLD THE FLAG LENGTHWISE AGAIN, WITH THE BLUE FIELD ON THE OUTSIDE.

4 MAKE A TRIANGULAR FOLD BY BRINGING THE STRIPED CORNER OF THE FOLDED EDGE TO MEET THE TOP EDGE OF THE FLAG.

5 TURN THE OUTER POINT INWARD, PARALLEL TO THE OPEN EDGE, TO FORM A SECOND TRIANGLE, AND KEEP FOLDING UNTIL THE ENTIRE LENGTH OF THE FLAG IS FOLDED, SO ONLY A TRIANGULAR BLUE FIELD OF STARS IS VISIBLE.

6 STUFF FLAG IN ATTIC, AND THEN FLY NOVELTY "MARTINI GLASS" FLAG, WHICH IS A LOT LESS HASSLE TO PUT AWAY.

JUNE 15, 1952
Ben Franklin Goes Electric.

STATESMAN, INVENTOR, WRITER, PRINTER, PHILOSOPHER, AND HORN-DOG Benjamin Franklin conducted perhaps his most famous experiment on this date when he flew a kite high into a stormy sky above Philadelphia.

Franklin had a theory that lightning was electricity, and planned to use a kite to attract sparks from a passing cloud. This would be the first and last time that the hobby of kite-flying would attract sparks from anything or anyone.

Franklin, accompanied by his twenty-one-year-old illegitimate son William—who was expecting another absentee-dad-pony-ride-and-ice-cream bonding session—went out with kite, kite string, key, and an early capacitor device known as a Leyden jar attached to the key by a thin metal wire. And when the contraption failed to serve as a conversation starter with a few passing ladies, they broke down and started with the science stuff.

A storm cloud passed over, and the negative charges in the cloud hit Franklin's kite and passed down to the key. The inventor was protected from the negative charges because he was holding a silk string that insulated him, but when Franklin reached out his finger to touch the key he received a shock because the negative charges in the key were strongly attracted to the positive charges in his body. Franklin's experiment successfully showed that lightning was actually static electricity, a triumph for science that his illegitimate son heralded with, "Yeah, Dad, great. Quit pretending to care."

Eventually, this led to Franklin's invention of the lightning rod, a simple device to protect homes and barns from being struck by lightning, and which you can buy today from Restoration Hardware to protect your 500K weekend place from seeming "unrustic."

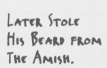

LATER STOLE
HIS BEARD FROM
THE AMISH.

JUNE 16, 1858
"Honest Abe" Lincoln Rips Off Bible.

A house divided against itself cannot stand. I believe this government cannot endure permanently half slave and half free.

SO SAID ABRAHAM LINCOLN on this date in 1858, addressing the Illinois Republican Convention and killing the buzz of attendees wearing gay, colorful, elephant-shaped hats and crocheted "USA" sweaters. Yet they had no choice but to listen to the succession of bummers being laid upon them by the man they just nominated for the Senate, who no doubt forgot to take his mood-leveling tincture of lead and wormwood that morning.

The man from Springfield, Illinois, borrowed "A house divided" from the Bible only after trying for hours to find that perfect line to warn of the dangers of a possible Civil War. A few of the lines Lincoln rejected were found on an envelope he discarded after the convention, more proof of the kinky thing he had for writing on the backs of envelopes. We list these alternate lines below.

- **A house divided against itself is like my house on a cloudy day. (This may have been a reference to Mary Todd Lincoln's emotional struggles.)**
- **A house divided against itself cannot stand, unless it's one of those sturdy log cabins, like the one I was born in. (This was not used because earlier that day an advisor told Lincoln he had the nomination locked and could go easy with the "hayseed log cabin crap.")**
- **If your house is divided, you better hope you're on the side with the crapper. (It took Lincoln a while to really nail "Folksy.")**

JUNE 17, 1775
The Battle of [Location TBD].

ON THIS DAY IN HISTORY, one of the bloodiest battles of the American Revolution took place at Bunker Hill. Actually, it wasn't at Bunker Hill at all, but at Breed's Hill, which is nearby. The British had planned on attacking Bunker Hill, but got off the wrong exit in one of the city's famed rotaries and, well, let's just say they got lost.

Revolutionary forces gunned down nearly one hundred redcoats, thanks in part to the order given by General William Prescott, "Don't shoot till you see the whites of their eyes." Although this led to the survival of one jaundiced British soldier named Corporal Nigel "Yellow Eyes" Worthington.

Unfortunately, the Americans ran out of ammo and had to engage the British in hand-to-hand combat. Some patriots found it hard to find an Englishman to take a swing at, however, after the order "Don't punch till you see the prominence of their strong chins" was given.

It was a victory for the British but a morale booster for the Americans, who managed to lose fewer men despite their defeat and retreat. This might explain why Philadelphia is called "The Cradle of Liberty" and Boston is called "The Bassinet of Spinning It Positive."

YANKEES SUCK!

122

Radio Day.

THIS IS A DAY OF SOME NOTE IN THE HISTORY OF RADIO, which, thanks to television and online music downloads, might soon be history itself.

JUNE 18, 1905 Bandleader Kay Kyser is born, later hosts a long-running comedy radio show called *Kay Kyser's Kollege of Musical Knowledge*. Supposedly never learned how to play an instrument, which is probably a load of krap.

JUNE 18, 1945 Nazi shock jock "Lord Haw Haw," aka fascist Irishman William Joyce, is charged with three counts of high treason by the British government. Joyce broadcast pro-Nazi and anti-Allied messages to England throughout the war, all of which were probably funnier than anything heard on *Kay Kyser's Kollege of Musical Knowledge*. To get a feel for what it must have been like to listen to Haw Haw's wartime broadcasts, have someone throw M-80s at you while you listen to Rush Limbaugh.

JUNE 18, 1984 Over-the-top Left Wing radio personality Alan Berg is shot twelve times by neo-Nazis in his driveway in Colorado. Later inspires Eric Bogosian to write the play *Talk Radio*, which later inspires Oliver Stone to make a movie of Eric Bogosian's play, *Talk Radio*, which later inspires the author of this book to leave the theater midway through and sneak into one next-door showing *Beaches*, which then made author wish he would suddenly be shot twelve times by neo-Nazis.

JUNE 19, 1885

Statuesque Woman Found Floating in New York Harbor.

OF COURSE, our title refers to the arrival in America of the separate pieces that would eventually make up the Statue of Liberty. It is not the opening line of description in a shooting script of *Law & Order: SVU*.

As the statue arrived via ship in over two hundred packing crates, the citizens of New York City gathered along the banks of the harbor and made a note to themselves that one day they would really have to go and visit the statue.

To this day, no citizen of New York City has ever made good on that pledge. ←

GIVE ME YOUR TIRED,
YOUR POOR, YOUR
HUDDLED TOURISTS.

JUNE 20, 1893
Lizzie Borden Gets Whack Jury.

Lizzie Borden took an ax,
Gave her mother forty whacks
When she saw what she had done
Gave her father forty-one.

THIS ONE NEEDS A BIT OF FACT-CHECKING.

FOR ONE THING, it wasn't her mother, it was her stepmother, a woman Lizzie referred to as "Mrs. Borden" and whom she deeply loathed, especially after finding out her miser father was going to leave the majority of his $500,000 estate to her. Also, it wasn't forty or forty-one whacks, but over a dozen and eleven, respectively (inasmuch as hitting anyone a dozen times with a hatchet can be "respective").

"When she saw what she had done, gave her father forty-one?" Well, it wasn't that spontaneous. The killer waited nearly two hours between the killings, suggesting she or he had easy access to the house that was also occupied by an Irish maid, who claims to have heard Lizzie laughing downstairs when the murders occurred. Shoddy fact-checking aside—who can argue with the joyful mirth provided to children by such a wonderful rhyme about patricide and step-matricide?

And it was on this day in 1893 that a jury in Fall River, Massachusetts, acquitted Miss Borden of murdering her father and stepmother, despite some overwhelming evidence against her. Many now say she was sprung because a jury of Victorian gentlemen couldn't imagine a woman ever committing such a shocking, deranged, and grotesque act. Keep in mind, this was over a hundred years before anyone witnessed Britney Spears entering a public restroom barefoot.

Lizzie used her inheritance to buy an enormous mansion in Fall River called Maplecroft, where her only violent acts consisted of brutally stomping out many bags of flaming dog crap left on her porch.

I WANT YOU . . .
TO ACCEPT MY APOLOGY
FOR BEING A JERK.

JUNE 21
Shame on You, America.

IN SOME RESPECTS, this heading could apply to nearly every day of the year, but that would make for a bummer of a book. Yet today really contains some fairly reprehensible events in the history of the (usually) Good ol' USA.

JUNE 21, 1639 The Puritan Reverend Increase Mather born in Massachusetts. He was one of the overseers of the Salem Witch Trials and, despite half-hearted efforts to stem the presentation of "spectral evidence," he spent the rest of his life justifying his involvement and refusing to renounce any of the judges or the trials themselves. One of the thousands of reasons why, even centuries later, boys named Increase probably had a pretty hard time at school.

JUNE 21, 1788 The United States ratifies the stupid Constitution. (That is a bone thrown to readers who work at the Department of Homeland Security.)

JUNE 21, 1877 Ten Irish immigrants, coal miners, and members of the Molly Maguires are hanged in Pennsylvania after being arrested by Pinkertons—not police—in a trial where Irish were not allowed on the jury and the judge was the head of the Philadelphia & Reading Railroad, which transported coal. It was a travesty of justice that makes you forget all about . . . the men the miners actually murdered.

JUNE 21, 1964 The Ku Klux Klan kills three civil rights workers who were registering black voters in Mississippi. Mississippi refuses to try the murderers in a state court, due to a lack of "spectral evidence," which is still admissible in the Mississippi judicial system.

JUNE 22, 1848
Hanson Gregory Invents Doughnut, Maybe.

GIVE YOURSELF AN EXTRA LONG DUNK OF THAT PASTRY and suck out a little celebratory strawberry jelly because today, according to many sources, is the birthday of the doughnut.

There are differing versions of the tale. In the dullest take, a fifteen-year-old Hanson Gregory was sitting in his family kitchen somewhere in New England and noticed that his mother's fried cakes were "wicked soggy" in the center. He poked a hole through the cake with a fork, and created a doughnut, or a "quit-playing-with-your-food cake." This version of the story was made popular on Paul Harvey's radio program, so feel free to reread the above inserting pauses that make the listener think he's lost reception, and offer up plenty of whistling sounds with your dentures.

In the more exciting version of the invention story, Captain Hanson Gregory found himself having difficulty steering his fishing ship and holding his olykoek, or oily cake, a Dutch dessert (and one of the few that is not 80 percent hashish).

The quick-thinking sailor impaled his cake on one of the spokes of his steering wheel. Happy with the result, he ordered the cook to prepare all oily cakes with holes in the center (pastry chefs only began to appear on ships after the invention of the Lido Deck). Unfortunately, sailors being sailors, many of them started calling the new invention "a shipboard wife" and began "loving" the pastries in a rather unholy manner.

TWO DAYS LATER, "AMERICAN OBESITY" WAS INVENTED.

DON'T ASK HIM TO
BLOW ANYTHING OUT.

JUNE 23, 1948

Supreme Court Justice Clarence Thomas Born.

THUS BEGINS THE COUNTDOWN to his sixty-ninth birthday, which he comments about inappropriately to all his female staffers.

JUNE 24, 1997

The Air Force Flies Right into Conspiracy Freak Danger Zone.

ON THIS DAY IN 1997, the United States Air Force (which in those days had a bit more time on their hands than they do now), having already closed the book on the Project Easter Bunny and Operation Your Girlfriend in Canada, released a report that no doubt upset many people who were not mentally or physically fit enough to join the air force and lodge a formal complaint.

The report, titled "Case Closed," stated that the supposed alien landing in Roswell, New Mexico, in 1947 was not an alien landing at all but a top-secret mishap involving balloons, a couple of male mannequins, and an injured airman with a badly swollen head. (He was injured in a typically homoerotic flyboy hazing, which required the presence of the male mannequins and balloons.)

The report was released on the fiftieth anniversary of the supposed alien landing and was 231 pages long. The main people interested in the report were not put off by the length, since most of them could polish off 251 pages of a *Dune* novel in the dull, twenty-four-hour break between *Star Trek: TOS* airings on the Sci-Fi channel.

JUNE 25

War. What Is It Good For? Making June 25 a Notable Day!

THIS DAY IN HISTORY IS USUALLY A GOOD ONE for fans of war and warlike people. Of course, those "fans" are usually people who have never been involved in a war themselves, apart from the violent struggle to get the remote control away from their wives so they can return to watching the History Channel's "Hitler Week."

JUNE 25, 1876 U.S. CAVALRY COMMANDER GEORGE ARMSTRONG CUSTER stops ←
standing when he is killed by a confederation of Native-American forces led by Sitting Bull
and Crazy Horse at the Battle of Little Bighorn. Tragedy of that day commemorated with free
second scoop at Custard's Last Stands across the American Midwest.

JUNE 25, 1940 France formally surrenders to the Germans. Everyone in France starts
rehearsing the story of their involvement in the Resistance so they can start telling it in 1945.

JUNE 25, 1942 General Dwight D. Eisenhower takes command of the U.S. forces in Europe,
despite having never seen combat after nearly thirty years in the army. The combat experience
he soon gets in the war, however, almost makes him ineligible to later run as the Republican
candidate for president.

JUNE 25, 1950 The Korean War begins as Communist North Korea invades South Korea.
Thankfully, war does not last nearly as long as the television series *M*A*S*H*, and North
Korea is never a problem again.

JUNE 26, 2003

Senator Strom "Highlander II: The Segregating" Thurmond Dies at One Hundred.

ON THIS DAY IN 2003, Senator Strom Thurmond (extremely R-SC) died after a
long battle with the forces at work in a fair universe. He had left the Senate a year
earlier, having then served longer than any other person in that storied institution.
His record was recently broken by Senator Robert Byrd, once a member of the Ku Klux Klan.
(This link between racism and longevity is explored in Dr. Nicholas Perricone's new best
seller, *The Wrinkle Cure: White Skin–Only Edition*. Apparently all you need to do is positively
envision a white America and eat fish twice a week.)

Thurmond's political career began in 1946 when he was elected governor of South Carolina.
He was famously pro-segregation, saying in a 1948 speech, "There's not enough troops in
the army to force the Southern people to break down segregation and admit the Negro race
into our theaters, into our swimming pools, into our homes, and into our churches." (Oddly
enough, he wasn't opposed to them entering his bedroom, but that's another story.)

In 1954, he ran for the United States Senate as a Democrat and became the only candidate
ever elected to the Senate by a write-in vote, which led to a severe shortage of crayons
throughout South Carolina for many weeks afterward.

Three years later, he staged a record-breaking one-man filibuster to defeat a civil rights
bill. It lasted more than twenty-four hours and was the first (but not the last) time the senator
was seen in the chamber fully diapered and not entirely aware of the time.

**STROM THURMOND
FUN FACT:**
HE'S DEAD!

JUNE 28, 1969
Over-the-Top Outrage at Stonewall Inn.

"You Have the Right to Wear a Tutti-frutti Hat."

ON THIS DATE IN 1969, a riot broke out in New York's Greenwich Village after police raided a gay bar known as the Stonewall Inn, kicking off the gay rights movement in America. The city had not seen such a violent outbreak of put-upon minorities with bushy mustaches since the 1863 New York City Draft Riots.

Early in the morning, police officers entered the Christopher Street "private club," which operated without a liquor license and was owned by the Mafia (which for many years controlled the city's lucrative Frozen Cosmo Trade).

IDs were checked, and cops took names but soon began letting patrons go. Before the violence, a crowd gathered outside to cheer every time a gay person emerged from the bar (the exact opposite intention of a typical Reverend Fred Phelps rally, but just as festive). But they grew angry when they saw three drag queens being hauled into a paddy wagon, although from their appearances, it was obvious they had already been Carmen Mirandized (sorry).

A few in the crowd uprooted a parking meter and used it to barricade the door, trapping the cops inside the bar, and forcing many of the Irish-American officers to undergo a horrifying ordeal known as being off-duty.

The rioting grew and lasted for three days. After this historic uprising, dozens of gay rights organizations emerged throughout the city and the nation, eventually numbering over four hundred. However, the Ladies Stonewall Society—a group of spinster descendants of the famed Civil War general—would like it known that they are not a gay rights organization and would prefer it if unruly "boot sluts" stopped attending their meetings and wreaking havoc on their finger sandwiches.

Globe-al Warming.

SHAKESPEARE'S BELOVED GLOBE THEATRE: Shall I compare thee to a smoldering wreck? Many might have done so on this day in 1613, when it burned to the ground during the opening night performance of the Bard's *Henry VIII*, which at the time made it a problem play but not in the way snooty academics describe Shakespeare's "problem plays."

Apparently a special-effects cannon ignited the building's thatched roof, and the fire then spread to a prop cabinet filled with an assortment of Henry VIII's greasy turkey legs.

The theatre burned to the ground in about an hour, and history does not record any fatalities, although Sir Henry Wotton wrote that "only one man had his breeches set on fire, that would perhaps have broyled him, if he had not by the benefit of a provident wit, put it out with a bottle of ale," which suggests that this date also marks the first recorded occurrence of a stunt by the *Ye Olde Jackass* crew.

The Great Blondin Crosses the Falls.

ON THIS DAY IN 1859, Jean-Francois Gravelet, a Frenchman known as the Great Blondin because of his blond hair (detractors called him the Great Blackroots), became the first daredevil to walk across Niagara Falls on a tightrope.

Wearing pink tights and a yellow tunic (a costume greeted with more tolerance on the Canadian side), Blondin crossed a cable about two inches in diameter and 1,100 feet long while holding a forty-pound balancing pole that was thirty feet long (overcompensation for the pink tights and yellow tunic).

He stepped onto the tightrope and started his long descent down the cable. Upon reaching the midpoint he stopped, dropped a bottle tied to a piece of twine into the river, hauled up some Niagara water, and drank it. The crowd went wild. They went less wild when, a few minutes later, he dazzled them with high-wire feats of stomach cramps and explosive diarrhea.

For two years afterward, Blondin performed above the Niagara. He crossed the Falls on a bicycle and on stilts, did somersaults, and stood on his head on a chair. He also once pushed a stove in a wheelbarrow and cooked an omelet, a feat recently duplicated on the Food Network program *Daredeviled Eggs*.

BLONDIN HAS MORE FUN.

July

JULY 1
FIGHT!

THIS DAY HAS SEEN THE START OF MANY A BLOODY CONFLICT, so if there is something that's been bugging you about the boyfriend/girlfriend, you might want to leave it lay until tomorrow.

LAZY!

JULY 1, 251 Decius became the first Roman emperor ever killed in combat during the Battle of Abrittus, but at least he died over a region that would one day vanish from every map. The Roman forces were defeated by the Goths, in a battle that gave birth to the cry, "Don't fight till you see the blacks of their eyeliners."

JULY 1, 1863 The American Civil War's **BATTLE OF GETTYSBURG** kicks off, and—without the soothing "Jimmy Crack Corn" Ken Burnsesque score underneath—one imagines it was pretty horrible. Fifty-one thousand men died in the three-day battle, which saw the retreat of the Confederate forces, thanks to the more effective Union battle cry, "Don't shoot till you see the fullness of their mullets."

JULY 1, 1898 **TEDDY ROOSEVELT AND HIS ROUGH RIDERS** (which didn't sound so gay in 1898) swung into action at the Battle of San Juan Hill in Cuba during the Spanish-American War. A month later, Cuba was captured, and it was never a problem for the United States ever again.

JULY 1, 1916 World War I's Battle of the Somme begins, and proves to be Somme kind of mess. (Note: That was the author's attempt to make a joke slightly more awful than the battle itself.) During the five months of the battle, over a million soldiers would be killed or wounded. But at least Germany would never be a problem for Britain ever again.

TEDDY'S BEARS.

WOULDN'T HAVE GOTTEN
BACKSTAGE AT A
SLAUGHTER CONCERT.

THE "RIGID BODY"
ZEPPELIN SOUNDS LIKE
A BIT OF A BOAST.

JULY 2
Hot Wings.

LOOK TO THE SKIES. Today is a day when famous aviation events have flown high, or come crashing down.

← **JULY 2, 1900** Ferdinand Adolf August Heinrich Graf von Zeppelin debuts his namesake invention, **THE ZEPPELIN**, after deciding not to call it a "Flying August Heinrich." His invention's days were numbered after the Hindenburg disaster, but his name lived on in the slightly more volatile creation, Led Zeppelin.

JULY 2, 1937 AMELIA EARHART goes missing over the Pacific ← Ocean while trying to circumnavigate the globe. Later honored in the song "Fly to the Angels" by the band Slaughter, a hair metal outfit that wanted more than anything to be like the band that took its name from Ferdinand Adolf August Heinrich Graf von Zeppelin.

JULY 2, 1947 Aliens supposedly crash-land in Roswell, New Mexico. People who believe in the occurrence of this event are also willing to believe that Amelia Earhart is still living on an island in the Pacific with Judge Crater, Ambrose Bierce, and Led Zeppelin drummer John Bonham.

JULY 2, 1982 A man in California named Larry Walters ties forty-five helium-filled balloons to a lawn chair and reaches an altitude of sixteen thousand feet. His story is later the inspiration for the movie *Danny Deckchair*, which starred Welsh actor Rhys Ifans, who was once in the rock band Super Furry Animals, to which making a Led Zeppelin comparison would be harder than getting sixteen thousand feet in a deck chair tied to balloons.

JULY 3
Mass Historia Mortality In and Out List:
Musical Edition.

LOTS OF LUMINARIES from the world of music heard either "Happy Birthday" or a funeral dirge on this day in history.

IN:

JULY 3, 1893 Blues legend Mississippi John Hurt is born. He is not to be confused with the British character actor John Hurt, who is already too busy being confused with American character actor John Heard.

JULY 3, 1957 Singer Laura Brannigan is born. She had a hit in the 1980s with the song "Gloria," which is not to be confused with the song "Gloria" by the Irish rock band Them, who are not to be confused with a movie about giant ants.

JULY 3, 1960 VINCE CLARKE, of both Depeche Mode and Erasure, is born. His ← fontanel was covered with the first in a series of asymmetrical haircuts.

OUT:

JULY 3, 1969 Rolling Stones guitarist Brian Jones dies of a drug overdose, a few weeks after being kicked out of the band for seeming like the kind of wussy who would allow himself to die of a drug overdose. His yellow, pudding-bowl haircut survived and later relocated to the top of Carol Channing.

JULY 3, 1971 "I'm the Lizard King, and I can do anything." Except breathe, apparently, because on this day Jim Morrison of the Doors died. His music survived him, thanks to the world's unending supply of moody male teenagers.

JULY 3, 1986 Vagabond lover and megaphone crooner Rudy Vallee dies. Was the 1930s answer to Jim Morrison, except he knew how to keep his penis from flying out when cops were in the audience. Or he at least knew how to conceal it (see megaphone).

Founding Fathers Celebrate Founding by Being Found Dead.

ON THE FIFTIETH ANNIVERSARY of the signing of the Declaration of Independence, two of that document's writers and former presidents John Adams and Thomas Jefferson died in what was either an ironic end or a bizarre, long-distance suicide pact between two closeted lovers (the rumor starts here!).

Adams, well into his nineties, supposedly uttered the last words "Thomas Jefferson still survives," although Jefferson had died a few hours before, his last words having been "I bet that dick Adams still thinks I'm alive."

To find out more about the relationship between Jefferson and Adams, rent the film version of the musical *1776*. Tell the video clerk you're a history buff, so he doesn't think you're a musical-loving closeted homosexual like Thomas Jefferson and John Adams (this rumor is going to be HUGE!).

MOLDERING FATHERS.

JULY 5, 1946
Itsy-Bitsy Teeny-Weeny Birthday.

THE WORLD'S BEACHES suddenly became havens for pervs with telephoto lenses on this day in 1946, when the French (of course) designer Louis Reard unveiled the two-piece bathing suit known as the bikini.

He named his suit after the Bikini Atoll, on which the United States had just conducted an atomic test. Thankfully, for the self-esteem of women everywhere, the U.S. opted not to conduct their experiment on nearby Fathips Island or on the Sagass Sandbar.

Ironically, Reard had trouble finding a model who would wear his design. Sadly, this European modesty all but vanished a few years later when the men's Speedo was invented.

JULY 6, 1946
George W. Bush Is Born (The First Time).

Note: This commemorates our forty-third president's first birth, which kicked off many years of partying, drinking, and failing upward. He was Born Again a few years later, and promptly became the giant nuisance he is today.

JULY 7, 1865
Respectable Lady Becomes Swinger.

THINGS GOT EVEN HOTTER on a very hot July 7, 1865, when the United States government hanged their first woman, forty-three-year-old Lincoln assassination coconspirator Mary Surratt.

Surratt owned a tavern and inn outside Washington where John Wilkes Booth and his other pro-Confederate plotters frequently met (this was years before the invention of the other favorite Confederate haunt, Hooters). Some believe that Mrs. Surratt thought the conspirators were only going to kidnap Lincoln, not kill him, although both options would have been preferable to sitting through the dull second act of *Our American Cousin*.

CAUSES OF DEATH:
AUTOEROTIC ASPHYXIATION.

Mrs. Surratt's fate was sealed when inn tenant John M. Lloyd testified during her trial that she had told him to have field glasses and weapons ready for Booth and David Herold when they arrived at the tavern after the assassination. Since they were hoping to escape through the south, she also requested that he supply them with "Git-R-Done" bug screens for the front of their horses.

Despite pleas for clemency, President Andrew Johnson signed her order of execution, declaring that she "kept the nest that hatched the egg." (Not as powerful as George W. Bush's "Wanted: Dead or Alive," but at least Johnson actually followed up on it.)

Surratt was led to the gallows, and her last words were "Don't let me fall," proving that while she may not have known of the plan to kill Lincoln, she certainly did not know anything about the mechanics of a hanging.

JULY 8, 1822

Percy Bysshe Shelley Dies, Takes Pronunciation Secrets of "Bysshe" with Him.

WHILE SAILING IN HIS SLOOP *Don Juan* (he thought the name *Poon Hound* might have been overdoing it) off the coast of Italy, the famed "infidel poet" Percy Bysshe Shelley drowned when he and his vessel encountered a violent storm on this day in 1822. Shelley had supposedly seen his doppelganger a few days before, which was considered by many at the time to be a harbinger of doom. (To be fair, the appearance of more than one poet under any circumstances is at least fatal to a "good time.")

When his body washed ashore a few days later, his friends Lord Byron, Leigh Hunt, and noted Romantic poet hanger-on Edward Trelawny burned it on a pyre on a beach in Viareggio. This, combined with the advanced state of decomposition of the corpse, made for the most repulsive sight ever seen on an Italian beach, until the invention of the Speedo in the twentieth century. (For more on the Speedo, see same exact joke on page 134.)

Lord Byron was supposedly sickened by the corpse and had to leave, calling into question the veracity of that whole "mad, bad, and dangerous to know" business. Trelawny, made of stronger stuff, reached into the flaming corpse and removed the heart, which he then gave to Shelley's widow, Mary Wollstonecraft "the original Anne Rice" Shelley. It was a tradition at the time that Victorian women not attend funerals, which made the other tradition of bringing home putrefied souvenirs from the funeral all the more special.

Note: Romantic poets demanded that mankind turn its back on the Industrial Revolution and return to nature; they also rebelled against the Enlightenment's "reason over emotion" as the basis of authority. If they were alive today, they'd probably be known as "A Bunch of Drama Queens."

Old Rough-And-Ready Turns Stiff-and-Gamey.

ON THIS DAY IN HISTORY, after a short illness, President Zachary Taylor died of either cholera, typhoid, gastroenteritis, or heat stroke. He had consumed large amounts of cherries, iced milk, and pickles, a mixture that also led to a diagnosis of the very rare "man pregnancy."

He had been president for only sixteen months when he attended Fourth of July celebrations on a sweltering day on the Washington Mall. He had ingested all the foods very quickly, but like every Fourth of July event involving very fast eating, he ultimately didn't eat as much as a nearby skinny teenager from Japan.

He took to bed and died after a few days of diarrhea, nausea, cramping, and vomiting, creating an atmosphere in the White House that was not seen again until the early twentieth century, a day after someone introduced President William Howard Taft to the concept of the Jalapeño Popper.

Since Taylor had been a hard-liner against slavery, and threatened to attack any state that might secede from the Union, some thought he might have been poisoned. In 1991, over 140 years after his death, his body was exhumed, yet no substantial traces of arsenic were found in the body. Still, conspiracy theorists believe Taylor was a victim of the massive Pickle Industrial Complex and mock the "Magic Cherry" theory.

THE STILL LIFE OF ZACK AND HORSEY.

This Day in Histor-SEA!

AHOY, MATEYS. Walk the gangplank and set sail for a briny exploration of various nautical-themed events that dropped anchor on this day in history.

JULY 10, 1797 The first U.S. frigate, named the USS *United States*, is launched. She would sail for nearly seventy years and count among her seamen noted author Herman Melville, who recounted his onboard adventures in his novel *White-Jacket*, which is not the one about the whale. Eventually, she was captured by Confederate forces who accidentally scuttled her by nailing Playboy Bunny mud flaps to the craft's hull.

"WAIT. WE HAVEN'T INSTALLED THE TRAILER HITCH!"

JULY 10, 1987 Greenpeace vessel *Rainbow Warrior* sinks in Auckland Harbor, New Zealand, after French Secret Service agents place a bomb on the hull of the ship, bringing most of the hippies on board dangerously close to water. Eventually, it was revealed that the French government had ordered the sinking of the ship because it had been disrupting French nuclear tests, setting back their "clean-fission brulé" program many years.

JULY 10, 1992 Exxon Valdez "Captain Blood (Alcohol Content)" Joseph Hazelwood—who was found guilty of negligence in 1989 after he befouled Prince William Sound with millions of gallons of crude oil—has his conviction overturned by the Alaska Court of Appeals on this day in 1992. Despite the fact that Hazelwood had been drinking heavily that evening, the court found that he was immune from the charges since he reported the spill to authorities twenty minutes after the ship had run aground. He would have called sooner, but he spent precious minutes drunk-dialing old girlfriends, with the ol' "I'm really in a bad place right now, I just need someone to talk to" chestnut.

JULY 11, 1804
Vice President Shoots Someone!

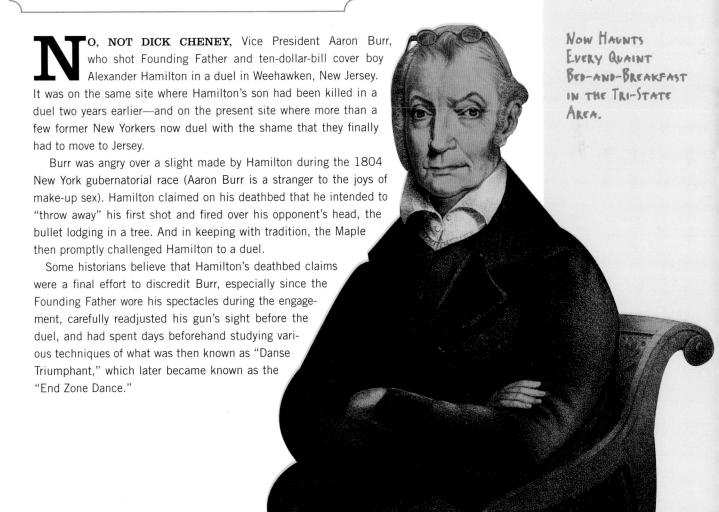

NO, NOT DICK CHENEY, Vice President Aaron Burr, who shot Founding Father and ten-dollar-bill cover boy Alexander Hamilton in a duel in Weehawken, New Jersey. It was on the same site where Hamilton's son had been killed in a duel two years earlier—and on the present site where more than a few former New Yorkers now duel with the shame that they finally had to move to Jersey.

Burr was angry over a slight made by Hamilton during the 1804 New York gubernatorial race (Aaron Burr is a stranger to the joys of make-up sex). Hamilton claimed on his deathbed that he intended to "throw away" his first shot and fired over his opponent's head, the bullet lodging in a tree. And in keeping with tradition, the Maple then promptly challenged Hamilton to a duel.

Some historians believe that Hamilton's deathbed claims were a final effort to discredit Burr, especially since the Founding Father wore his spectacles during the engagement, carefully readjusted his gun's sight before the duel, and had spent days beforehand studying various techniques of what was then known as "Danse Triumphant," which later became known as the "End Zone Dance."

NOW HAUNTS
EVERY QUAINT
BED-AND-BREAKFAST
IN THE TRI-STATE
AREA.

JULY 12
A Day of Good News, Bad News.

JULY 12, 1543 **The good news?** England's King Henry VIII weds his sixth and final wife, Catherine Parr. The king's clever methods for avoiding alimony payments from previous unions ensure that couple has a secure financial future. **The bad news?** Mass production of toothbrushes in England does not begin until 1780, leaving the couple unable to handle perpetual intimacy crisis of king's mutton breath.

↜ **JULY 12, 1859** **The good news?** William Goodale of Massachusetts patents machine to manufacture **PAPER BAGS**. Cheapos around the world now get phrase "brown bagging it" to soften distasteful personal stinginess. **The bad news?** Brownness of paper bags causes Massachusetts residents to shun the product far longer than the rest of the nation.

JULY 12, 1902 **The good news?** Australian parliament says "G'day" to equality and agrees to allow women to vote. **The bad news?** Severe crowding at polls because everyone in Australia traditionally considered a "woman" until their first beer-fueled blackout killing.

JULY 12, 1933 **The good news?** Congress passes first minimum wage law of 33 cents per hour. Also authorizes employers to enforce strict "paper hat, name tag, and polyester smock" codes so workers don't get too full of themselves. **The bad news?** Thirty-three cents an hour truly appreciated by the four people in the nation who have jobs.

JULY 12, 1962 **The good news?** At the Marquee Club in London, the Rolling Stones give their first public performance. Bassist Dick Taylor later leaves to form the Pretty Things, and drummer Mick Avory later joins the Kinks. Bill Wyman and Charlie Watts soon recruited from the nearby Home for Charmless Unrhythmics. **The bad news?** After the show, Mick Jagger doesn't run over to the group and say "Hey, that was great. But whaddya say we only do this for twenty years and then call it quits?"

JULY 13
What a Riot!

TODAY IS A DAY when people stop counting to ten, tensions bubble over, and a lot of stuff gets smashed up.

JULY 13, 1863 New York City's Draft Riots begin, as a primarily Irish mob revolts over unfair conscription policies during the Civil War, which saw mostly poor people going off to fight (never happened again). Hundreds were killed and property damage was estimated at over a million dollars, so it was slightly less tame than a modern-day Saint Patrick's Day Parade.

JULY 13, 1967 Race riots erupt in Newark, New Jersey, after police beat up an African-American cabdriver and a rumor spreads that he died in custody (a cabbie willing to pick up other blacks is still a rare and precious resource not to be squandered). The riot lasted for five days, and the National Guard was called in. On the plus side, a lot of Newark burned down.

JULY 13, 1977 New York City has a **BLACKOUT**, and thousands of people start looting and burning buildings. On the downside, none of the fires spread to Newark. (It should also be noted that this is a rare occurrence of something first becoming popular in New Jersey and THEN spreading to New York.)

LIGHTS OUT!

JULY 14, 1834
Painter James McNeill Whistler Born.

IT WAS A GOOD DAY, since it marked the first meeting with his most famous subject.

JULY 15, 1606
Rembrandt Born
(the Artist, Not the Smoker's Toothpaste).

FUG!

THIS DAY MARKS THE BIRTH of Dutch painter Rembrandt Harmenszoon Van Rijn (obviously, those guys who sang the theme from *Friends* knew which part of this man's name was the most radio-friendly). Unlike James McNeill Whistler, he never painted a portrait of his mother, because that would have taken precious easel time away from yet another study of himself.

A most prolific painter, Rembrandt created around six hundred canvases, and over one hundred of those were self-portraits, showing a remarkable ego that nowadays would manifest itself with a MySpace page and a whole bunch of self-taken cell phone photos. And who could blame him?

Early in his career, he was a wealthy man but began to live beyond his means. Eventually, he died in poverty, after overestimating the art-buying public's fondness for having a bloated, balding, unhandsome man with a mustache staring down at them from over their mantel. (See Sotheby's recent failure to secure any bidders for Leroy Neiman's celebrity portrait *Dennis Franz #7.*)

JULY 16, 1945
Boom Time for the United States.

ON THIS DAY IN 1945, America becomes a superpower when the first-ever atomic bomb is set off in Los Alamos, New Mexico, at 5:30 a.m. The detonation at the crack of dawn is the reason behind the saying, "The early bird gets the horribly damaged thyroid gland."

Albert Einstein had first suggested an atomic bomb in a letter to FDR, in which he explained that massive destructive power could result from an uncontrolled nuclear chain reaction. Roosevelt didn't know what the hell he was talking about, but figured that since he was some kind of Einstein, he might have a point.

This led to the formation of the Manhattan Project in 1942, and scientists gathered to start working. (This is not to be confused with the vocal group Manhattan Transfer, whose presence in the CD changer at a party can result in a nuclear winter that will slowly kill anyone's chance of getting laid.)

By July of 1945, they had successfully tested a prototype in the desert near the research facility. Project head Dr. J. Robert Oppenheimer supposedly quoted a line from the *Bhagavad Gita*, "Now I am become death, destroyer of worlds." (Note: When Dr. J. Robert "Chuckles" Oppenheimer opened his mouth at a party, it was nearly as lethal as putting on Manhattan Transfer.)

JULY 17, 1955
Arco, Idaho, Gets Nuked.

ON THIS DAY IN HISTORY, a small community in Idaho named Arco became the first community anywhere to be powered by nuclear energy. It was a first for the world and a first for the desolate, potato-growing state, whose towns are usually fueled by the clean-burning rage of White Supremacy.

On the evening of July 17, the power lines to the town were disconnected, and the lights were lit for a full hour by nuclear energy. This is proudly proclaimed on a sign you can see at the city limits, reading "First City in the World to Be Lit by Atomic Power." (Although frustrated members of the Chamber of Commerce a few years ago attempted to change the city slogan to the more practical "It's called a man-tentacle (mantacle)—now stop staring!")

The power was supplied by a reactor called the Experimental Breeder Reactor I, located eighteen miles southeast of Arco, which is now on the National Register of Historic Places and open for tours in the summer. The Breeder Reactor's other claim to fame is that it is also the site of the nation's first nuclear accident, which claimed the lives of three men who later had to be entombed in lead caskets, their hands buried separately at a nuclear waste dump site.

Needless to say, this attraction is a must-see pick in the pages of the beloved tourism guide *Let's Go! As Far Away As We Can From Arco, Idaho.*

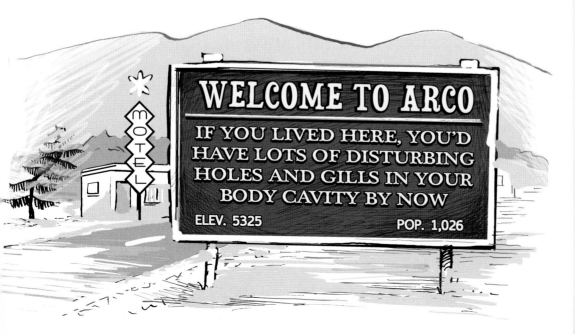

WELCOME TO ARCO
IF YOU LIVED HERE, YOU'D HAVE LOTS OF DISTURBING HOLES AND GILLS IN YOUR BODY CAVITY BY NOW
ELEV. 5325   POP. 1,026

JULY 18, 1969
Chappaquiddick and Kopechne Make for Hard-to-Spell Scandal.

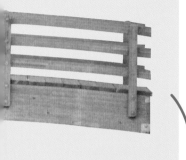

SPLASH!

ON THIS DAY IN HISTORY, Senator Edward Kennedy made a big splash on the national scene after driving off a one-lane wooden bridge on Chappaquiddick Island, with a twenty-eight-year-old passenger named Mary Jane Kopechne on board. Kennedy ran to get help, while Kopechne made the unfortunate decision to stay with the car.

After the car went underwater, the married Kennedy dove down to rescue the single Ms. Kopechne, but to no avail. He then walked back to the party he had attended earlier, grabbed a cousin and lawyer named Joe Gargan, and another lawyer named Paul Markham, and the three walked to the crash site and took turns diving under to save the woman. It may have been a half-hearted effort, but by removing two lawyers from a barbecue, Kennedy probably managed to save other party guests from drowning in dull conversation.

Giving up, Kennedy then went to the ferry landing, hopped into the water, and swam the mile back to Martha's Vineyard. Conspiracy theorists say he was hoping the impact of his large cranium on the water would cause a tsunami that would destroy all the evidence on Chappaquiddick.

Kennedy eventually walked back to the place he was staying and changed his clothes. Apparently, his lucky "police interview shirt" was at the bottom of the hamper, because instead of going to the authorities, he approached the front desk clerk and made up some story about being woken up by a noise. He also asked where the ice machine was because he needed a place to forever store his presidential aspirations.

Ten hours later, Kennedy managed to get himself to a police station to report the accident, which led Martha's Vineyard police to pull a few of their best men off their "Norman Mailer Drunken Cookout" riot squad.

JULY 19, 1958
World's Fattest Man Stops Eating.

ON THIS DAY IN HISTORY, Robert Earl Hughes, famed World's Fattest Man in the *Guinness Book of World Records*, died in Bremen, Indiana. At his height—not his most noticeable attribute—Hughes weighed in at 1,069 pounds, which, in modern measurements, clocks in at around Wal-Mart boys' XL. He was Guinness's "Heaviest Authenticated Human," a title that had been previously held by the very slim but exceedingly "heavy" Eugene O'Neill.

Hughes weighed eleven pounds at birth, but was 203 pounds by age six and nearly four hundred pounds by age ten. So even if he were a four-hundred-pound ten-year-old today, he would still be eight years away from legally enjoying a one-on-one session of sobbing and hand-holding with a satin-shorted Richard Simmons.

The saddest thing about the tale of Mr. Hughes is that in the intervening years, his 1,069-pound record has been broken by at least seven people, although one of those "people" was unmasked as merely a pile of everything that has been liposuctioned out of Kenny Rogers since 1988.

OTHER FAMOUS HISTORICAL THINGS THAT WEIGHED 1,069 POUNDS:

1. The missing corn from military stores shipped by W. S. Shrewsbury at the center of 1874's Supreme Court Case *U.S. v. Shrewsbury*.

2. W. S. Shrewsbury, after a depressive 1873 popcorn binge following a day of hauling military stores.

JULY 20, 1969
Neil Armstrong: Giant Screwup.

ON THIS DAY IN 1969, Carol Mann's win of the LPGA Danbury Lady Carling Golf Classic was unjustly overshadowed by the achievement of a MAN—as astronaut Neil Armstrong hopped out of the lunar landing module Eagle and became the first man to set foot on the moon.

(Edwin "Buzz" Aldrin Jr. was soon the second man on the moon. He could have been the first but, well, there's a reason they call him "Buzz." Someone needed to sleep off his series of guzzled TANGquerays.)

Armstrong apparently is not a guy you want in a pressure situation, because he then botched his big line, "One small step for man, one giant leap for mankind." What he meant to say was "One small step for a man . . . " And if you are reading this from your basement bedroom/conspiracy study lair, feel free to characterize this as a gaffe that really should have been caught by whoever was directing the moon-landing hoax.

More than a billion people on Earth were watching or listening to the landing. It was such an overwhelming moment of inspiration and joy that some then felt the need to come down by watching a sobering, mirth-free hour of *Laugh-In*.

JULY 21, 1861

General Jackson Gets a New Nickname.

ON A SWELTERING JULY DAY IN 1861, as the first major land battle of the Civil War was fought, Confederate General Thomas Jackson became easier to find on antebellum Google searches when he earned the nickname "Stonewall" due to his inspiring bravery in battle. This was a relief to Mrs. Jackson, who felt that his previous nickname, "Kegger," was kind of juvenile and something he should have dropped when he graduated West Point.

As the battle began some twenty miles outside Washington, D.C., the Union forces quickly pummeled the Confederates, and their lines began to break. (To imagine this in a Ken Burns style, read that sentence using your best Sam Waterston impression and go to iTunes to download "Turkey in the Straw.")

Jackson remained cool-headed during the battle, and as troops began to scramble, another general, Barnard Bee, shouted to his men, "There stands Jackson like a stone wall. Rally behind the Virginians." Over the din of gunfire, however, some rebel troops heard it as "There stands Jackson with his one ball." It unfortunately filled them with empathy and admiration, not the most useful qualities on the battlefield.

Two years later, on his deathbed, Jackson's last words were "Let us cross the river and rest in the shade of the trees." A gorgeous and evocative statement becoming of a true Southern gentleman, which was sadly marred by its addendum, "Tell my slave Erastus to fetch us a boat."

JULY 22

Bad Guys Stop Being Bad Guys.

THIS IS A DAY WHEN MANY killers, criminals, and strongmen got themselves caught, gunned down, or captured.

JULY 22, 1934 Take the "One" in Public Enemy Number One, and times it by a thousand, and you'll get the number of bullets that were pumped into John Dillinger by Federal Agents on this date in 1934. He was a wanted man because his ability to escape capture had gotten FBI head J. Edgar Hoover's panties in a bunch . . . literally. Dillinger had just exited the Biograph Movie Theater in Chicago, and even as he lay dying, he realized it was preferable to still being inside the theater watching a Ritz Brothers short.

JULY 22, 1991 Milwaukee police officers stop by the apartment of a loner named Jeffrey Dahmer and smell something they at first think is just Milwaukee. Eventually, they discover the remains of eleven men scattered around the candy-factory employee's apartment: Several corpses were in acid-filled vats, severed heads were found in his refrigerator, and an altar of candles and human skulls were found in his closet. Dahmer was later sentenced to fifteen life terms and totally lost his security deposit.

JULY 22, 2003 Saddam Hussein's chips off the old chopping block, Qusay and Uday Hussein, two men known for torture, cruelty, and not attacking the United States on 9/11, are killed after a three-hour firefight with U.S. forces in the Iraqi city of Mosul. (Qusay's fourteen-year-old son was also killed, but forget you read that.) A few thousand miles away in Pakistan, Osama Bin Laden sat in a tent and, while absolutely safe from harm, wondered just what he had to do to get the United States to pay attention to him. He felt awfully unpopular and fat.

JULY 23
Hooray (?) for Hollywood.

TODAY MARKS MANY SIGNIFICANT EVENTS in the lives of showbiz figures whose careers started out strong, and wound up more than a little depressing by the time their end credits rolled.

JULY 23, 1884 Actor Emil Jannings is born. He was the first-ever Best Actor Oscar winner, yet later his German accent made the talkies a problem, and he wound up appearing in pro-Nazi productions for Hitler. (Almost as bad an Oscar rebound as Halle Berry in *Catwoman*.) As the Allies invaded, he supposedly waved his Oscar to show them who he was. It didn't help him escape prosecution, although it did help him get a better table at some of Berlin's midlevel nightspots.

JULY 23, 1948 Pioneering film director and inventor of the "close up" D. W. Griffith dies in a seedy Los Angeles hotel at age seventy-three, after not having made a film for over fifteen years (he was put off by advancements in "color" filmmaking). His highly controversial but technically important film *Birth of a Nation* is in the Library of Congress, despite protests from Spike Lee, who was hoping in vain to see some shelf space saved for his film *She Hate Me*.

JULY 23, 1966 Actor Montgomery Clift dies at age 45 from complications related to being Montgomery Clift. A drunken, disfiguring car crash a few years earlier had made D. W. Griffith's "close up" a liability for the once-handsome actor, and he sank deeper into alcohol and drug addiction. Unfortunately, the rehab clinic Promises had not yet opened, so the actor's final days could not be spent "recovering" (i.e., shopping, tanning, and emerging from limousines without any underwear).

+

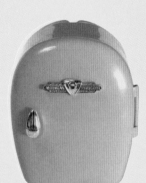

=

Fugly

See Dick Argue.

ON THIS DAY IN HISTORY, Vice President Richard M. Nixon got into a heated argument with Soviet leader Nikita Khrushchev (see Sting's *Russians*, if you are an idiot) while standing in a model "kitchen of tomorrow" at the American National Exhibition in Moscow. For many years, it was the most famous kitchen-based argument in pop culture, until 2004 when rotund celebrity chef Mario Batali throttled his pastry chef for "not letting Mario lick the spoon. Mario always licks the spoon!"

Nixon was proudly showing off a display of what was described as a typical American kitchen—but without the family silently eating in the middle of it, no longer able to communicate with one another—when the two began to mix it up over Communism versus capitalism. This was despite some common ground discovered just moments before, when both concurred that the avocado-colored appliances throughout the kitchen were "**FUGLY**" and probably wouldn't age well.

As cameras rolled, the two did a lot of finger-pointing and, through interpreters, shouting. Nixon snapped at Khrushchev, telling him to "not be afraid of ideas. After all, you don't know everything." Khrushchev retorted with "You don't know anything about Communism—except fear of it." Nixon attempted to end the debate with a humiliating, verbal knockout punch, but the translator was unable to find the Russian words for the query, "Homosayswhat?"

It Could Have Been Worse.

JULY 25, 1832 First recorded railroad accident in the United States occurs, when one person is killed in a wreck on the Granite Railway in Quincy, Massachusetts. **It could have been worse:** Airplanes had not yet been invented, so victim could not have been afraid to fly, and is therefore spared an ironic death. (He was, however, deathly afraid of horseback riding and his own two feet.)

JULY 25, 1965 Bob Dylan plugs in electric guitar at Newport Folk Festival and gets boos from always-tolerant hippies, the same people who now regularly vent outrage by swatting people with their woven manbags if they feel they've been cut in line at the wheatgrass bar. **It could have been worse:** Harsh lesson of that day means Dylan eventually became the only artist in mid-1980s to never risk plugging in an electric keytar. (See *Mass Historia*, April 4, 1984: Pete Seeger Pummeled While Performing "Puff, the New Wave Dragon.")

JULY 25, 1990 Roseanne Barr aka Roseanne Arnold aka Roseanne aka "That Crazy Lady Who Used to Be on That Depressing Sitcom" is booed off the mound while singing the National Anthem before a San Diego Padres game. Irreverent song-stylings lead to outrage from Americans, who had not yet seen the horrors of "Skinhead O'Communist's" pope-shredding stunt. **It could have been worse:** Tom Arnold, a barnacle attached to Roseanne's hull at the time, actually foregoes camera time and doesn't opt to bellow harmonies.

JULY 26, 1775
America Goes Postal!

ON THIS DAY, Congress established the United States Post Office and named Benjamin Franklin the first U.S. Postmaster.

While this is happy and important news, it should be said that a few people were later injured when Franklin attempted to get a patent for his "Pot-bellied Shooting Spree."

WHAT YOUR GRANDPARENTS USED BEFORE E-MAIL.

Bob Hope Dies (Literally).

VETERAN COMEDIAN BOB HOPE embarked on the Road to Heaven on this day in 2003, a few weeks after his one hundredth birthday, which he celebrated by taking an extra-long ogle of Barbara Mandrell.

Here are some fun facts about the comic. To get a feeling for what it was like to have been Bob Hope on stage, blow them up and read them on cue cards. If you want to feel like an older Bob Hope, blow through them quickly so you can get to the important business of ogling Barbara Mandrell.

HOPE WAS BORN LESLEY TOWNES HOPE IN ENGLAND AND EMIGRATED TO THE UNITED STATES WHEN HE WAS SIX. HE OGLED THE STATUE OF LIBERTY.

HE MADE SEVEN "ROAD" MOVIES WITH BING CROSBY AND DOROTHY LAMOUR. BEFORE CROSBY DIED, THE THREE SEPTUAGENARIANS WERE PLANNING TO MAKE ANOTHER ONE, WITH THE WORKING TITLE *The Road to Really Embarrassing Ourselves*.

His USO PERFORMANCES WERE BELOVED BY THOUSANDS OF TROOPS, ESPECIALLY THE PARTS WHERE HE'D GET OFF THE STAGE AND EVERYBODY WOULD GET SOME NANCY SINATRA UPSKIRTS.

AN ACT OF CONGRESS IN 1997 MADE HOPE AN "HONORARY VETERAN," WHICH IN WASHINGTON USUALLY REQUIRES AT LEAST A WEEK OR TWO IN THE TEXAS AIR NATIONAL GUARD.

JULY 28
Be-heady Times.

TODAY SAW THE NOTABLE BEHEADINGS of two notable men. It might be a good day to avoid pissing off kings or people who had previously pissed off kings.

JULY 28, 1540 Thomas Cromwell, the first Earl of Essex, aka "the Leo McKern Guy" in *A Man for All Seasons*, finally got his comeuppance on this day after pressing Henry VIII into marrying Anne of Cleves, whom Henry found so repulsive that he had the union annulled six months later. (She was known as "An Uncomely Maiden Who Doth Requiredeth Not a One But a Two Goodly Bags.") Henry deliberately hired an inexperienced executioner who botched the job on Cromwell with several blows, and the damaged head was boiled and placed on a pike facing away from the city of London, as a warning to all who might ever utter the phrase "She has a great personality."

JULY 28, 1794 French revolutionary and "Reign of Terror" terrorizer Maximilien Robespierre got "*Le* taste of his own *Le* medicine" (close enough) on this day, when he was guillotined without a trial in front of a cheering crowd. He had grown so despised that he was the only person in the French Revolution to be guillotined face up. This brutal, spiteful punishment was never seen in France again, except for a time in 1991 when an American tourist named Byron Frizell ordered a "Chardonnay Spritzer" while dining near "the Loover."

JULY 29, 1981
The Fairy-Tale Wedding of Prince Charles and Lady Diana.

AND BY "FAIRY TALE," we mean the Frog Prince and Sleeping (with everyone) Beauty.

JULY 30, 1864
A Hole-y Mess.

TODAY MARKS THE INFAMOUS BATTLE OF THE CRATER during the Civil War. (Note: This is not to be confused with the "Battle of the Craterface," which saw Confederate Major Nelson "Pimples" McLean finally blow up after his men had hidden his "Clearisil Postule Solution" for the tenth time.)

At Petersburg, Virginia, the Union forces were at a stalemate with the Confederates and had dug a tunnel beneath the rebel lines. This is the only hole dug during the Civil War that was not later mislabeled as a spot on the Underground Railroad by nearby bed-and-breakfast owners in an attempt to make their moldy old homes seem more historic.

A month earlier, a Union regiment from Pennsylvania, with many miners from the coal regions there, set upon the task of digging the tunnel, and then packed it with four tons of gunpowder—which, if anything, made the tunnel safer than your average Pennsylvania coal mine.

When the charges were blown, it resulted in a crater that was 170 feet long, eighty feet wide, and thirty feet deep, or roughly the size of two fairly svelte Confederate Civil War reenactors.

While over 1,000 Confederate soldiers were immediately killed, the Union forces poured into the crater to fight but were then picked off by rebels gathered at the rim of the blast site, which is the meaning behind the beloved Dan Ratherism "Like Shooting Yankees in a Smokin' Crater-Hole."

Henry Perky Ruins Breakfast.

ON THIS DAY IN 1893, a lawyer named Henry Perky, whose last name also described his bowel functions, patented a machine for the manufacture of shredded wheat. He originally displayed the invention at Chicago's 1893 World's Columbian Exposition in the "Coarse and Dry Wonders of Tomorrow Pavilion."

Perky suffered rather severely from heartburn, and one morning in a hotel lobby in Nebraska, he started up a conversation with a similarly afflicted stranger who claimed that a soothing boiled-wheat-with-cream breakfast was a reliable cure. Desperate to end the conversation, Perky began to experiment.

He referred to his invention as "little whole-wheat mattresses." (Perky later referred to Cheerios with an even less appealing nickname, "the little sugared-doughnut pillows.")

The fifty-year-old Ohio native began handing out shredded wheat from the back of a horse-drawn wagon in Denver, Colorado, and the breakfast item proved very popular. (To Denver residents accustomed to the 5,200-foot altitude, the product was deemed "wondrously moist.")

Soon, he opened up the Shredded Wheat Company in Boston, where the motto "Constipation is Wicked Queehah" became very popular—and soon his "cookless breakfast food" was being sold across the world. Although once the non-English-speaking world realized the biscuits were not intended to scrub stubborn stains off pans, sales dipped somewhat.

Yuck.

August

AUGUST 1, 1876

Welcome Colorado.

OUR PRETTIEST AIRLESS STATE with the largest population of wealthy and leathery skiers entered the union on this day. Settle back in your fuzzy après ski boots and enjoy these fun facts.

- In Spanish, Colorado means "colored red," which is what most out-of-towners are after they've attempted to walk two blocks in the high altitude.

- Colorado has the highest mean altitude of all fifty states. The thirteenth step of the state capitol building in Denver is exactly one mile above sea level. The Dwight Eisenhower Memorial Tunnel across the Continental Divide is the highest auto tunnel in the world. Leadville is the highest incorporated city in the United States at 10,430 feet. The tallest sand dune in America is in Great Sand Dunes National Monument outside of Alamosa. And despite all these facts, not surprisingly, Colorado has a tiny penis.

WHEEZE!

- Colorado boasts the world's largest flat-top mountain in Grand Mesa, while Colorado Springs' Air Force Academy hosts the largest concentration of flat-top haircuts.

- The LoDo region of Denver stands for Lower Downtown, which is in the horribly uncomfortable statewide LoOx region (Low Oxygen).

- The United States federal government owns more than one third of the land in Colorado, which mostly contains monitoring stations to check on all the mountain men who feel the federal government owns too much of Colorado.

- Each year Denver hosts the world's largest rodeo, the Western Stock Show. Every cowboy in America attends, because the hopelessly out-of-breath cattle are pretty easy to rope.

AUGUST 2

A Day of Good News, Bad News.

AUGUST 2, 1776 The good news? Fifty-six delegates from the thirteen colonies sign an enlarged copy of the Declaration of Independence before it is shipped off to England for review by a crazy king who probably then coated it with his own blue urine. **The bad news?** John Hancock's July 4 signing of the document used up all the ink reserves in the nation, making delegates wish they too had blue urine like Crazy King George.

THE LOST ART OF TINY, VOLATILE HANDWRITING.

AUGUST 2, 1869 The good news? Mary Ann Evans, writing under the name George Eliot, begins work on her epic masterpiece *Middlemarch*. **The bad news?** She finished it, and now all of us are expected to read it.

AUGUST 2, 1932 The good news? Acclaimed actor Peter O'Toole is born in County Galway, Ireland. Eventually goes on to star in *Lawrence of Arabia* (which few people have watched all the way through) and *Caligula* (which people have watched more often than they care to admit). **The bad news?** The baby O'Toole was then forced to endure one whole year of sobriety until the birth of drinking buddy Richard Harris.

AUGUST 2, 1934 The good news? German President Paul Von Hindenburg, known as the "Wooden Titan" for his impressive facade rarely backed up by meaningful action, dies. The senile Von Hindenburg, actually a staunch monarchist, had held the office—which he never really wanted—for years. **The bad news?** His successor, Adolph Hitler, proves somewhat more goal-oriented.

AUGUST 2, 1962 The good news? The Beatles play their first-ever gig at Liverpool's Cavern Club, which is later torn down and divvied into over a million collector's bricks—one of which you were lucky enough to snag on eBay. **The bad news?** For what you spent on your authentic collector's brick, you could have hired **RINGO** and his All Star Band to play—and strip—in your den-turned-Beatles Room.

STARKEY NAKED!

AUGUST 3, 1941

Hitchhikers Forced to Pony Up More Grass or Ass.

ON THIS DAY IN 1941, even though the United States had not yet entered World War II, gas rationing began in the eastern part of the country. (This would mark the last time Americans would ever have to sacrifice something for a war.) Thankfully, modern wars are usually fought to obtain more oil, which provides the petroleum needed to fuel our important wartime plastic yellow ribbon industry.

AUGUST 4
When Bad Things Happen to Historic People.

↓ **AUGUST 4, 1875** Danish fairy-tale author **HANS CHRISTIAN ANDERSEN** dies at age seventy. Most of his stories are now seen as allegories for the pain he suffered from his homosexuality. Fortunately, he died many years before the invention of the masters degree in Literature, so he never got to hear anyone proclaim that his stories were allegories for the pain he suffered as a result of his homosexuality.

AUGUST 4, 1944 Anne Frank discovered, but not in a good way. Diary later found, makes her famous and forever loathed by bloggers whose daily musings have not catapulted them to the big time.

AUGUST 4, 1962 Nelson Mandela thrown in jail in South Africa. Released nearly thirty years later to the shock and horror that problematic wife Winnie did not leave him.

AUGUST 4, 1964 The bodies of missing civil rights workers Michael Schwerner, Andrew Goodman, and James E. Chaney discovered in an earthen dam near Philadelphia, Mississippi. In that same town in 1980, Ronald Reagan kicked off his presidential campaign with a speech about states' rights. America feels good about itself again.

AUGUST 4, 1970 The Doors' Jim Morrison arrested for public drunkenness, later arrested for his more deviant and shocking act of "brief public sobriety." Also joined in lockup by bandmate Ray Manzarek, who was in on a lesser charge of "excessive keyboard tinnyness."

ANDERSEN AWAITING
HIS "SWAN" STAGE.

Lincoln Becomes First Tax 'n Spend Republican.

BACK IN THE OLD DAYS, deficits in Washington, D.C., were a big concern and not something to ignore until a Democrat took power. President Abraham Lincoln, with no clue how to pay for the Civil War, decided that it was time to levy an income tax. (Of course, even though California was only ten years old and sparsely inhabited, Californians were pissed off about it and demanded a recall.)

Once it passed Congress, an annual income tax was put in place on incomes over $800. Of course, as in today's America, those making over $900 quickly figured out a way to not pay any tax at all.

Keep in mind that someone making $800 in 1861 was the equivalent of someone making $16,000 now, although we finally decided to stop calling those people "slaves," and instead just call them whatever is written on the name tag on their smock.

The law was repealed in 1871, and our nation's wealthy reclined easily on their money-stuffed swooning couches until 1913, when the Sixteenth Amendment was ratified, establishing the income tax that we all enjoy today. (SHHHH—just play along. Those rubes making sixteen grand a year think the rest of us pay taxes. Ha!)

WARHOL AND
TENNESSEE WILLIAMS
DO THEIR EXPLODING
PLASTIC BLIND GUY
IMPRESSIONS.

Andy Warhol Pops From the Womb.

POP ARTIST ANDY WARHOL, the reason most people go to art school nowadays, and the reason most of them are currently unemployable, was born Andrew Warhola on this day in Pittsburgh, Pennsylvania, and was promptly wrapped in his first swaddling toupee.

After working for a dozen or so years as an illustrator in New York, he received notoriety in 1962 when his paintings of Campbell's soup cans were exhibited in Los Angeles and New York (the usual second and third choices when all the gallery space in the city of Suckerville, U.S.A., is booked). Later, he began mass-producing multicolored, silk-screened images of such celebs as Marilyn Monroe and Jackie Kennedy, perfect for any home unencumbered by portraits of actual friends and/or loved ones.

Warhol is perhaps most famous nowadays for his statement, "In the future, everyone will be famous for fifteen minutes," which is now the first sentence heard in any pitch meeting for a new VH1 show.

AUGUST 7, 1944

Calculation Sensation.

IBM, THE COMPANY THAT EVERYONE'S DAD WORKED FOR IN THE 1970s— even though dad couldn't really explain what it was he did for a living—made great strides toward eliminating the need for simple math skills on this day in history with the dedication of the first calculator.

The Automatic Sequence Controlled Calculator, or the Harvard Mark II (which sounded cooler, although perhaps too much like a disposable shaving product), was considered by some to be the first universal calculator, and it began the modern computer age, while giving hope to the world's "abacus nerds" that they might some day make a lucrative living.

The calculator, housed at Harvard, was fifty-one feet long, eight feet high, and weighed over 10,000 pounds, making it nearly impossible to flip upside-down and snicker at the word "BOOBLESS" on its main screen.

The machine was devised by Howard H. Aiken and built by IBM. However, at the Harvard dedication ceremony, Aiken failed to mention the company in his speech, which lead IBM execs to sever their ties with him. He had meant to give them a shout out, but halfway through his speech some members of Harvard's rugby team barged in and promptly hung him from the toilets by his underwear strap.

CALCULATOR FUN FACT:
THE EARLIEST CALCULATOR WAS THE BABYLONIAN SAND ABACUS, IN WHICH NUMERALS WERE DRAWN IN SAND RESTING ON A FLAT ROCK. THE SAND WOULD SCATTER, HOWEVER, WHEN ANCIENT BABYLONIAN GEEKS WOULD TRY TO CLIP THIS DEVICE TO THEIR BELTS.

AUGUST 8, 1974

Dick Nixon No Longer "Kick-Aroundable."

PRESIDENT RICHARD MILHOUS NIXON, who—as a long national nightmare—rose to fame as a Red baiter before becoming a scandal-plagued vice president, then a failed presidential candidate and a failed gubernatorial candidate, before eventually being elected and then reelected after stealing information from his opponent's campaign, FINALLY left public life, when he announced his resignation from the presidency of the United States of America just as he was about to be impeached. He is the only man in history to have resigned from the office, which sometimes overshadows his other notable achievement as the only man in history to ever be named "Milhous."

SMILE AND SAY
"MILHOUS!"

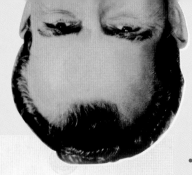

FOLLOWING ARE A FEW FUN FACTS ABOUT ONE OF OUR MOST INFAMOUS PRESIDENTS.

- He was an avid bowler who once bowled a perfect game, after G. Gordon Liddy and several others leaned on the 7 and 10 pins to make sure no splits happened.

- He was an accomplished musician who in 1963 played one of his own piano compositions on *The Tonight Show*. The piece is notable for its John Cage–influenced eighteen-and-a-half-minute gap of silence in the middle.

- His library contains only pre- and post-office papers, since his presidential documents are still held as evidence. (And no, that's still not a good excuse for why your homework essay about the Nixon administration only got a C.)

- There's a famous photo of him and Elvis Presley together in the Oval Office. (Or at least it's famous among those with a very narrow frame of "ironic" reference.)

- When JFK was assassinated, Nixon was attending a Pepsi Conference in Dallas, which is the most "refreshing" aspect of any conspiracy theory.

AUGUST 9, 1969
A Manson Family Affair.

ON THIS DAY IN HISTORY, while thousands of American boys were off getting killed in Vietnam, America showed its usual keen sense of perspective by flipping out over the discovery of five murdered bodies in a home in Hollywood.

The five people were murdered by the Manson family, a cult of hippies operating under the influence of career criminal and sometime-musician Charles Manson (for a picture, look to the T-shirt of the belligerent skater kid who works at your video store).

It was a shock to easy-living Angelinos, and author Joan Didion wrote, "the 1960s abruptly ended on August 9, 1969," probably because in addition to scrawling "Kill the Pigs" and "Helter Skelter" in blood on the walls of the crime scene, one of the killers added, "Joan Didion's *Slouching Towards Bethlehem* is a bit of a downer." (It's really amazing that someone was able to scrawl in italics.)

Manson's group of followers was convinced that the murders would spark a race war and that their cult would rule the new world order that would then take shape. If that didn't work, they would have settled for another stab at city council on the "Acid and Hippy Group Sex" ticket.

Manson insisted that his prophecy for world domination was easily explained by listening closely to the Beatles' *White Album*. The Beatles denied this, although even they admitted that enough listens to "Ob-La-Di, Ob-La-Da" could drive someone to violence.

Anarchy in the N.J.

ON THIS DAY IN 1934, the first International Anarchist Convention was held in Stelton, New Jersey, to discuss the creation of an anarchist newspaper.

Of course, the convention fell apart during the registration check-in because none of the names had been entered into the clipboard and the goodie bags/welcome kits were at best scattered and not very well organized.

In short, it was anarchy.

Right You Are!

PIN YOUR AMERICAN FLAG to your lapel and crank up the Toby Keith because today is a day of famous Right-Wing milestones.

AUGUST 11, 1927 The Reverend Jerry Falwell is born in Virginia to a mother he never slept with, despite Larry Flynt's insistence to the contrary. He became a Baptist minister and in 1979 formed the Moral Majority, whose greatest lasting achievement was getting liberals to replace their "You Can't Hug a Child with Nuclear Arms" bumper stickers with those "The Moral Majority is Neither" bumper stickers.

AUGUST 11, 1984 Six-hundred-and-eight-year-old President **RONALD REAGAN**, aka "the Great Communicator," did a great job ← of communicating how nuanced his world view was when he joked during the taping of a radio address that, "My fellow Americans, I am pleased to tell you today that I've signed legislation that will outlaw Russia forever. We begin bombing in five minutes." Many were outraged, while others knew it was a joke— especially the whole part where a president's signing of legislation leads to "action" within five minutes. Apparently, Reagan saw a dip in popularity after the remark, plunging him into the basement of a 90-to-95 percent approval rating.

AUGUST 11, 2000 Far-Right journalist, author, and most beady-eyed member of the Nixon team, Pat Buchanan becomes the Reform Party candidate for president, because that party's usual parade of porn stars and professional wrestlers didn't get their paperwork in on time.

THE GOP's "DUTCH" TREAT.

AUGUST 12, 1851
Singer Sews Up Patent.

HERE'S A STORY FOR THE LADIES—or the boys who are forced to take a Home Economics class in high school and wind up making a crappy cloth tennis racket cover they will never use. On this day in 1851, Isaac Singer (not the guy with all the Jewish short stories) obtained his patent for the Singer Sewing Machine. It was the biggest success in nineteenth-century mass manufacturing since the invention of the child laborer.

Singer did not invent the sewing machine and never claimed to do so, probably because he'd worked for many years as an actor, and that had already cast enough aspersions on his masculinity.

In 1839, he had made $2,000 after selling his patent for a rock drill, which is certainly a very manly device. But it was with his sewing machines that he achieved his greatest success, although the fact that he named his first model after the singer and "Swedish Nightingale" Jenny Lind was certainly, well, a little suspect.

So to counteract all this innuendo, the actor/inventor embarked on a mission to become an actor/inventor/bigamist, with four different wives at the same time and eighteen children, which is why his original patent listed the sewing machine as the Singer Diaper Churner-Outer.

AUGUST 13, 1899
Hitchcock Makes First Cameo Appearance.

FILM DIRECTOR AND NOTED MASTER OF SUSPENSE Alfred Hitchcock was born on this day in England in 1899, and probably made his first unfortunate associations with women and pain. Let's look at some fun facts about this famous director.

• His films are dark expressions of his Catholic guilt and manifestations of his mother complex and voyeuristic obsessions. If you have ever sincerely written that statement, then you are one of the thousands of people who wanted to work in the movies but then just settled on getting your master's degree in Film Studies.

• His 1929 film *Blackmail* was the first British "talkie," and it marked the first time that people with degrees in film studies would get overexcited about a movie just because it had British accents in it.

- He left England and went to work in Hollywood in the 1940s, where he made such classics as *Rebecca*, *Shadow of a Doubt*, and *Notorious*, all of which were wisely remade as TV movies in the 1990s. (All of the other Hitchcock films have been remade by Brian DePalma.)

- Some of his silent movies are now lost. Sadly, none of the work of Brian DePalma enjoys the same status.

- In the 1950s and 1960s, he was embraced by the directors of the French New Wave, despite his own work's insistence on being entertaining.

- When Melanie Griffith was a little girl, he gave her a small wooden casket containing a doll that looked just like her mother, actress and Hitchcock muse **TIPPI HEDREN**. ← One imagines it still was not as creepy for Griffith as having to work with director Brian DePalma on his *Rear Window/Vertigo* rip-off, *Body Double*.

IT ALSO CAME WITH A MALIBU DEATH HOUSE.

AUGUST 14, 1935

Social Security Act Signed, Kicking Off Illustrious Month or Two of Solvency.

ON THIS DAY IN 1935, Franklin Delano Roosevelt created a new reason for young people to feel hostile toward their elders when he signed into law the Social Security Act, after a study showed that over half the nation's elderly lacked the means to support themselves—a fact they did not give up easily, since the elderly traditionally aren't big complainers.

The bill called for a "contributory system" in which taxes were taken out of paychecks (or "contributed") and put into a joint pension fund, which we came to believe was in some sort of "lock box" during the 2000 presidential election. The lock, however, might need to be changed to accommodate all the keys gripped in the hands of our nation's rapidly aging baby boomers.

In the intervening seventy years, the fund has collected over $4.5 trillion and paid out nearly as much, but don't worry—that $2,000 you put into an IRA six years ago has already grown to $2,600, and by the time you retire it will have blossomed into . . . a tremendous cloud of devastating regret.

SOCIAL SECURITY

I.M. Busted
000 00 0000

I'LL GIVE HIM
SOMETHING TO
SMILE ABOUT.

AUGUST 15, 1961

Soviet Union Tired of Iron Curtain Being Metaphorical.

ON THIS DAY IN 1961, it became a little harder to enjoy all the sun and the fun of East Berlin, as the Soviet Union began to construct what would be known as the Berlin Wall.

In 1948, the British and French sectors joined together to form West Germany, which led the Soviets to form a blockade around the city. With the blockade rendered unsuccessful by the Berlin Airlift (not your band in college), and after the slow realization by the East Germans that life under Soviet rule was rendering their women unattractive after the age of twenty-five, people began fleeing to the west through Berlin. This eventually led to Nikita Khrushchev's call to build the wall in 1961.

The long, grim structure became a symbol of Soviet oppression, unlike a wall that was later built in Israel, which became a symbol for the way American politicians sometimes call a wall a "fence" so as not to be called "anti-Semitic."

This barrier remained up until 1989, when Eastern German officials finally opened up the checkpoints. Depending on who you talk to, this was thanks to either Ronald Reagan, George H. W. Bush, or David Hasselhoff. (If you believe the last one, it means you talked to David Hasselhoff.)

AUGUST 16

Legends Take a Fall.

IF YOU ARE AN ICON, either in film, literature, sports, or music, you might want to check your vital signs today, because chances are you might make the transition from "icon" to "late icon."

AUGUST 16, 1948 Yankee slugger **BABE RUTH** ← points to heaven's nosebleed seats and dies of cancer at age fifty-three. He was a home run king back in the days before steroids, when baseball players gained mass by drinking massive quantities of beer. Later proved that Red Sox fans could hate a white man as much as any black man.

THE SULTAN OF RIP.

162

AUGUST 16, 1949 Margaret Mitchell, the author of *Gone with the Wind*, goes down at age forty-eight, after being run over by a drunk driver. Her Pulitzer Prize–winning novel still sells thousands of copies a year, and the film version is one of the highest-grossing movies of all time, so it's pretty apparent why she didn't give a damn about ever publishing another one. Two hundred million people have supposedly seen the movie, but only 20 million would sit through it again, since only 10 percent of all people are gay.

AUGUST 16, 1956 Dracula portrayer Bela "Dracula" Lugosi proves that heroin is a little more fatal than a stake through the heart, as he dies on this day at age seventy-three, having spent many years battling poverty and addiction. His son and wife decided that he should be buried in his Dracula cape, so that he might be more swiftly typecast in the afterlife.

AUGUST 16, 1977 Singer and actor Elvis Presley revives his career by morphing into a hunka hunka bloating corpse. Upon his death, President Jimmy Carter said "Elvis Presley's death deprives our country of a part of itself." Although his death did give the country back its surplus prescription painkillers and white-fringed pleather parts.

AUGUST 17, 1987
Last Superman Standing.

Hess Spent His Days Reading and Growing His Eyebrows.

ON THIS DAY IN 1987, inside West Berlin's Spandau Prison, guards found that Adolph Hitler's last surviving henchman, ninety-three-year-old Rudolph Hess, had strangled himself to death with an electrical cord. Hess was the only prisoner in Spandau and had been there over forty years, so he opted to avoid the other suicide option of suffocating himself under his nearby mountain of used Kleenex.

While most Nazis were crazy, Hess was bat-crap crazy, having parachuted into Scotland (with a tartan aero-kilt) in 1941 to arrange a treaty with England that would stop the fighting and give the rest of Europe over to Germany. And while his hopes for the war's outcome were exactly the same as those held by Britain's lovable royal family at the time, he was arrested as a prisoner of war.

He was tried at the Nuremberg Trials, where he talked to himself, giggled uncontrollably, and claimed he had no memory of his involvement with the Nazis—meaning his testimony was one Band-Aid-on-the-nose short of being just as crazy as Michael Jackson's at his last molestation trial.

Hess's life was spared by the authorities because he wasn't found guilty of crimes against humanity, since he'd left Germany before the genocide started (he was to the Nazis what Pete Best was to the Beatles, although had Rudolph Hess been in the Beatles, he would have surely given Ringo a hard time for his Semitic features).

THE MEMBERS OF THE FAIRER SEX get their due on August 18, a day which has seen many a first in the history of women.

AUGUST 18, 293 BC The oldest-known Roman temple to the goddess Venus is declared on this day, no doubt a happy event for all, unless you were a chicken whose entrails were about to be scattered around for luck. Venus, of course, is the goddess of love and a Bananarama song many are ashamed to admit is on their iPod.

AUGUST 18, 1587 Virginia Dare is born in Virginia, making her the first female child of English descent born in the colonies. Unfortunately, she was born in the ill-fated colony of Roanoke, which also made her the first missing teenage girl in the colonies.

AUGUST 18, 1920 American ladies finally have their opportunity to be disenfranchised and/or cheated by the broken Electoral College system, when the Nineteenth Amendment to the Constitution is ratified, granting women the right to vote. It's a very important event, yet it is buried on this list of trivial items, because the male author is sexist.

AUGUST 18, 1928 Cincinnati Reds owner Marge Schott is born and later goes on to become the first woman to buy a major league baseball team. (She had been able to make the purchase once she cashed in several "million-dollar n*ggers" she had in savings.)

AUGUST 18, 1933 Acclaimed director Roman Polanksi born. Was many a woman's "first."

AUGUST 19, 1946
Bill Clinton Born!

AND THANKS TO THE PRESENCE OF AMNIOTIC FLUID, the baby—for the first time in his life—was declared as "slick" by onlookers.

HORNY.

AUGUST 20
Popes Get Really Elevated.

THERE'S GOOD NEWS AND BAD NEWS TODAY if you are a pope. The bad news is you might die. The good news? You finally get to meet that God you talked about so much.

AUGUST 20, 984 Pope John XIV dies. He was only pope for a few months, having been placed in the job by Holy Roman Emperor Otto II (the "science" of selection by White Smoke was still in its infancy). However, Otto II dies a few weeks later, leaving in charge three-year-old Otto III, who was unable to protect "Uncle Pope John XIV" from the powers of antipope Boniface VII, who placed John XIV in prison, where he died of starvation (the science of preventing "manorexia" was still in its infancy).

AUGUST 20, 1823 Pope Pius VII, who was pope for nearly a quarter of a century, dies at eighty-one years of age. He excommunicated Napoleon, probably because of a Catholic compulsion to manipulate anything boy-sized. Napoleon wound up kidnapping him and holding him prisoner for six years. This confinement, along with that of Pope John XIV, shows that while God may have created the universe in seven days, he has never mastered a technique for baking a file inside of a cake.

AUGUST 20, 1914 Pope Pius X dies, having never spent any time in the lockup, so who cares about a pope so obviously "un-gangsta?"

THE HOLY PRISON
SHANK OF
POPE PIUS VII.

AUGUST 21, 1959
Hawaii Messes Up the Flag.

ON THIS DAY IN HISTORY, in an attempt to fulfill his prediction of a Happily Mauied T-shirt Industrial Complex, President Dwight D. Eisenhower signed a proclamation admitting Hawaii into the Union as the fiftieth state. Fortunately, he still had enough ink in his pen to write "Eat it" on a paper airplane that was then sailed toward Puerto Rico.

Eisenhower also issued an executive order to remake the American flag with fifty stars instead of forty-nine, thus taking the sheen off Alaska as the newest state. (This day also marks the anniversary of the creation of Grudge #621 on the official registry of *100,000 Irrational Alaskan Grudges Toward the Lower Forty-eight*.)

In the early eighteenth century, American traders came to Hawaii to exploit the islands' sandalwood. All the islands' sandalwood oil was entirely depleted in the 1960s when used to tame the hairscape of *Hawaii Five-0* star Jack Lord.

Eventually, the sugar industry took hold on the islands and, in the 1840s, a constitutional monarchy was established. This monarchy lasted until 1893, when Queen Liliuokalani was deposed by a group of American ex-pats, sugar planters, and forward-thinking spell-checker fetishists.

HAWAII

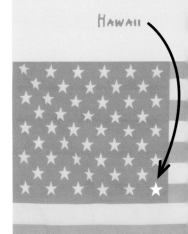

AUGUST 22, 1902

Teddy and the Cruiser.

AMERICA'S (ABUSIVE) LOVE AFFAIR with the car got itself a little more speed on this day in 1902, in Hartford, Connecticut, when President Theodore Roosevelt became the first president to ride in a car. It is the most famous presidential car ride ever (that did not take place in Dealey Plaza).

He also invented the phrase "Shotgun!" on this day, not because he wanted to sit up front but because the conservationist in him wanted a weapon handy in case he needed to euthanize any native Hartford species dying from boredom.

Roosevelt rode in a purple Columbia Electric Victoria car, followed by twenty carriages, on a tour of the city. If you've ever wondered whatever happened to this particular kind of vehicle, see the shocking documentary exposé *Who Killed the Columbia Electric Victoria Car?*

Consequently, Roosevelt was the first president to also own a car. Historians note that he found a "No Credit? No Problem" 0 percent APR deal to be most "Bully."

In a few short years, autos became more popular, and in 1909, President William Howard Taft converted the White House horse stables into a four-car garage. (Although many at the time felt it was unnecessary for Taft to ceremoniously cook and eat all the horses beforehand.)

Honk If You're Bully!

AUGUST 23, 1927

Anarchy in the AC (Alternating Current).

ON THIS DAY IN 1927, Nicola Sacco and Bartolomeo Vanzetti were put to death in the electric chair, ending the lives of the last two anarchists on Earth who weren't easily identifiable by their bumper stickers reading "Skateboarding is not a crime."

Theirs was one of the most notorious murder cases of the day, but they are not to be confused with homosexual thrill-killing contemporaries Leopold and Loeb, although both pairs of men often pop up in that beloved parlor game "1920s Murderers or Comedy Team?"

Both were accused of murdering Frederick Parmenter and Alessandro Berardelli, employees at a South Braintree, Massachusetts, shoe company, and absconding with over $15,000. The money was never recovered, but Vanzetti was subsequently found with over 15,000 one-dollar tubes of Cherrybomb Mustache Wax: For the Anarchist Who Wants to Topple Flyaway Facial Hair.

While their sensational trial and the lack of evidence against them spawned outrage throughout the world, experts now believe that while Vanzetti had nothing to do with the murders, Sacco was involved and owned the gun used in the shooting. Although there was some confusion recently when JonBenét Ramsey perv John Mark Karr announced he murdered Parmenter because "I love him." Karr later recanted, saying he meant to confess to the murder of fourteen-year-old Leopold and Loeb victim Bobby Franks, adding "I love him . . . but I hate how I always confuse Leopold and Loeb with Sacco and Vanzetti."

AUGUST 24
DUCK!

YEP, TODAY IS ONE OF THOSE HIGH BODY COUNT DAYS. Be careful out there.

AUGUST 24, 79 AD Mount Vesuvius erupts, and thousands in the nearby cities of Pompeii, Herculaneum, and Stabiae suddenly realize that sandals are pretty crappy for running. The cities are excavated nearly 2,000 years later, and a technique of filling voids in the ash layer with plaster reveals outlines of bodies frozen in their final moments, providing postmortem embarrassment for noted Pompeii pervert Augustus, Citizen-Onanist.

AUGUST 24, 1349 Thousands of Jews in Germany are killed after they are blamed for having started the Black Plague. Fortunately, this provides Germans an opportunity to get those kind of feelings out of their systems.

AUGUST 24, 1572 King Charles IX of France, at the behest of his mother, Catherine de'Medici, launches the St. Bartholomew's Day Massacre, in which thousands of Huguenots across the country are killed. Some Huguenots later flee to America and found the village of New Paltz in upstate New York. The local high school football team is known as the Huguenots, and many of its members massacred the self-esteem of this author during the 1980s.

AUGUST 24, 1814 The British set fire to the **WHITE HOUSE** in Washington, ← D.C. While this isn't nearly as severe as the other events on this list, it did happen in America, whose inhabitants have little sense of tragic perspective and are very self-centered, and sometimes even hold grudges for years against King Charles IX of France because of some gentle ribbing received in the 1980s.

It Is Illegal to Wish for This.

Webb's Feat!

ON THIS DAY IN HISTORY, Matthew Webb became the first person to do what many people wish they could do when stuck on the Chunnel train next to some loud American students on vacation: He swam the English Channel.

Webb was a twenty-seven-year-old British merchant seaman, and this was his second attempt. He was followed by three boats with men on board who kept him plied with brandy, coffee, and beef tea. The beef tea was a symbolic reminder that while the swim would be rough, dinner in France would be much better than the breakfast he had had in England.

He eventually arrived on the shores of Calais over twenty-one hours later, and the following day announced that "the sensation in my limbs is similar to that after the first day of cricket season," which must mean he had to be treated for acute muscular boredom.

Webb became famous for the swim, but eventually was reduced to doing various swimming stunts for money. He died while trying to swim the rapids at Niagara Falls in 1883, many years before aquatic achievements led to a secure future of Tarzan movies, Wheaties box appearances, and *Playboy* spreads.

Note: Although getting confused and appearing nude on a Wheaties box might lead to a costly lawsuit or two.

Yugo Crazy for America!

ON THIS DAY IN HISTORY, the Yugo, a compact, low-cost car built in Yugoslavia, became available for sale in the United States.

ALSO ON THIS DAY:

AUGUST 26, 1985 First Yugos available in the United States break down and have to be towed back to the dealer.

← Taken August 27, 1985

BATTLE OF BROOKLYN

This is the site of the Battle of Brooklyn, where in 177--

Hey, look behind you!

First Exit From Brooklyn.

THE ILL-FATED BATTLE OF BROOKLYN, which commenced and ended on this day in 1776, was the first battle in the Revolutionary War, the first clash that the organized U.S. Army ever engaged in, and the first time pro-U.S. pundits employed the term "strategic retreat" in place of the usual downer, "big failure."

The British forces, 4,000 strong and under the command of Lieutenant General Sir William Howe, landed in Gravesend Bay a few weeks previous, where nowadays the abundance of pleasure craft with names like *Admiral Agita* and *Workaholic* would have certainly blocked their entrance. Soon there were over 30,000 British troops throughout Brooklyn and Long Island. This huge concentration of Englishmen threatened not only liberty, but scores of New York men whose girlfriends were suckers for those fruity accents.

General Washington's forces engaged the British in what is now Brooklyn's Prospect Park and suffered a loss of 1,000 men. (There is a marker commemorating the battle in a deserted part of the park. Nowadays, if you stare at it long enough, some local teens will declare you independent of your bike, wallet, and watch.)

The Americans were pushed back to Brooklyn Heights, and Washington ordered a retreat back to Manhattan via boat, one stable enough to allow the general to stand up in case there were any portrait painters nearby.

A Day for Dream Believers.

MARTIN LUTHER KING JR. gave his famous "I Have a Dream" speech on the Washington Mall on this day in history. Nowadays, it might be hard to understand and appreciate the context in which the speech was given and its impact at the time. So just skip ahead to tomorrow, August 29, to see what kind of goofball the civil rights movement was fighting against. (Hint: The goofball stuck around long after Dr. King did.)

I HAVE A DREAM . . . AND A PODIUM!

Racist Races to Nearby Toilet.

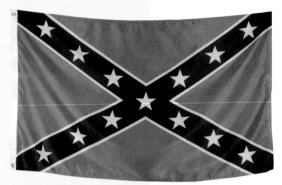

DEMOCRAT-TURNED-DIXIECRAT-TURNED-REPUBLICAN-TURNED-DELICATE-MADE-OF-PARCHMENT-CRYPT-KEEPER Senator Strom Thurmond ended his famous twenty-four-hour filibuster to block the Civil Rights Act of 1957 on this day in history. It was the dullest, lengthiest race-related ordeal Washington has ever seen, if you don't count a 1999 unabridged White House reading of *How Stella Got Her Groove Back* by Ossie Davis and Ruby Dee.

Thurmond prepared for the event with throat lozenges and energy-boosting malt tablets, and flushed all the excess fluids out of his body with a visit to the Senate steam room. He also practiced his filibustering skills in the steam room by coming up with a variety of different verbal excuses to turn down the many "come-ons" he encountered in there.

The Senator eventually droned on against civil rights for twenty-four hours and eighteen minutes. He planned on going longer, but he had to run to the bank before closing to make sure he transferred some hush money into the account of his black daughter.

During the filibuster, Thurmond recited the voting rights laws of every state and the entire Declaration of Independence, and discussed the history of Anglo-Saxon juries. He also holds the record as "The Only Person from South Carolina Who Has Read the Voting Rights Laws of Every State, the Entire Declaration of Independence, and Knows What 'Anglo-Saxon' Means."

Mass Historia Mortality "In and Out" List.

IN:

AUGUST 30, 580 Mohammed, the famed prophet, founder of Islam, and Right-Wing blogger "slow news day" target. Fortunately, he was born 1,835 years before the invention of the Sears Baby Portrait, so no one was stoned that day for blasphemy.

AUGUST 30, 1930 Warren Buffett, American businessman, philanthropist, and Right-Wing blogger "slow news day" target. Even as a baby, he was most popularly (and incorrectly) known as Jimmy Buffett's cousin, even though Jimmy Buffett would not be born for another sixteen years.

AUGUST 30, 1943 R. Crumb, cartoonist of big-breasted women with chunky legs, is born in Philadelphia. Hopefully, he will not be joined on his birthday by any fans of his work, because even he finds them a little too creepy.

OUT:

AUGUST 30, 30 BC CLEOPATRA commits suicide with bite from asp (but you already knew that if you've ever done a *New York Times* crossword). Heavy use of eyeliner coupled with early death at own hand, plus name "Cleopatra," suggests that she may have been the first-ever "Goth." ←

AUGUST 30, 1930 William Howard Taft, twenty-seventh U.S. president who later served on the Supreme Court, dies at age seventy-three. While it is a sad day, many observe that Taft had finally found a diet that works.

AUGUST 30, 1970 Abraham Zapruder dies at age sixty-five. He was the president of Jennifer Juniors, a manufacturer of ladies' garments. Best known for one very violent movie.

AUGUST 30, 2003 Charles Bronson, tough-guy actor, proves somewhat untough and dies at age eighty-one; his surviving mustache chides press over "Death Wish" headlines. Best known for one very violent movie.

THE BITE WAS PART OF SOME WEIRD "VAMPIRE" THING.

AUGUST 31, 1897
Edison Invents the Movies!

OF COURSE HE DIDN'T INVENT THE MOVIES, but he did file a patent on this day in 1897 for a movie camera called the Kinetograph, which means—in the world of Thomas Edison—that HE INVENTED THE MOVIES. (After all, that's much more pleasant than writing the more accurate "Edison rushed to the patent office to claim the idea of someone he either crushed financially, outright robbed, or maybe even had killed.")

The film shot in the Kinetograph was exhibited in a large and cumbersome device called a Kinetoscope—a cabinet that housed gears moving along a strip of film, which could be watched through a small window while manually cranked. Thankfully, the crank could be operated with one hand, because by the end of the day on August 31, 1897, someone had already figured out a way to use both the Kinetograph and Kinetoscope for porn.

Like pretty much all of Edison's inventions, this one found its way to a battle in front of the Supreme Court after a lawsuit by a rival inventor had been filed against the Wizard of Menlo Park. The court found that Edison only owned the rights to the sprocket system that moved the film inside the camera, but not to the camera itself. Edison was a good sport, but before sacrificing his rights to the patent, he made one more humorous film with the device, entitled *The Wizard of Menlo Park Teabags the Supreme Court Water Fountain.*

September

TONIGHT ON THE HISTORY CHANNEL:

8 pm	Hitler: The Rise to Power
9 pm	Hitler: The Years in Power
10 pm	Hitler: The Power Walker
11 pm	Hitler:

The Nazi leader was susceptible to shin splints

Germany Gets the Party Started.

ON THIS DAY IN HISTORY, British Prime Minister Neville Chamberlain looked at the "BFF" signed next to Adolph Hitler's name on the Munich Agreement and sighed. German forces had invaded Poland, effectively kicking off World War II and eventually providing all the future television programming on the History Channel.

Hitler made no apologies for the invasion, and merely said that the German people needed Lebenstraum, or "living space." (This is the closest any German has ever come to telling an effective joke.)

Eventually, the Allies (SPOILER ALERT) defeated Hitler, but not before the Führer and his gang worked hard to ensure that Poland—of all the nations involved in World War II—lost the highest percentage of its citizenry, around 6 million people. And after the war, they were handed over to Stalin. So yes, in case you were wondering, Poles can handle your dad's stupid Polish jokes.

September 1 is a pretty good day in general for crappy events.

SEPTEMBER 1, 1914 Martha, the last surviving passenger pigeon, dies in captivity at the Cincinnati Zoo. (Cause of death: autoerotic asphyxiation.)

SEPTEMBER 1, 1923 The Great Kanto Earthquake kills over 100,000 people in Japan. Now quit feeling sad about the passenger pigeon.

SEPTEMBER 1, 1983 The Soviet Union shoots down Korean Airliner Flight 007, killing all 269 on board. Seriously, there's nothing like a good animal autoerotic asphyxiation joke, but it really doesn't belong on this list.

London Bridge Is Burning Down.

COR BLIMEY! (Translation pending—we assume that is some sort of appropriate exclamation.) Things got hot in London on this day in 1666 (they would not be "hot" again until the mid-1960s invention of the "Twiggy") when Thomas Farrinor, a baker for Charles II, failed to extinguish one of his ovens before bed, and started a fire that eventually destroyed more than four-fifths of London. What's worse, he was baking scones, which the people of England still refuse to admit never taste as good as they look and are really not worth all the trouble.

In the course of three days, the blaze destroyed over 13,000 buildings, 87 churches, the old St. Paul's Cathedral, and the homes of 70,000 of the city's 80,000 inhabitants.

Fortunately, even back then, male Londoners could escape to the colonies and use their accents to find accommodations for the evening with American girls who really knew how to hurt their boyfriends' feelings.

Word spread throughout the city that the fire was started by foreigners. In fact, the monument commemorating the fire had an inscription on its side that blamed the blaze on "the treachery and malice of the Popish faction," although one imagines the word "Irish" would have saved the stonemason a little time with the chisel.

In 1986, however, an organization called Members of the Worshipful Company of Bakers erected a plaque on Pudding Lane, the site of Farrinor's bakery, which acknowledged his role in the fire. Their penance was complete when they then consumed a few of their own scones. Seriously—those things are dry as hell and not worth the effort!!!

SEPTEMBER 3, 1777
Stars and Stripes First Time Ever!

THE FLAG OF THE UNITED STATES was flown for the first time on this day in 1777, during the Battle of Cooch's Bridge, which was nestled in Delaware's beloved Vagina-Slang Valley.

American General William Maxwell ordered the flag—which had recently been approved by Congress—to be raised when his men met a battalion of British and Hessian troops. Sadly, the eye-catching new banner did not prove enough of a distraction for the enemy, and they instead concentrated on defeating the patriots, all of whom were wishing that Congress had approved a slightly more threatening flag. (See *Mass Historia*, August 1, 1775: Congress Rejects **BETSY ROSS'S FLAMING SKULLS AND STRIPES**.)

LIBERTY GETS EXTREME!

SEPTEMBER 4, 476
Rome Moves Past Decline Stage.

ON THIS DAY IN HISTORY, after a 1,000-year-run that saw major advancements in every aspect of human existence (except pants), the Roman Empire officially fell, as the thirteen-year-old Emperor Romulus Augustus was deposed by the Germanic chieftain Odoacer.

Romulus had been installed as a figurehead by his father, head of the Roman Army, Falvius Orestes, who had overthrown the previous emperor, Julius Nepos. And while the thirteen-year-old was a puppet autocrat, he did pass a law making it illegal for citizens to comment on his acne "cover" medication, and anyone who called it "makeup" was thrown to the lions.

There are few achievements of note during his nine-month rule, unless you count his repeated claims of having lost it to a girlfriend who lived in Narbonensis. Odoacer spared him because of his age and because he didn't want to touch any little pervert wearing makeup, and Romulus was sent to live with family in Campania. After this, he vanished entirely from history. He left no monuments, and the only likeness of him appears on a coin, marked with the legend *"Is eram a numerus virgo,"* which loosely translates to "He was a total virgin."

Coveted by Coin Collectors, Who Are Usually Virgins, Too.

SEPTEMBER 5, 1698

Moscow Does Not Believe in Beards.

ON THIS DAY IN 1698, **TSAR PETER I** continued his efforts to Westernize his nation ⬆ (after years of it seeming too Country-Westernized, apparently) by imposing a beard tax on all Russian men.

Men throughout Russia who wanted to keep their beards had to pay an annual tax of 100 rubles and were forced to wear a medal that read "Beards are a ridiculous ornament." (Something that sadly wasn't enacted in the United States during the hipster goatee surge of the early 1990s.)

To set an example, Peter himself shaved off the beards of all the noblemen in his court, an action similar to later Russian leader Boris Yeltsin's obnoxious habit of shaving the head of whatever cabinet member was unfortunate enough to pass out first.

The only men in the nation exempt from this tax were the clergy and peasants from the lowest classes, so as not to interfere with the country's lice-herding industry.

Many historical events involving our friends/enemies in Russia occurred on this day.

Sadly, No Tax on Silly Hats.

SEPTEMBER 5, 1857 The father of space travel, Konstantin Tsiolkovsky is born. The basic mathematical formula for rocket propulsion is called the Tsiolkovsky rocket equation, although many wish he had offered a basic mathematical formula for pronouncing his last name.

SEPTEMBER 5, 1905 The Russo-Japanese War ends with the signing of the Treaty of Portsmouth, mediated by Teddy Roosevelt. This won him the 1906 Nobel Peace Prize, which he probably celebrated by going out and shooting as many animals or Cubans as he could.

SEPTEMBER 5, 1958 Boris Pasternak's *Doctor Zhivago* is published in the United States. Those with a lot of time on their hands can ignore the book and just spend a few weeks watching the David Lean movie version.

SEPTEMBER 6, 1901
Most Memorable Moment of the McKinley Administration.

IN AN ATTEMPT to make the notion of a Pan-American Exposition in Buffalo even drearier, anarchist Leon Czolgosz shot President William McKinley on this day in 1901.

McKinley had been shaking hands on a receiving line when Czolgosz approached him with a revolver wrapped in a handkerchief. (Note: This was a risky act in those days, since "white-hanky-wrapped-around-fist" used to be code for "Anarchist Bottom.")

Czolgosz fired twice, hitting McKinley in the chest and stomach, but he was then pounced upon by an African-American waiter named James B. Parker, who prevented the assassin from firing a third shot. As a reward, Parker only received a "suspended lynching" for assaulting a white man.

The city's top surgeon was unavailable, so a gynecologist named Dr. Matthew Mann operated on McKinley. Mann was unable to find the bullet in the president's abdomen, but since he also couldn't find any ovaries, gave the dying McKinley a comforting pep talk about adoption opportunities.

McKinley died a week later, and Czolgosz died a month later in the electric chair. His last words were "I killed the president because he was the enemy of the good people. I am not sorry for my crime." He also added "But I am sorry about all that funnel cake I ate at the Pan-American Expo. Funnel cake is an enemy of the small intestine."

SEPTEMBER 7, 1776
War is Shell—The *Turtle* Debuts!

THE WORLD'S FIRST-EVER SUBMARINE ATTACK took place on this day in New York Harbor, aided by none other than Ben Franklin, who ultimately was disappointed to learn that the offer to participate in a "sub mission" wasn't the elusive kink he had always wanted to try out.

The *Turtle* was a wooden submersible craft invented by David Bushnell (with help from Franklin) in 1775, years before it became standard to name war machines after things that are fast, scary, and not easily captured and then starved by ten-year-olds.

FEAR THE TURTLE!

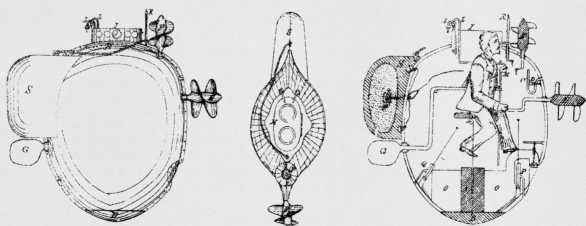

176

The one-man craft was 7.5 feet long and three feet wide, made of wood, and sealed in tar. It submerged by allowing water into the hull, rose by forcing water out through a hand pump, and was propelled by hand-cranked propellers. (It was not unlike one of those personal submarines one sees in the Hammacher Schlemmer catalog, except the mission of this craft was not to escape your too-privileged dysfunctional family for a few hours.)

The *Turtle*'s mission was to float into New York Harbor and drill a hole into the hull of a British ship, the HMS *Eagle*. The mission failed, and the *Turtle* wound up sinking, making it the only submarine mission in history that Tom Clancy won't turn into a long, overly technical beach-read.

SEPTEMBER 8, 1966
Star Trek Boldly Begins Three-Year Ratings Slump.

HAPPY FORTY-SECOND BIRTHDAY, *Star Trek*!
Note: To make the above statement hopelessly tragic, please add the word "Fan" to the end of the sentence.

On this star date in 1966, the science-fiction program *Star Trek* debuted on NBC. It never got above number fifty-two in the ratings and was given the ax after only three seasons, which made the show about as popular as most of its fans were back in high school.

This cancellation was an injustice many have attempted to right over the years with volumes of continuing-adventure fan fiction, usually published on the Internet. (Be warned though, most of this fiction contains more gay sex than George Takei's "reality.")

The show proved a hit in syndication, however, and has seemingly never gone off the air. Nowadays, most people refer to *Star Trek* by the retronym *Star Trek: TOS*, or *Star Trek: The Original Series*, since the show eventually spun off into other shows. Among these are *Star Trek: The Next Generation* (the one with the bald guy), *Star Trek: Deep Space Nine* (the one with the black guy), *Star Trek: Voyager* (the one with the hot chick with the metal on her face), *Star Trek: Enterprise* (the one with the *Quantum Leap* guy), and the upcoming *Star Trek: Gratuitous Use of Colons*.

STAR TREK
GIRLFRIEND QUEST

(THIS MISSION MIGHT TAKE LONGER THAN FIVE YEARS.)

SEPTEMBER 9, 1976
Mao No Mo'.

CHINA'S COMMUNIST LEADER CHAIRMAN MAO TSE-TUNG opted for "Better Dead Than Red" and made a Great Leap Forward into the Great Beyond on this day, when he died in Beijing at the age of eighty-two.

Mao is still a pop-culture icon, despite having killed somewhere in the neighborhood of 38 million people. That's probably because in China, that's not called genocide, but "getting a little more elbow room."

Safe for Speed, Any Kind.

TODAY IS A DAY to rev up our engines and drive down the highway of automotive history.

SEPTEMBER 10, 1897 George Smith is arrested behind the wheel in England after police notice his vehicle swerving. His is the first recorded drunk-driving arrest in history, and thankfully he didn't kill either of the only two drivers on the road at that time, who might not have been able to get out of the way of an 1897 model car.

SEPTEMBER 10, 1913 The Lincoln Highway, the first coast-to-coast paved road in the United States, opens for traffic. That same day, first adventurous teen who travels the highway in search of America later becomes first teenager who realizes that a lot of America is flat and not very interesting and turns back at Franklin Grove, Illinois.

SEPTEMBER 10, 1921 Germany's Autobahn, the only highway in the world with no speed limit, opens. Sammy Hagar's application for German citizenship later denied after performance of shoddy, keyboard-free cover of Kraftwerk's *Autobahn*.

SEPTEMBER 10, 1934 Famed television newsman Charles Kuralt is born. Later became known for his *On the Road* reports, in which he would travel the nation profiling regular people, back in the days before all regular people made it on TV by eating raw pig ass on reality shows.

SEPTEMBER 10, 2006 Michael Schumacher, the most successful driver in Formula One history, announces his retirement. Apparently, he felt his career was going around in circles.

Other Stuff Happened, Too!

ALSO THE FIRST
MAN TO LOOK
DOWN ON
NEW JERSEY.

← **SEPTEMBER 11, 1609 HENRY HUDSON** lands on Manhattan. Like most foreigners, he tries to blend in, but fanny pack and denim overmatching give him away.

SEPTEMBER 11, 1847 At Mountain Meadows, Utah, Mormons murder 120 settlers from Missouri and Arkansas. Most disturbing Mormon-related atrocity that does not involve gratuitous Bill Paxton *Big Love* butt-shots.

SEPTEMBER 11, 1922 The British Mandate of Palestine begins. So far, so good.

SEPTEMBER 11, 1943 Jack Ely, lead singer of the Kingsmen ("Louie Louie" and many, many other hits) is born. Will mumble a version of "Happy Birthday" to himself today that people will immediately assume is dirty.

SEPTEMBER 11, 1970 Ford introduces their compact car, the Pinto, knowing full well it contains a design flaw that causes the fuel tank to explode upon rear impact of 20 mph or higher. What they didn't know was that the subsequent explosions would vastly improve the appearance of the car.

SEPTEMBER 11, 1973 Chilean General Augusto Pinochet comes to power after successful coup, with some alleged U.S. backing. Fortunately, U.S. actions in the Third World never come back to bite us in the ass.

SEPTEMBER 11, 1978 President Carter, President Sadat, and Prime Minister Begin meet at Camp David and agree upon peace plan between Israel and Egypt. So far, so good!

SEPTEMBER 12, 2001

President Bush Finally Stops Reading *My Pet Goat* to Group of Schoolkids.

C'MON, he just wanted to see how it ended.

SEPTEMBER 13, 1899

First American Dies in Auto Accident, Insurance Skyrockets.

ON THIS DAY IN HISTORY IN 1899, sixty-eight-year-old New Yorker Henry Hale Bliss was struck by a car. He died a day later, making him the first person in America killed in an auto-related accident. This is not to be confused with the first person in America killed in an autoerotic accident. That, of course, was flag maker Betsy Ross. (The rumor starts here.)

Bliss, a realtor, got off a streetcar on West 74th Street and Central Park West, and was hit by an electric-powered taxicab. One imagines that, as an Upper West Sider, he promptly began legal proceedings against the cabdriver, the city, and against the owners of the SRO on his block (just for good measure).

The driver of the taxi was arrested and charged with manslaughter but was later acquitted, despite the fact that he was distracted by high jinks in his backseat resulting from a **"Victorian Taxicab Confession,"** when two young drunk ladies flashed him some ankle before both admitting to "being under Sappho's spell" while in college.

SEPTEMBER 14, 1814

Francis Scott Key Becomes One-Hit Wonder.

FRANCIS SCOTT KEY, in an effort to provide descendant F. Scott Fitzgerald with more time to grab a beer or six before the first inning, composed "The Star Spangled Banner" on this day in 1814.

Key, a lawyer, had composed the lyrics after seeing the British assault on Maryland's Fort McHenry in the War of 1812. The violence seemed unnecessary, because even by 1814, the entire world had already forgotten what the War of 1812 was about or that it had ever happened.

Key witnessed the carnage while detained on a British prison ship, unaware of the carnage about to take place on his person once word got round among the other prisoners that a lyricist was on board. He was inspired by the fact that despite the assault, the American flag still flew over the battered fort. Of course, soldiers being soldiers, their "No Fat Wenches" barracks banner also survived but never found proper tribute in song.

The lyrics were published in a Baltimore newspaper on September 20, and eventually set to the tune of an English drinking song called "To Anacreon in Heaven" by British composer John Stafford Smith. This anecdote is always of some small comfort to Sammy Hagar, who wishes that the tight melody line of his "Mas Tequila" might someday be used for a higher purpose.

MUSIC'S MAJOR KEY.

Happy Birthday, William Howard Taft.

OUR TWENTY-SEVENTH PRESIDENT OF THE UNITED STATES, William Howard Taft, was born on this day and one assumes he began nursing immediately. Here are some fun facts about our fattest chief executive.

READING A MENU, PRESUMABLY.

- As mentioned, Taft was our heaviest president, weighing in at 340 pounds. He is not to be confused with our phattest president, Calvin "Master C" Coolidge.

- Was the only president who later became a Supreme Court Justice. He lobbied hard for the construction of the Supreme Court Building after the Congress refused to allow him to hear cases in the dining room at the nearby Wing Lo's All You Can Eat Chinese Buffet.

- Taft was the first president to throw out the first pitch at the beginning of baseball season. He was also the first president to be censured by Congress for throwing like a girl.

- He was the last president in office to have facial hair. (Jimmy Carter's 1978 "soul patch" was grown during a brief overseas vacation.)

- He dramatically called the White House the "Loneliest Place in the World," although during his administration, the White House Cookie and Fudge Pantry was the "Most-Visited Place in the World."

- His funeral in 1930 was the first to be broadcast on radio. And once again, presence of radio tap dancers and ventriloquists seemed inappropriate for the medium.

- Taft was the last president to keep a cow at the White House for fresh milk, a tradition that ended when he became the first president to eat an entire cow as a prebreakfast warm-up.

TODAY, HE WOULD BE NICKNAMED "SLIM."

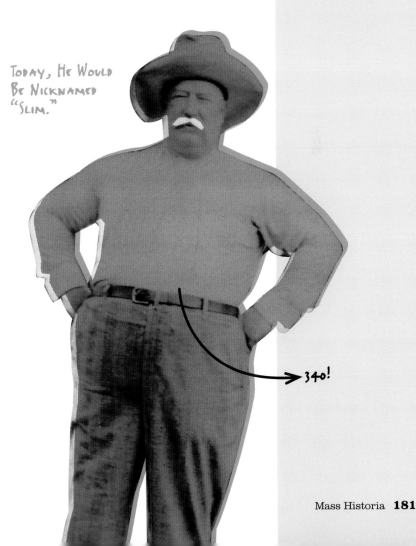

340!

DICK CHENEY, RIGHT, SEEN HAVING HIS FIRST HEART ATTACK.

The "Come Back" Kid.

GERALD FORD, our most forgiving president (although he held a grudge against that airplane staircase for many years), extended yet another olive branch to the world on this day in 1974, when he announced a conditional amnesty program for Vietnam deserters and draft dodgers who agreed to perform at least two years in public-service jobs.

To show he meant business, he then hired Dick "Five Deferrals" Cheney to be his deputy chief of staff.

Flying Ace Becomes Dying Ace.

MANFRED VON RICHTHOFEN, aka the Red Baron (after "Manny the V" was deemed not intimidating enough), shot down his first plane on this day. The person he killed is lost to history, but that's what you get for not having a cool nickname.

After this kill, Richthofen had a jeweler create a silver cup engraved with the date of the fight and the type of plane. Eventually, he amassed sixty cups, which were great conversation pieces, especially since they caught all the spittle one encounters when having a conversation with a German.

The Red Baron's career was a fairly short one, and in 1918 he was shot through the abdomen by an anti-aircraft machine gunner while flying over France, and the machine gunner was later killed when running to the silversmith's to have his own cup made.

Von Richthofen managed to land the plane, and his last word was allegedly "*Kaput*," which in English means "kaput."

Richthofen has become a pop-culture legend over the years and is the only German war enemy who has a frozen pizza named after him, now that General Mills no longer makes the "Goebbels Supreme: You'll Gobble It Up."

WORLD'S BIGGEST FLYING KILLER

Mass Historia Mortality In and Out List.

IN:

SEPTEMBER 18, 1905 Nine months of blessed alone time in the womb ends as actress Greta Garbo is born. If you already knew this date, you need to get down and open the boutique where you sell *I Love Lucy* fridge magnets and *That Girl* T-shirts.

SEPTEMBER 18, 1933 Actor Robert Blake born in Nutley, New Jersey. Best known for *Baretta*, and for allegedly yielding a similar weapon to dispatch his grifter/wife.

SEPTEMBER 18, 1951 Ramones bassist Dee Dee Ramone born in Fort Lee, Virginia. Among the Ramones, he was known as "the Cute One."

SEPTEMBER 18, 1958 Rocker Lita Ford born. Considered a hot chick, which in the rock world means she's slightly prettier than Dee Dee Ramone.

OUT:

SEPTEMBER 18, 1949 Actor Frank Morgan dies. Most famous for playing the title character in *The Wizard of Oz*. If you already knew this, you need to get down and open the boutique where you sell *I Love Lucy* fridge magnets and *That Girl* T-shirts.

SEPTEMBER 18, 1961 Dag Hammarskjöld, U.N. Secretary General and Nobel Peace Prize winner, dies in a plane crash in Zambia. Along with former secretary generals Boutros Boutros-Ghali and U Thant, has yet to make peace with most spell-check programs.

SEPTEMBER 18, 1970 Guitar hero Jimi Hendrix dies of a drug overdose at twenty-seven years of age, or the same number of years it has taken your bachelor uncle to learn how to play the intro to "Purple Haze" (the very slow version).

SEPTEMBER 18, 2004 Camp movie director Russ Meyer dies. And if you knew that— seriously, that boutique where you sell *I Love Lucy* fridge magnets and *That Girl* T-shirts isn't going to open itself!

SEPTEMBER 19, 1881
Garfield's Big Fat Hairy Death.

HIS DEATHBED VIGIL WAS SHORTER THAN THE TIME IT TOOK TO BUTTON THIS COAT.

ON THIS DAY IN 1881, nearly three months after being shot in the back and in the arm, President James Garfield died from complications from blood poisoning, bronchial pneumonia, and a ruptured splenic artery aneurysm. He was the second president assassinated and, like Lincoln, also born in a log cabin. (Let that be a warning to you folk out there who live in log cabins. "Style" might not be your only "curse.")

He was shot by Charles Julius Guiteau on July 2, 1881, while walking through a Washington D.C., train station. After the shooting, Guiteau excitedly said, "I am a Stalwart of the Stalwarts. I did it and I want to be arrested. Arthur is president now." (The 1880s equivalent of "In Your Face!")

(Note: Garfield was a member of the GOP's Half-Breeds, who supported Civil Service Reform and a lenient treatment of the South, while his former adversary and eventual Vice President Chester Alan Arthur was a Republican Stalwart, who favored a retention of the patronage system, a harder line on the former Confederate states, and, most importantly to Arthur, a stronger union between mustache and sideburn.)

Guiteau had been demanding a civil service job for weeks and wanted to be appointed the United States consul in Paris. While not qualified for the job, his subsequent actions suggest that he might have had a promising career with the post office.

Chauvinist Riggs.

ON THIS DAY, BILLIE JEAN KING mopped up the court with elderly moptop and tennis legend Bobby Riggs during the so-called Battle of the Sexes, after Riggs declared that even the best female tennis player wasn't as good as a fifty-five-year-old senior male player. And while Riggs's tennis skills were still pretty sharp, he displayed a slightly clouded gaydar when accepting the challenge from his assumably too-feminine rival King.

The match was played before a crowd of 30,000 at the Astrodome in Houston, where the turf was slightly more natural than the aging Riggs's "youthful" haircut. King was carried out on a sedan chair held aloft by oiled musclemen, much like Cleopatra, if Cleopatra's heavy eyeliner allowed for a lot of ironic lesbian eye-rolling at the sight of the oiled men. Riggs was brought out on a rickshaw pulled by scantily clad women, subsequently offending Asians, feminists, and fans of traditionally boring tennis.

King beat Riggs 6–4, 6–3, and 6–3, and kept him running all around the court (once again, startling fans of traditionally boring tennis). The event drew more attention to women's tennis than any other event in the game's history until the release of the four-hundred-page coffee table book, *Anna Kournikova Bends Over to Pick Up a Ball*.

Nathan Hale, Failure.

ON THIS DAY IN HISTORY, America's first spy, Nathan Hale, became America's first captured spy, when he was arrested by British forces in a tavern in Flushing Bay, Queens, New York. The name of this tavern is lost to history, but if it was in Queens, it was probably called Shamrock-something-or-other, and filled with old men nursing both a glass of Wild Turkey and a severe contempt for any sunlight streaming through the window.

Hale volunteered to go behind enemy lines during the Battle of Long Island (which, in case you're reading, Great Britain, you can take back anytime), disguised as a Dutch school teacher. He was revealed as a fraud when unable to fake any knowledge of the best places to buy "Ye Olde Space Cakes" in Amsterdam.

The following day, he was taken to another bar called the Dove Tavern, at what is now Third Avenue and 63rd Street in Manhattan, to be tried and hanged—on the second stop of what has become Nathan Hale's Depressing Pub Crawl of Failure.

Before being strung up, he was heard to say, "I only regret that I have but one life to lose for my country." He added, "But I also regret wearing those wooden shoes in my Dutch school teacher's disguise. Authentic, yes, but not the best thing to wear if you have to make a quick escape."

Four or five different locations in Manhattan lay claim to being the spot where Hale was hanged. This is because the British found hanging the patriot so much fun, they decided to do it four more times.

President Kennedy's Most Sought-After "Peace."

THE LEGACY OF PRESIDENT JOHN F. KENNEDY took a turn for the crunchy on this day in history when he signed legislation establishing the Peace Corps. It was a plan to reinvigorate foreign policy that sadly left our nation's food co-ops and alternative bookstores dangerously understaffed.

Kennedy envisioned his Peace Corps as an army of volunteers sent off to aid poor people in underdeveloped countries, which would in turn aid American college students who didn't want to start their postgraduate work right after their graduate work. Ideally, this would also lessen the possibility of smaller nations succumbing to Communism, by filling them with young people who were already considered Communists by most Americans.

The first director of the organization was Kennedy's brother-in-law, Sergeant Shriver, whose daughter Maria would go on to marry a man who would one day save the Third World from the Predator.

Since that day, over 187,000 volunteers have been sent overseas to help make a difference in over 139 countries, once they were taught and had safely memorized the native expression for "No, no, I am one of the *good* Americans."

USEFUL PHRASES FOR PEACE CORPS VOLUNTEERS:
1 WHICH WAY TO THE BATHROOM?
2 SERIOUSLY, I NEED A BATHROOM.
3 WHAT THE HELL IS WRONG WITH YOUR WATER HERE?

John Paul Jones Finishes Fight That He Had Not Yet Begun.

JOHN PAUL JONES, piloting the *Bonhomme Richard*, defeated two British warships, the *Seraphis* and the *Countess of Scarborough* on this day, making him the first American naval hero (not counting the time **BEN FRANKLIN** invented the ← belly-shirt).

HE HAD A THING FOR POT-BELLIED INVENTIONS.

During the engagement, **JONES**, who was only thirty-two at ← the time, was asked by the British captain if he wanted to surrender, to which he replied "I have not yet begun to fight!" His less graceful addendum, "So shove it up your ass, Nigel," was blessedly drowned out by cannon fire.

(Note: This hero of the Continental navy is not to be confused with Led Zeppelin bassist John Paul Jones, whose only remotely nautical adventure involved a groupie and a shark. No notable quotes from that incident are known to have been uttered.)

SEPTEMBER 24
A Boom in Boomer Milestones.

MORE STORIES OF INTEREST TO THE BABY BOOMER GANG, who might not be reading this book but are certainly not reading any of that crap the traitor Tom Brokaw writes about the so-called "greatest" generation of war mongers. Ungroovy.

SEPTEMBER 24, 1936 Beloved boomer puppeteer and creator of Kermit the Frog, Jim Henson is born. His and Kermit's song, "(It's Not Easy) Bein' Green," was covered by Frank Sinatra, Van Morrison, and Ray Charles (like he would know).

SEPTEMBER 24, 1941 Photographer, vegetarian, musician, and rock-and-roll wife Linda McCartney is born. Despite these credits, in life she was best loved for not being Yoko and in death for not being Heather Mills.

SEPTEMBER 24, 1964 *The Munsters* debuts on CBS. Two years later, it was canceled, and monster-filled families went unrepresented on television until the 2002 debut of *The Osbournes*.

SEPTEMBER 24, 1968 Famed news program *60 Minutes* goes on the air, ten years before they try to pander to the youth market with the addition of Andy Rooney. Mike Wallace has been on the program since its debut, and is nowadays best loved for not being his weasel son, Chris Wallace.

SEPTEMBER 24, 1991 Theodore Geisel, aka Dr. Seuss, dies at age eighty-seven. His stories were beloved by boomer children, until the late 1960s when they realized that a handful of mescaline and *The Lorax* television special was not an easy mix.

SEPTEMBER 25, 1976

U2 Born.

ON THIS DAY IN HISTORY IN 1976, seven Dublin teenagers gathered in the house of fourteen-year-old Larry Mullen Jr., in what would be the first-ever meeting of the band U2. The seven members were soon whittled down to four, after sixteen-year-old Paul Hewson, aka Bono, won the wrestling match to see who would get to wear the group's sole pair of giant, buglike, Jackie Onassis sunglasses.

The band was originally called the Larry Mullen Band, and they soon set out on the important task of growing their hair long in the back. Once that goal was achieved, the band changed its name to Feedback. Unfortunately, they didn't call themselves Feedback after the looping signal noise a guitar makes through an amplifier, but rather "the process of communication whereby a person can disagree, ask a question, repeat information for understanding, or otherwise talk back in the communication process." It was the only name less rock and roll than the Larry Mullen Band, so they then changed their name to the Hype, which is what U2 would later coast on during the unfortunate MacPhisto Period.

This lineup—**BONO** on vocals, Dave "the Edge" Evans on guitar and knit hat, group leader Larry Mullen on drums, and Adam Clayton on bass and the lion's share of groupies—eventually signed to Island Records and in 1980 released their first single, "11 O'Clock Tick Tock," and if we have to hear the story about how you used to "own the 45 but lost it, and man, would it be worth something now," you are going to get a kick in the teeth.

"Am I Buglike? Sorry, I Didn't Mean to Be Buglike."

SEPTEMBER 26, 1982
America Falls in Love with Snooty Talking Car!

ON THIS DAY IN 1982, after a sixteen-year effort to purge the Nielsen system of the viewers who scuttled *My Mother the Car*, the television show *Knight Rider* debuted and became an instant hit. The program featured a Pontiac Firebird named KITT, which was able to intelligently communicate with humans, and David Hasselhoff, who appeared to be able to do so as well. The magic of television!

During the course of the show, Hasselhoff released an album called *Night Rocker*, the cover of which featured the actor standing on the hood of a car holding a guitar. You can find it in the record collection of any hipster whose sense of irony is probably long overdue for a tune-up. (Hasselhoff often claims to be very popular in Europe, which is the musical equivalent of having a "girlfriend in Canada.")

As the show went on, KITT squared off against an evil version of himself named KATT, while Hasselhoff later vanished and was replaced by a winking, evil replicate who was diabolically too "in" on his own joke to be any fun.

HASSELHOFF FUN FACT:
DAVID HASSELHOFF'S HAIR ALSO DOUBLED AS A CRASH HELMET ON THE SERIES.

SEPTEMBER 27, 1590
Urban Blighted.

POPE URBAN VII (yes, there were six other guys who thought "Urban" was the best pope name to choose from) died on this day of malaria, after having been pope for only two weeks. His reign is the shortest of any pope, unless you count the three-day reign of Stephen II, but he hasn't been recognized as a true pope by the Catholic Church since the Second Vatican Council, which was the gathering that made loonies like Mel Gibson refuse to recognize any subsequent pope since 1961. (Go ahead and name yourself pope. Most people won't recognize it, but hey—you never know. You can even use it as an excuse for your perennial datelessness.)

Needless to say, he didn't accomplish much during his short reign, but he is credited with having launched the first-known smoking ban, threatening anyone who smoked in a church with excommunication. Many heralded this healthy initiative at the time, without realizing it was just another creepy attempt to make Catholic houses of worship more kid-friendly.

Radiant Gwyneth Paltrow Born, Radiantly.

On this day in 1972, the radiant actress Gwyneth Paltrow was born to famous parents who would become more famous once she became famous. Shortly after the birth, the doctor announced, "It's a girl," and quickly added "She's radiant." (Although there was some debate in the delivery room as to the baby's "willowiness" and "luminosity.")

After a brief stint in the mid-1990s as "the new Grace Kelly," the actress quickly moved into more radiant starring roles. She played the radiant muse in *Shakespeare in Love*, a radiant head in a box in *Se7en* [sic], and later, a radiant-yet-retarded stewardess in that comedy that's always on HBO.

She is currently radiant and married to the lead singer of the band Coldplay, whose music is as "sweeping" and "shimmering" as Paltrow is "radiant."

ALSO ON THIS DAY:
SEPTEMBER 28, 1994 Film critics enter into Anti-Thesaurus Agreement to describe "the new Grace Kelly."

Don't Support the Troops.

ANDRÉ'S HANGING
AROUND, PRE-HANGING.

TODAY HAS TRADITIONALLY BEEN a bad day for men in uniform. Military uniform. (Men in uniforms at theme parks and fast-food restaurants have bad days every day.)

SEPTEMBER 29, 1780 Thirty-one-year-old British spy **MAJOR JOHN ANDRÉ** is sentenced to die for aiding in Benedict Arnold's treason. As a soldier, he asks to be shot by firing squad rather than hanged. As an Englishman, he asks to be shot because his lack of chin makes hanging a bit of a crapshoot. General George Washington tries to spare André's life by arranging a swap for Arnold, who was fighting for the British. The British wouldn't hand him over, since they were "most enraptured with his rarest of chins most protruded!"

SEPTEMBER 29, 1862 Union General Jefferson C. Davis, probably already tense from sharing his name with the leader of the Confederacy (see *Mass Historia*, April 19, 1943: *Private Adolph Hitler Once Again De-pantsed by Fellow American Soldiers*), kills his commanding officer, General William Nelson. Nelson had slapped Davis in a hotel lobby in Louisville, Kentucky, so Davis shot him. Due to political connections in the Union forces at the time, Davis was never court-martialed, and went on to serve with distinction at several battles—but only after another officer would slap him and get him ready to kill en masse.

SEPTEMBER 29, 1965 Hanoi announces that all downed U.S. fighter pilots will not be treated as POWs, and instead will be treated as war criminals, meaning they'll miss out on all the cushy treatment that American POWs were enjoying at the time.

SEPTEMBER 30, 1955
Rebel Without a Pulse.

TWENTY-FOUR-YEAR-OLD JAMES DEAN died in a car accident on this day in 1955, with only three films to his credit, and a burgeoning reputation as one of the finest actors of his generation. Where he would have gone in his career is one of Hollywood's biggest "What ifs?" And we would like to answer "What if?" with this speculative entry from a 1978 *TV Guide* that might have appeared had the young star been tooling around in a slow-but-steady Nash Rambler rather than a Porsche 550 Spider.

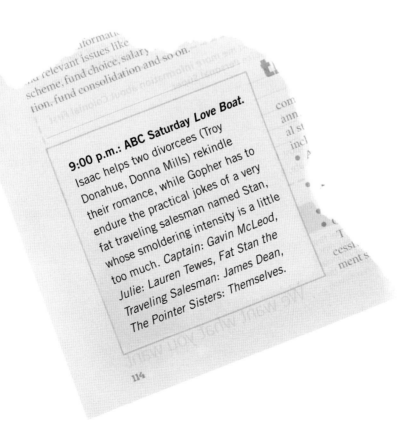

9:00 p.m.: ABC Saturday Love Boat. Isaac helps two divorcees (Troy Donahue, Donna Mills) rekindle their romance, while Gopher has to endure the practical jokes of a very fat traveling salesman named Stan, whose smoldering intensity is a little too much. Captain: Gavin McLeod, Julie: Lauren Tewes, Fat Stan the Traveling Salesman: James Dean, The Pointer Sisters: Themselves.

October

OCTOBER 1, 1955

The Honeymooners Debuts.

THE CLASSIC SITCOM *THE HONEYMOONERS* debuted on this date in 1955 on CBS. The show followed the adventures of a grossly overweight loser bus driver living in what appeared to be a kitchen somewhere in Brooklyn, stuck in a loveless marriage to a cold shrew who never supported any of his endeavors to better himself. His only friend is a retarded sewer worker who barges into his home occasionally, and who may or may not have a wife named Trixie. Oddly enough, they were only able to produce thirty-nine episodes from this rich comic premise, and the show was not a hit during its original run.

Despite this setback, Gleason went on to have a varied and successful career in TV, film, and music, and was dubbed "the Great One" by Orson Welles. (To be fair, Welles called anyone "the Great One" if they had a "slimming" effect on him.)

MEMORABLE LINES FROM *THE HONEYMOONERS*:

"One of These Days . . . One of These Days . . . POW. Right in the Kisser!"

"You're Going to the Moon, Alice!"

"You're a Riot Alice, a Regular Riot!"

"Well, What's Stopping You from Making Money? I'm Going to Beat the Living Crap Out of You, You Goddamned, Cold Shrew!"

(THIS IS FROM ONE OF THE "LOST" EPISODES.)

Mass Historia Mortality In and Out List.

IN:

OCTOBER 2, 1800 Nat Turner born. Led famous slave uprising in Virginia in 1831 after witnessing a solar eclipse, which he took as a sign. Probably also took the regular beatings and the whole "slave thing" as signs that an uprising might be called for too.

OCTOBER 2, 1904 British novelist Graham Greene born. Conversion to Catholicism has major impact on all his novels, especially in the "laugh quotient."

OCTOBER 2, 1937 Famed O. J. Simpson defense attorney Johnny Cochran born. First words were "If the diaper fits, I'll take a sh—."

OCTOBER 2, 1945 Singer and songwriter Don McLean born, famous for 1971's "American Pie." A hip English teacher once played it for you as an example of "Allusion," and of his/her own "Squareness."

OCTOBER 2, 1951 British musician and actor Sting born. Once worked the phrase "a murder of crows" into a song, the penalty for which should be "a murder of Sting."

OUT:

OCTOBER 2, 1803 SAM ADAMS dies. American patriot ← who helped organize the Boston Tea Party, and later had a beer named after him, probably to end sissy associations with "tea parties."

OCTOBER 2, 1850 Armless and legless British painter Sarah Biffen dies at age sixty-six. Overcomes biggest physical handicap in painting history, until the emergence of cripplingly dorky Bob Ross Afro.

OCTOBER 2, 1968 Leading Dadaist artist Marcel Duchamp dies. Once signed his name to an actual urinal and called it *Fountain*, which is why our dads say embarrassing things when they go to the modern art museum.

OCTOBER 2, 1985 Actor and sex symbol Rock Hudson dies of AIDS at sixty, becoming the first major American celebrity to do so. His television series *McMillan and Wife* renamed *McMillan and "Wife"* in syndication.

Sam He Was.

OCTOBER 3
Ouch.

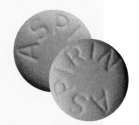

TODAY HAS HISTORICALLY BEEN A DAY of the physically painful and unpleasant. Take a few aspirin before reading.

OCTOBER 3, 1873 The United States military hangs four Indians found guilty of murdering the Civil War hero General Edward Canby during the Modoc War in Oregon. The alternate sentence of "life on a reservation" was deemed too cruel.

OCTOBER 3, 1981 The IRA hunger strike in the Maze Prison called off after seven months and ten deaths. On the plus side, the prisoners blessedly had avoided all food prepared for them by their British captors.

OCTOBER 3, 1995 Guilty football hero O. J. Simpson is found "not guilty" of being guilty of murdering his wife Nicole (married to a guilty man) and her male friend, Ron Goldman (famous for being carved up by O. J. Simpson).

OCTOBER 3, 2003 Magician Roy Horn, of Siegfried and Roy, celebrates his fifty-ninth birthday by allowing his tiger Montecore to try and devour his head. It is another accident that shows the limited protective power of the glittery aqua codpiece.

OCTOBER 4, 1983
Hooters Pops Out!

ON THIS DAY IN HOT-WINGSTORY, the first-ever Hooters restaurant opened in Clearwater, Florida, and to this date, they have still not changed the fry oil. The restaurant was housed in what used to be a large, trash-processing center, but that was "not casual enough" for most of the traditional Hooters clientele.

The chain is now twenty-five years old, the same age most Hooters waitresses are relegated to "kitchen work." In that time, it has blossomed into over four hundred branches in the United States, Mexico, Singapore, Australia, and Canada, where the waitresses are known for their fetching orange quilted snowpants.

The eateries feature the novelty of large-breasted women in short shorts sitting at your table while you order your food—all of which is considerably spicier than the relationship you have with your wife, who is sitting next to the waitress, her head buried in a copy of *O* magazine.

Chester Alan Arthur Born!

PRESIDENT CHESTER ALAN ARTHUR was born on this day in 1829 in a small town in northern Vermont. He was only president for three-and-a-half years and his party refused to nominate him for a second term, but there is more to the man than meets the eye-catching sideburns.

- Arthur insisted that people pronounce his middle name with the accent on the second syllable, Al-LAN. This precious affectation led people to call him Fat-TY behind his back.

- Arthur changed his pants several times a day, and supposedly owned over eighty pairs. This was a marked change from the previous president, the dowdy James "Sans-a-Belt" Garfield.

- He didn't make an inaugural address, which was just as well since he was planning on rereading his totally unoriginal high school valedictory speech entitled "Our Duty to Tomorrow."

- His favorite food was mutton, which once led to the accidental consumption of his facial hair.

- Arthur's citizenship was questioned when political opponents alleged he was born across the Vermont border in Canada. This wasn't true, because if he were a Canadian living among Americans, he would have insisted on working it into every friggin' conversation.

Be Arthur.

THE CUBS GOT BLEAT.

Goat Gets Goaded, Cubs Get Clubbed.

AT GAME 4 OF THE WORLD SERIES between the Chicago Cubs and the Detroit Tigers at Wrigley Field, a local Greek immigrant and bar owner named Billy Sianis sat in his box seat with a pet goat. (Among Greek immigrants at the time, this was called "accessorizing.") Sianis, a Cubs fan, had placed a blanket over the animal that read "We Got Detroit's Goat."

The goat became a hit with the Chicago fans that day, especially since the animal seemed mentally sharper and more worldly than your average White Sox fan. But the tide began to turn when Andy Frain, head of stadium security, held up Sianis's ticket stub in the air and announced, "If he eats the ticket, we win." (Believe it or not, there was a baseball game or something going on at the same time.) The goat refused to eat the ticket, even though it was more nutritious and flavorful than the hot dogs being munched all around him.

Eventually, Cubs owner and gum magnate Philip Knight Wrigley had the animal ejected because of its odor, which infuriated Sianis. He supposedly cursed the Cubs, who then lost the game and eventually the World Series, and they have never made it to another. (Note: Many Red Sox fans over the years have dismissed this curse as "too rational.")

After the loss, Sianis wrote Wrigley and asked, "Who stinks now?" At first, Wrigley thought it was yet another complaint letter over his family's ill-advised experiment with the loathsome gum, "Kippers and Tripe Juicy Fruit."

Take That, Osama!

MAKING GOOD ON PRESIDENT BUSH'S PLEDGE of "Wanted Dead or Alive," the United States military begins the assault on Afghanistan, in hopes of catching Osama Bin Laden, the mastermind behind 9/11. How does it turn out? *See October 8, 2001.*

Attack on Afghanistan, Day 2.

WHATEVER BECAME OF OSAMA BIN LADEN? GOOD QUESTION!

THE ATTACK EFFECTIVELY ENDS, as Secretary of Defense Donald Rumsfeld informs the United States Military not to unpack its bags, and to head down to the Kabul post office to fill out forms so their mail can be forwarded to Iraq.

Che Guevara Embarks on Journey to Your T-Shirt.

THERE IS PROBABLY A PRETTY LOUD SALSABRATION going on at anti-Castro Sound Machinist Gloria Estefan's house today, because it is the anniversary of the murder of Cuban Revolution figure Ernesto "Che" Guevara.

Guevara was born in 1928 in Argentina to a wealthy family. Unlike most rich kids who become Marxist, however, he didn't immediately lose interest once he got his undergraduate degree and/or his Marxist girlfriend broke up with him.

In his late twenties, he met Fidel Castro in Mexico and decided to join the anti-Batista/pro–scraggly beard forces. After the revolution, he oversaw the execution of "political dissenters," and later claimed that had he been in charge of the Soviet nuclear arsenal on the island, he would have deployed it against American cities. Ironically, this would have annihilated the infant members of Che-friendly Rage Against the Machine, but thankfully they do not appreciate or understand irony.

Later, captured and wounded by Bolivian special forces, he was heard to shout, "Do not shoot! I am Che Guevara and worth more to you alive than dead!" Of course, as a rich kid, Che didn't really understand the "worth" of anything, and was rather shocked when he was executed the next day.

A CIA agent named Felix Rodriguez stripped Guevara's body of its belongings (the "C" in CIA stands for "Classy") and among the revolutionary's possessions was a Rolex watch. This is an extravagance, but in order for a Communist revolution to survive, it needs to keep precise track of every minute and the suckers born therein.

OTHER T-SHIRT-WORTHY OCTOBER 9 NOTABLES ARE:

John Lennon, who was born on this day in 1940, and reggae legend Peter Tosh, who was born on October 9 in 1944. Both were shot to death. If your birthday is October 9, it might be better to live the rest of your days in relative obscurity.

YOUR PROBLEMATIC IDOL HERE

OCTOBER 10

A Couple of Sorry Republicans.

OCTOBER 10 IS NOTABLE BECAUSE it marks two separate instances of Republicans doing something they don't do anymore: resigning after screwing up, and apologizing.

OCTOBER 10, 1957 On this day, President Dwight D. Eisenhower apologized to Ghanaian Finance Minister Komla Agbeli Gbdemah, who had been refused service at a restaurant in Dover, Delaware. The name of the establishment is lost to history, but it should be said that Ghanaians everywhere like nothing more than waking up to an artery-clogging bout of Moons Over My Hammy. (Note: The Eisenhower 1950s were later celebrated by the TV show *Happy Days*, and they were indeed happy days for any person whose complexion was lighter than the Ghanaian finance minister's.)

OCTOBER 10, 1973 Spiro Agnew (the second-most-popular *Mad* magazine go-to guy in the early 1970s), vice president to Richard Nixon (the first-most-popular *Mad* magazine go-to guy in the early 1970s), resigned on this day after pleading No Contest to criminal charges of tax evasion and money laundering. He was hit with a $10,000 fine and three years probation, although nowadays these crimes would have earned him the much harsher "Demotion to Senate Majority Leader."

He was later disbarred in Maryland (a state whose only significant legal moment came in the 1954 landmark *Crab v. Cake*), and his resignation led to the first use of the Constitution's Twenty-fifth Amendment, in which the president must choose a successor who is then confirmed by a majority vote in the Senate and the House. This was all once explained to you by the famous *Schoolhouse Rock!* cartoon "Succession Successor (I'm Just a Ford)."

OCTOBER 11

A Good Day to Die!

PLENTY OF FAMOUS ICONS departed this mortal coil on this day in history.

OCTOBER 11, 1308 Pope Boniface VIII dies. Was believed to have made such statements as "The dead will rise just as little as my horse which died yesterday" and "Mary, when she bore Christ, was just as little a virgin as my own mother when she gave birth to me." Later considered a heretic by scholars until they realized that he actually thought his mom was a virgin and that zombie horses would one day roam the earth.

OCTOBER 11, 1963 French chanteuse and icon Edith Piaf dies at age forty-seven. You have heard her music if you have ever been to a French-style bistro, or had a friend in college who started wearing velvet blazers and smoking clove cigarettes junior year.

OCTOBER 11, 1965 American photographer Dorothea Lange dies at seventy. She took photos for the Farm Security Administration during the 1930s and snapped this image ← (right) of a starving Okie mother named Florence Owens Thompson. Thompson became an icon of the Great Depression, although she was bummed to learn that icon status did not include a complimentary boxed lunch.

OCTOBER 11, 1978 Nancy Spungen elevated to icon status by knife-wielding boyfriend Sid Vicious. Your friend with the velvet blazers and clove cigarettes had a T-shirt with both of them on it during sophomore year.

OCTOBER 12, 1492
Christopher Columbus Discovers Americans! You're Welcome, Rest of the World!

THE WORLD WASN'T FLAT, NEITHER WAS HIS HAIR!

ON THIS DAY IN HISTORY, Italian explorer Christopher Columbus (and if he didn't want us to create an Anglicanism for his name, he shouldn't have discovered us), landed on an island in the Bahamas, and in the process, discovered America. (He was also the last Italian to land on a Bahamian island in a boat without the words "Carnival," "Stugots," or "Poppa's Toy" painted on the side.)

Technically, the Americas had already been discovered by the Vikings about five hundred years before. And they were discovered by all the folks who trotted across the Bering Strait about 1,000 years before that. And the folks who had been living here for as long as mankind has existed probably own some claim to discovery as well. Columbus probably realized this, which is why he promptly set about killing and/or infecting everyone who might lay claim to his "discovery."

Either way, his accomplishments are celebrated throughout our nation every year with multicity Columbus Day Parades, in which Italian-Americans set out to discover new routes toward behaving as loutishly in public as Irish-Americans.

Note: The accomplishments of the Vikings in the discovery of America should be revisited and celebrated. Especially since Viking-Americans would probably throw one hell of a parade. ←

Milestone in Cornerstones!

ON THIS DAY IN 1792, the cornerstone of the White House was laid in the nation's brand-new capital, Washington, D.C. It was the most important laying the White House would see until 1961, when John F. Kennedy _____. (Please feel free to write your own joke. Angie Dickinson is a good go-to.)

At One Time, Only Horses Stunk Up the Place.

The mansion was designed by Irish-born architect James Hoban, which explained the original's Stout-and-Spirits Chamber, which vanished once outgoing president and dipsomaniac Franklin Pierce sealed himself up inside of it. In 1800, President John Adams and his wife Abigail were its first residents, but they lived there less than a year before Thomas Jefferson moved in. And as a widower, he promptly set about leaving his clothes all over the floor and piling up racing forms.

HERE ARE OTHER WHITE HOUSE FUN FACTS:

• During the War of 1812, British troops set fire to the White House in an attempt to do something that would make people remember the War of 1812. It didn't work.

• Grover Cleveland stopped the tradition of opening the house on inauguration day, and it wasn't until 1993 that the Clintons invited in 2,000 citizens who had been chosen by lottery— a lottery of girls ages sixteen to twenty-one.

• Woodrow Wilson kept a flock of sheep on the White House grounds as a way to support the war effort. The animals saved manpower by keeping the lawn short, and they raised over $50,000 for the Red Cross when their wool was auctioned off. This was similar to President Bush's symbolic war effort gesture, when he kept a yellow Support Our Troops Humvee idling in the driveway while a Lee Greenwood cassette played nearby on a coal-powered boom box.

HISTO-POURRI: Manly Men Things.

BUTCH IT UP, and enjoy this collection of incredibly manly, virile things that happened on this day. But don't let anyone know you're a "reader," sissy!

OCTOBER 14, 1912 During a campaign stop in Milwaukee, **PRESIDENT TEDDY ROOSEVELT** ← is shot in the chest by a saloon-keeper with a .32. He still finishes his speech, from which originated his second-most-famous phrase "Speak Softy and Carry A . . . Ow! What the hell?!" Fortunately, the bullet was slowed by a copy of his speech in his breast pocket and his glasses case, which is by far the most macho event ever associated with a spare glasses case, outside of a few episodes of *MacGyver*.

OCTOBER 14, 1944 General Edwin Rommel, aka the Desert Fox, commits suicide when his role in the failed assassination of Hitler is revealed. He is probably the most admired of the German leadership during World War II, despite Goebbels's attempts to fashion himself as the "cool Nazi" by giving his son's friends beer and letting them watch R-rated movies.

OCTOBER 14, 1958 "She Blinded Me with Science" singer and new-wave nerd Thomas Dolby is born. He is only included in this list of bullet points so that the other bullet points may tease it and beat it up.

GO AHEAD! CALL HIM "FOUR-EYES"

KING IN 1963, ANNOUNCING PLANS TO MARCH ALL OVER FIVE-YEAR-OLD THOMAS DOLBY'S ASS.

← **OCTOBER 14, 1964 DR. MARTIN LUTHER KING JR.** wins the Nobel Peace Prize. Actually, this is more inspirational and brave than manly. We'll let it slide. (Still, this bullet point plans on making the Thomas Dolby bullet point cry once the page is turned and no one is watching.)

A Day for the Death Penalty.

TODAY TRADITIONALLY HAS NOT BEEN THE GREATEST OF DAYS for history's spies, traitors, and Nazis, because it usually ends with a stroll to the gallows—a fairly peaceful stroll, unencumbered by the sounds of sobbing mourners.

OCTOBER 15, 1917 Hot spy Mata Hari is executed by a French firing squad. A dancer-turned-courtesan (one of those French words that makes even terrible things sound nice), she supposedly slept with generals on both sides during World War I, and revealed the secrets of the "tank" to German officials (which indicates that her "pillow talk" might have been a little under-sexy).

OCTOBER 15, 1945 Once again, those bloodthirsty French showed their itchy trigger fingers by dispatching puppet Vichy leader Pierre Laval, who found that the collaboration between bullets and chest cavity was even more regrettable than his collaboration with the Nazis.

OCTOBER 15, 1946 Commander in chief of the Luftwaffe, head of the Gestapo, prime minister of Prussia, drug addict, and gender-bending he-she Hermann Goering pulls a fast one on the executioner and kills himself a day before he was to be hanged. Apparently, the consoling words from the Nuremberg authorities that he just imagine the noose as a "string of lovely pearls" was not enough to sooth him.

OCTOBER 16, 1793
Marie Antoinette Gives France Head.

(WARNING: Spoilers ahead for Sofia Coppola's movie *Marie Antoinette*. Although unlike that film, this entry will not be scored by the Shins.)

ON THIS DAY IN HISTORY, the queen of France was beheaded by French revolutionaries for the crime of treason. Never particularly popular with the people, the Austrian native supposedly said "Let them eat cake!" of the peasants during a severe bread shortage. Of course, there is no evidence she ever said this. (Actually, she didn't say "cake," but "my dick." Either way, the sentiment was the same.)

The slogan of the French Revolution was "Liberty, equality, fraternity, or death" and the royals, apparently, were only allowed to choose from Column D. Her husband, Louis XVI, had met with the guillotine ten months earlier, and her son, the eight-year-old Louis XVII had been imprisoned in solitary confinement in a "Time Out" dungeon.

Marie was tossed in a slow-moving cart and paraded through Paris for an hour, stripped naked, and beheaded, and her severed head was held up to the cheers of thousands. Among first-time tourists to the nation, this is considered VIP treatment.

Le Bummer!

Longest Cab Ride Ends.

A BRITISH CABBIE NAMED JEREMY LEVINE returned to London on this day after making a round-trip to Capetown, South Africa, which is shocking just for the fact that a cab driver was willing to drive to a black neighborhood.

He was paid 40,000 pounds for the trip, which, in American dollars, is like a gazillion or something. He traveled 21,000 miles, and saw at least 300 erotic *Taxicab Confessions* confessed.

This is technically the longest trip ever made in a cab. To experience the Longest-Seeming Cab Ride ever, just enjoy any ride in New York where the cabbie begins to rant about the psychic impotence he feels when the CIA blasts signals into his teeth fillings.

TAXI FARE	
$3.50	First 1,000 miles stuck in traffic

Another Bad Day for Mapmakers.

OCTOBER 18, 1767 Surveyors Mason and Dixon (see where this is going?) finish mapping out their Mason-Dixon Line, which is still shorter than Thomas Pynchon's novel about the two. Most Northerners and Southerners still wish that instead of drawing a line, Mason and Dixon had built a very long and high wall.

OCTOBER 18, 1867 The United States takes control of Alaska, paving the way for mid-1990s annexation of America's Quirky Bone by television series *Northern Exposure*. Current Alaskan senator, Ted Stevens, then twenty-seven, begins to feel first pangs of hostility toward lower forty-eight.

OCTOBER 18, 1898 With Alaska being chilly and showing no signs of producing decent baseball players, the United States takes control of Puerto Rico. Possibility of statehood still a hope for Puerto Ricans, because U.S. response of "snowball's chance in hell" does not have a Spanish-language equivalent.

OCTOBER 18, 1908 Belgium takes control of the Congo Free State, after feeling that the phrase "free state" was really rather presumptuous. Sadly, despite their efforts there, Belgium is still better known for chocolate than they are for their brutality in the Congo.

OCTOBER 18, 1944 The Soviet Union invades Czechoslovakia. The first case of writer's block suffered by fifteen-year-old budding author Milan Kundera is suddenly cured.

> ## OCTOBER 19, 1812
> # Nyet, Shorty!

ON THIS DAY IN HISTORY, teensy French Emperor Napoleon I, suffering from what he called a Me Complex, began his retreat from Russia. This was the first of a series of Waterloos for the leader, which would ultimately culminate at Waterloo.

A month earlier, Napoleon and an army of 700,000 had reached Moscow, hoping to stock up on supplies, but the entire city was deserted. (They were, however, able to pick up a bunch of those little nesting dolls to give to their family and friends back home, along with the explanation that "those big fuzzy hats were too expensive." Their friends and family would try and hide their disappointment. They would fail.)

Instead of engaging Napoleon's forces, the Russian Army kept retreating, yet not surrendering. (Note: If you ever date a nineteenth-century Russian Army, you will be the one who has to initiate the break up.) Napoleon never got his surrender, but with the harsh Russian winter approaching, and his troops starving (in the French Army, starving equals forgoing the cheese course), Napoleon began his retreat.

The Russian Army then began to mercilessly attack the French from the rear (nope—we ran out of clever with "*Nyet*, Shorty"), and by the time the emperor made it back to France two months later, he was down 400,000 soldiers. Thankfully, the gravity of this tragedy could not be fully pondered because the French had not yet manufactured their first existentialist.

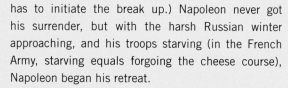

> ## OCTOBER 20, 1964
> # Hoover Sucks Up Dirt.

THAT'S A CRUDE WAY OF SAYING IT, but **PRESIDENT HERBERT HOOVER** died on this day in 1964 at age ninety. Here are a few fun facts about a one-term president who presided over one of America's least-fun economic disasters.

Speeches and Herb.

- The Iowa native was the first president to be born west of the Mississippi, and the last Republican president born west of the Mississippi who didn't feel the need to bring it up every five minutes to establish "aw shucks cred."

- After becoming wealthy as a mining engineer, the Quaker Hoover engaged in many famine-relief activities during the First World War, and was named one of the Ten Most Important Living Americans by the *New York Times*. Since such accolades violated the Quaker principles of "plainness," he decided to bring his reputation down a notch by going into politics.

- He was our only president who was able to speak Chinese, although recognizing an irreparable economic slide was decidedly Greek to him.

- He was the first president to have a telephone on his desk.

- He received eighty-four honorary degrees, keys to dozens of cities, and seventy-eight medals and awards, including Biggest Gossip (as a result of having the first telephone on desk).

- Encampments full of homeless during the Depression were known as Hoovervilles. A "Hoover Blanket" was a newspaper used as a blanket, and an empty pocket turned inside out was a "Hoover Flag." A "Herbert Hoover" was anyone named Herbert who was affected by the crash, and a "Hoover Hoover" was any makeshift means of getting dust off a carpet during the Depression. (Those last two didn't really catch on.)

OCTOBER 21, 1944

Potent Cocktail of Vodka, Triple Sec, and Lime Juice Gets Nickname.

KAMIKAZE =
1 OZ VODKA
1 OZ TRIPLE SEC
1 OZ LIME JUICE
1 OZ DEATH!

ON THIS DAY IN 1944, the warship HMAS *Australia* was damaged in what was believed to be the first-ever kamikaze attack, when a Japanese plane carrying a four-hundred-pound bomb smacked into the ship, killing thirty crewmembers.

Fortunately, the bomb didn't go off, which was not the case with two much larger and more horrific bombs detonated about nine months later over Japan, an event whose justification has been debated by many people ever since. With the exception, one assumes, of those who served on board ships like the HMAS *Australia*.

OCTOBER 22, 1797

Groundwork Laid for Charlie Sheen Vehicle, *Terminal Velocity.*

THE FIRST RECORDED PARACHUTE JUMP was made on this day by André-Jacques Garnerin, who leapt from a hydrogen balloon 3,200 feet above Paris. Many French onlookers viewed this as a bold step in the study of "Escaping via your mistress's boudoir window after the early arrival home of her husband."

In 1797, Garnerin completed his first parachute, a canopy attached to a basket with suspension lines, which was attached to another basket holding the crucial French survival items of cigarettes and overpriced wine (lest he be stranded somewhere for over five minutes).

His jump was a hair-raising one. Later parachutes had vents cut into them to keep them from spinning, but Garnerin's did not, although his wildly flailing and dangerous drop did lead to the invention of ESPN2's all–extreme sports programming schedule (which did not come fully into bloom until the invention of the Shred Guitar Lick.)

In 1802, Garnerin made a jump from 8,000 feet during an exhibition in England, but he was later killed in a balloon accident while trying to test a new parachute design. (SPOILER: The new parachute design didn't work.)

OCTOBER 23, 1921

Unknown Soldier Becomes Famous! For Being . . . Unknown.

ON OCTOBER 23, 1921, the first Unknown Soldier was selected in France to represent the approximately 77,000 United States servicemen killed on the Western Front during our nation's brief foray into World War I. (By the way, 77,000 is what England lost on the first day of the Battle of the Somme between lunch and tea.)

Four unknown corpses were placed in four caskets in a hotel in Chalons-sur-Marne—a hotel that obviously had a little trouble booking any decent convention traffic. A sergeant named Edward Younger was chosen to place a spray of white roses on one of the four caskets at random, in what must have seemed like the most gruesome episode of *The Bachelor* ever.

The chosen casket was then shipped to the United States and the soldier was entombed in Arlington National Cemetery outside Washington, D.C., where the remains were eventually joined by a World War II unknown, a Korean War unknown, and a Vietnam War unknown whose remains were later identified through DNA analysis. The other three will be the subject of a CBS summer replacement series, *CSI: Arlington*, once the proper song from The Who's catalog is selected and exploited.

Annie Fall.

ON OCTOBER 24, 1901, something very exciting happened at Niagara Falls, which in itself would be a remarkable event worthy of celebration. On this day, Annie Edson Taylor became the first person to ever ride over the mighty falls in a barrel.

She selected a pickle barrel made of oak and iron, with an inside lined with pillows and leather restraints. Unfortunately, no lonely and masochistic men were willing to pay the stout Annie to truss them up in it, so she figured she needed a new way to earn back her investment in the contraption.

At sixty-three, gravity had already done some rather cruel things to her, so she figured the odds of surviving a drop were pretty good. She was sealed in the barrel, which was then towed out into the middle of the Niagara River, before being cut loose and sent over the side of the Horseshow Falls. (Had anyone thought to add a blindfold, a greased hot dog, and a loaf of bread to this stunt, Miss Taylor would have automatically been inducted into any frat at the nearby University of Buffalo.)

After the drop, and fifteen minutes of being slammed by the rapids and rocks, Annie's barrel was snagged and towed into the Canadian side of the Falls. After the interior was thoroughly searched by a customs officer who thought he smelled pot for the ninth time that day, the lady daredevil staggered out and exclaimed, "No one ought ever do that again!" (The 1901 equivalent of "I'm going to Disneyland!")

It Almost Seems Exciting Here!

A Face Only a Modernist Mother Could Love.

OCTOBER 25, 1881
Picasso Born, Promptly Becomes PICASSO!

Pablo Picasso, the man who inspired your college series of acrylic-on-canvas *Poem Paintings (in Green)* (and your folks would really like you to get them out of their house already), was born on this day in Málaga, Spain, in 1881. Art historians call Picasso's labor and subsequent birth his Loud and Bloody Period.

Despite immense talent, Picasso became a popular artist and has been called the most influential painter of the twentieth century, but try telling that to someone who has glued, framed, and hung their most recently finished Thomas Kinkade Painter of Light jigsaw puzzle over their fireplace.

One of his best-known works is the mural *Guernica*, which depicted the bombing of the tiny Basque hamlet by Hitler's forces. It debuted at the 1937 World's Fair, at the famed Depressing Dorm Room Posters of Tomorrow Pavilion.

OCTOBER 26, 1881
OK Corral Shootout Livens Up Boring Day.

ON THIS DAY IN HISTORY, a thirty-second shoot-out between a group of thugs, another slightly less-thugy group, and an alcoholic doctor with tuberculosis in Tombstone, Arizona, forever entered the public imagination.

And why has America been so fascinated with this brief skirmish involving the Earps? Well, because everything else that ever happened on this day has been somewhat snoozy. Take a look.

OCTOBER 26, 1776 Benjamin Franklin sets sail for France to obtain support for the upcoming Revolution. Probably a two-week trip, in which Franklin didn't "get any." Even *he* probably wanted to forget about this voyage.

OCTOBER 26, 1825 The Erie Canal opens. It brought commerce deeper into the West, and helped open up this great nation of ours—with slow-moving boats pulled by donkeys.

ZZZZZZZZZZZ

OCTOBER 26, 1900 EDITH WHARTON sends her first letter to Henry ←
James, kicking off their correspondence, perhaps in an effort by both to
find a new written form in which to bore the world with.

OCTOBER 26, 1985 Squeaky-clean pop singer Whitney Houston scores
her first number-one hit. Years later she scores her first coke, and becomes
a little more interesting.

OCTOBER 27, 1904

New York City Subway Be(unintelligible)s Oper(unintelligible).

ON THIS DAY IN 1904, a New York City institution was born (no, not columnist
Cindy Adams). Mayor George McClellan (known for his Ed Kochesque Victorian-era
catchphrase "How'm I doin', my good man?") hopped behind the controls of a
train at City Hall Station (now sealed up, unlike Cindy Adams, unfortunately) and officially
opened the New York City subway system.

A SECOND LATER, IT SMELLED LIKE URINE.

McClellan operated the train, full of top-hatted city dignitaries, all the way up to the end of
the line at 145th Street, where everyone then got off, became very nervous that they were at
145th Street, and promptly got back on. Most never returned, although a few later bought
cheap real estate as part of an overestimated renaissance, and a couple others later visited a
soul food restaurant with a pack of friends and then always bragged about it a little too much.

Before the end of the day, nearly 100,000 people paid a nickel for the opportunity to ride
on the subway. Some of them even got the opportunity to use the subway station bathrooms
that day. (See *Mass Historia*, October 28, 1904: New York City Subway Bathrooms Close for
Repairs. Never Reopen.)

TODAY IS A GOOD DAY, GOOD DAY IN GENERAL FOR EVENTS CENTERED AROUND NEW YORK, NEW YORK.

OCTOBER 27, 1858 Macy's department store opens on 14th Street and is soon a huge success. Store eventually moves uptown, because up until the 1990s, a "Miracle on 14th Street" referred to one's ability to spend more than a day there without getting pricked by a syringe.

OCTOBER 27, 1858 Future president Theodore Roosevelt born. Parents run to opening-day sale at Macy's to buy a tube of Baby's First Mustache Wax.

OCTOBER 27, 1963 Trump trophy Marla Maples born. She once announced that her relations with the Donald constituted "the best sex I ever had," which was slightly more nauseating than a trip inside a subway restroom.

OCTOBER 28
A Monumental Day for Monuments.

BREAK OUT THE CHAMPAGNE and start cutting ribbons, because big monuments have a tendency to be dedicated and/or completed on this day in history.

OCTOBER 28, 1886 President Grover Cleveland presides over the dedication of the Statue of Liberty, saying "We will not forget that Liberty has here made her home; nor shall her chosen altar be neglected." Ironically, when he was governor of New York, Cleveland had vetoed a bill to pay for the statue's pedestal. His statement this day forced New York to pay for a pedestal to support the president's enormous balls.

OCTOBER 28, 1965 St. Louis's famed "Gateway Arch" is completed, as part of the Jefferson Expansion Memorial, which commemorates the Louisiana Purchase and the city's subsequent role in America's Western expansion. This expansion was due in part to the fact that until the Gateway Arch was completed, there wasn't much reason to stick around in St. Louis for any length of time.

Glenn Flies Like (an Early) Bird (Special).

NEARLY FORTY YEARS AFTER BECOMING THE FIRST AMERICAN IN SPACE, seventy-seven-year-old John Glenn becomes the oldest man ever in space as he blasts off on board the space shuttle *Discovery* for a nine-day mission.

Due to his advanced age, he also broke the record for Longest Orbit Around Earth with the Turn Signal Blinking.

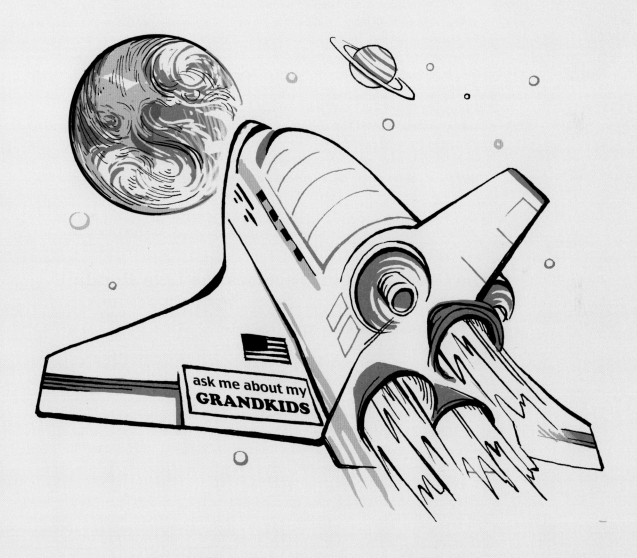

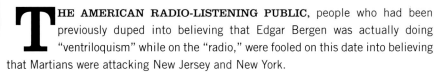

Welles's Wells Broadcast Doesn't Go Well.

THE AMERICAN RADIO-LISTENING PUBLIC, people who had been previously duped into believing that Edgar Bergen was actually doing "ventriloquism" while on the "radio," were fooled on this date into believing that Martians were attacking New Jersey and New York.

Nearly a million-and-a-half people went into a panic over Orson Welles and the Mercury Radio Theater's documentary-style production of H. G. Wells's *War of the Worlds*. And by a "million-and-a-half people," we mean "folks in the vicinity of New York and New Jersey." Like on September 11, the rest of the country at the time just planted a flag on their front lawn while secretly believing the attack was God's payback for all the homo stuff.

Welles and company told the story as a series of fake news reports interrupting a supposed live musical broadcast from New York City. (Nowadays, "fake news" is an effective comedic tool, although newspaper columnists can really take the fun out of it with their endless "Where Young People Get Their News" articles.)

Listeners tuning in heard that aliens had landed in Grover's Mill, New Jersey. The creatures then realized the small township was too close to Trenton, so they decided to head to the safer environs of Manhattan, where they unleashed a poison gas attack, much like the one Welles unleashed on Los Angeles in the 1970s after a late-night binge visit to Pink's hot dog stand.

RAISED A
LITTLE KANE.

The Great Houdini Becomes the Late Houdini!

ON THIS DAY IN HISTORY IN 1926, famed escape artist and bondage perv Harry Houdini was placed in a sealed wooden box and buried under six feet of earth. His eventual failure to emerge was a disappointment to his fans yet still less off-putting than the condition of David Blaine's skin after a week in his water-filled bacne ("back acne") incubator.

Earlier in the week, Houdini had performed at McGill University, and while reclining backstage, a student named Jocelyn Gordon Whitehead entered the room and asked Houdini if it was true that he could take any punch to the stomach. Before he could answer, Whitehead socked the magician several times. (Whitehead was in the habit of punching things, because his parents named him Jocelyn.)

This pain masked an already burst appendix, and the magician died of peritonitis a week later. He was laid to rest in a cemetery in Queens, New York, and every November members of the Society of American Magicians hold a "Broken Wand" ceremony at his gravesite. Then, after boarding the 7 train in their wizard hats and spandex unitards, local youths help them participate in "Broken Glasses" and "Broken Femur" ceremonies.

Some Set of Balls on This Guy!

OTHER MAGICAL EVENTS HAVE TRANSPIRED ON OCTOBER 31, AKA HALLOWEEN, AKA SATAN'S HOLIDAY (FOR OUR SOUTHERN READERS):

OCTOBER 31, 1517 Martin Luther magically creates Protestantism when he posts his ninety-five theses on the door of Castle Church in Wittenberg. Last bit of magic ever associated with Protestantism.

OCTOBER 31, 1864 Nevada is entered into the Union as the thirty-sixth state. In the city of Las Vegas, paychecks and sobriety pledges often vanish before one's very eyes!

November

Michelangelo's Roof the Hit!

ON THIS DAY IN HISTORY, art-loving folks in Rome saw the painted ceiling of the Sistine Chapel for the very first time. And like at today's art openings, the experience was ruined by an abundance of sweaty cheese cubes and white wine of dubious quality. Overall, reaction was mixed, particularly to the *Creation of Adam*. All the Italian men who saw the work felt a little bit better about themselves, while all the women just felt very sorry for Mrs. Michelangelo.

IN OTHER NAKED NEWS:

NOVEMBER 1, 1896 *National Geographic* magazine runs its first photo of naked female breasts. An entire generation of men are then shocked on their wedding nights to discover that their wives' breasts are neither brown, pendulous, nor attached to an African child.

Happy Birthday, Warren G. Harding!

G. WHIZ!

ON THIS DAY IN 1865, Warren Gamaliel Harding (often called our worst president by people who died before the year 2000) was born in Ohio in the town of Corsica. The town later changed its name to Blooming Grove as a tribute to its favorite son's lush and dense eyebrow shrubs.

Harding is probably best known today for having invented the word "normalcy" with a pledge to move away from the turmoil of the First World War (which he dubbed "Nastysy"). Such wordplay was nothing new to the man, who at age six invented his middle name, Gamaliel, which replaced the less exotic "Steve."

OTHER ASSORTED WARREN HARDING FUN FACTS:

- Harding was the first president to ride to his inauguration in a car, which he dubbed a "Vroom Vroom Go Go."

- Harding wore size fourteen shoes, making him the president with the largest feet, which he called "baddle-waddles."

- As senator he skipped two-thirds of his votes while in office, which he called "being a United States senator."

- Harding was the first candidate to use celebrity endorsements and received the support of such stars as Douglas Fairbanks, Mary Pickford, and Al Jolson, although the latter's use of blackface during a campaign stop lost Harding some votes in the South.

The Right Rrufff!

WHO'S A DEAD DOG?! Who's a Dead Historic Dog?!
Laika, that's who, the poor canine launched into space on this day in 1957 by the Soviet Union. The dog was the first living creature to ever be launched into orbit, if you don't count the time in 1956 when Aldous Huxley got the day started with a mescaline smoothie (with mescaline boost) and huevos con mescaline (with extra mescaline).

Laika was found on the streets of Moscow as a stray. She received training at the hands of Soviet scientists—hands filled with rolled-up copies of *Pravda*—and was launched inside of *Sputnik II*.

Laika's heartbeat was 103 bpm before the launch, and got up to around 240 bpm at maximum acceleration. Based on average dog heart rates, Soviet scientists then concluded that space travel was no more stressful than seeing a squirrel.

After about five hours, the cooling system malfunctioned, and Laika died. The original plan was even crueler: Laika was either supposed to starve to death in space, or go through a wormhole to the present day and be adopted by one of those sobbing, fat nuts featured on *The Dog Whisperer*.

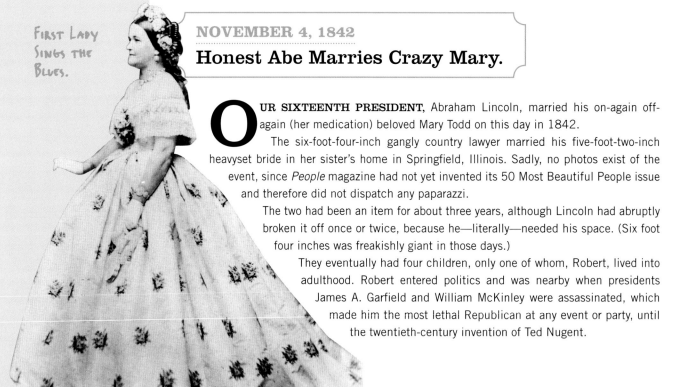

FIRST LADY
SINGS THE
BLUES.

NOVEMBER 4, 1842

Honest Abe Marries Crazy Mary.

OUR SIXTEENTH PRESIDENT, Abraham Lincoln, married his on-again off-again (her medication) beloved Mary Todd on this day in 1842.

The six-foot-four-inch gangly country lawyer married his five-foot-two-inch heavyset bride in her sister's home in Springfield, Illinois. Sadly, no photos exist of the event, since *People* magazine had not yet invented its 50 Most Beautiful People issue and therefore did not dispatch any paparazzi.

The two had been an item for about three years, although Lincoln had abruptly broken it off once or twice, because he—literally—needed his space. (Six foot four inches was freakishly giant in those days.)

They eventually had four children, only one of whom, Robert, lived into adulthood. Robert entered politics and was nearby when presidents James A. Garfield and William McKinley were assassinated, which made him the most lethal Republican at any event or party, until the twentieth-century invention of Ted Nugent.

Gunpowder Plot Takes a Powder.

GUY FAWKES AND HIS BAND OF CATHOLIC COCONSPIRATORS were discovered trying to blow up Parliament on this day in 1605, which is the basis for all that weird mask and nursery rhyme stuff in the movie *V for Vendetta*, which kept interrupting the far more interesting subplot about Natalie Portman in a T-shirt standing in a rain shower.

This day is commemorated in England, appropriately, with fireworks. The day marking the grotesque hanging, drawing, and quartering of Fawkes is commemorated a few days later in England, appropriately, with trying to consume British food.

Saxophone Inventor Adolph Sax Born, Gives Cry That is Slightly Easier on Ear Than the Soprano Saxophone.

ON THIS DAY, the man who invented the instrument you picked up for a few weeks in middle school because you liked the way Bruce Willis scatted with it in that wine cooler commercial, was born. He was a Belgian named Adolph Sax, and he invented the saxophone.

Sax's father was an instrument maker, and had eleven children, so it is obvious what the elder Sax's favorite instrument was. Adolph began working for his father at an early age, inventing a bass clarinet when he was twenty years old—or two years older than most people are when they stop playing the bass clarinet, vowing to leave their "nerdom" behind forever in high school.

Sax seems to have been a sort of antagonistic, tortured fellow (as opposed to noted saxman Kenny G., who antagonizes others to the point of torture) and lived a life of poverty in Paris while working on his saxophone, which he eventually patented in 1846. It combined the single reed of the clarinet with the bore and fingering patterns of the oboe, producing a sound all its own, but with a name that lends itself to sex puns and therefore seems somewhat cooler. (See sexy saxophonist Candy Dulfer's 1990 album *Saxuality*. It's probably sitting in a 99-cent bin somewhere.)

ALSO BORN ON THIS DATE:

NOVEMBER 6, 1948 Eagle and rocker Glen Frey, whose 1984 song "The Heat is On" is enough to make you hate Adolph Sax and his stupid invention forever.

SAXUAL SIZE.

Never Forget the Elephant.

BEFORE THE SYMBOL OF GOP LEADERSHIP was a "once-great, bitterly divided country now loathed by the rest of the free world," it was the Elephant, which debuted as a representation of the Republican Party in an editorial cartoon by Thomas Nast on this day in 1874.

STILL FUNNIER THAN ZIGGY.

The cartoon was called *The Third-Term Panic*, and was subtitled "An Ass, having put on the Lion's skin, roamed about in the Forest, and amused himself by frightening all the foolish Animals he met with in his wanderings." Needless to say, the cartoon wasn't designed to make you laugh, it was designed to make you think . . . about how unfunny Thomas Nast was.

The panel, printed in *Harper's Weekly*, was a reaction to a series of editorials in the *New York Herald* that condemned the possibility of Republican Ulysses S. Grant running for a third term. (At one time, New York papers would fight about things other than their alleged circulation figures or the validity of their scratcher tickets.)

The anti-Grant *Herald* newspaper is represented here as an ass in wolf's clothing, scaring away a unicorn (the *New York Times*), a giraffe (the *New York Tribune*) and an owl (the *New York World*, which was staunchly anti-owl. That one really hurt).

Meanwhile, Grant's administration was represented by the elephant (although a more accurate representation of the hard-drinking Grant would have been a pink elephant). The administration was about to tumble into a pit labeled "Southern Claims, Chaos, and Rum," beneath a precarious bridge labeled with the words "Inflation," "Repudiation," and "Reconstruction." (To put all of this into a simple, modern context, replace these words with "Iraq.")

NOVEMBER 8, 1923

Hitler Seizes Power!

ON THIS DAY IN HISTORY, Adolph Hitler, the most Hitleresque of all twentieth-century figures, launched his Beer Hall Putsch in an attempt to seize control of the German government, and to cause havoc for any bartender who in previous years had not been generous enough to the fascist leader during buyback time.

Hitler planned a coup against the state government of Bavaria, to topple the International Pretzel Index and spark the German army into rebelling in Berlin. A group of Nazi thugs under Goering—not really "under" him, that would have been painful—surrounded a Munich beer hall where Bavarian government officials were meeting. (Since the windows of the beer hall weren't painted black, Goering realized it wasn't his kind of place, and then took some time to remove his usual abundant applications of lipstick and rouge.)

Hitler ran into the hall, fired a pistol into the air and shouted, "The national revolution has begun!" The beer hall patrons then asked if it could wait until after their songs came on the jukebox.

The Bavarian leaders then agreed to support Hitler's new regime, anything to get him to shut up and quit killing their buzz.

And how did this turn out? See tomorrow.

"Chaptuh One: in Duh House of Moi Parents."

NOVEMBER 9, 1923

Hitler Loses Power!

UPON SOBERING UP, Bavarian officials ordered a crackdown on the Nazis, and a few hours later, sixteen Hitler supporters were shot by government forces. Goering got a bullet to the groin, which puts one in the unfortunate situation of briefly feeling sorry for a Nazi.

Hitler was arrested and began what would be a nine-month stint behind bars, where he began work on his autobiography, *Mein Kampf*.

Note: *Mass Historia* doesn't recommend reading this tome, but the book-on-tape as read by Tony Danza will help pass time on a long car trip.

NOVEMBER 10, 1975

Edmund Fitzgerald Wrecks, Spawns More Tragic "The Wreck of the Edmund Fitzgerald."

WE WON'T SPEND TOO MUCH TIME on the sinking of this freighter on Lake Superior, since it already spawned a six-and-a-half-minute hit song by morose Canadian singer/songwriter Gordon Lightfoot. The sinking was a tragedy that saw the deaths of twenty-nine crewmen, who at least died before they could hear themselves referred to on the radio as "Good Men-a-Shippin'."

The *Fitzgerald* left Superior, Wisconsin, and was headed for Detroit, although Lightfoot in his song chose Cleveland because it sounded better. (An odd show of fussiness from a man who took on the absurd meter challenges of working "Edmund Fitzgerald" into a song.) The craft encountered a terrible storm and was most likely hit with a series of rogue waves, which swamped the hold and quickly plunged it to the bottom of the lake, without her captain even making a distress call. Although chances are the captain greeted the promise of a watery grave with more enthusiasm than the idea of spending a day or two in Detroit.

The *Edmund Fitzgerald* was the largest vessel ever lost on Lake Superior, and in addition to the Lightfoot dirge, it has also inspired a piano concerto, a musical, a brand of beer, and the joke about the two gay Irishman lost at sea onboard the *Edmund Fitzgerald/Gerald Fitzedmund.*

NOVEMBER 11

HISTO-POURRI: Military Edition.

WAR? What is it good for? Well, for starters, making November 11 somewhat memorable.

NOVEMBER 11, 1864 Union General George Sherman heats up Atlanta by setting it on fire as part of his grueling March to the Sea. Atlantans still pissed off, despite later adoption of nickname "Hotlanta" to commemorate nightlife and grueling pub crawls.

WELL, THEY AT LEAST LEFT A FEW PEACH TREES!

↞ **NOVEMBER 11, 1885 GENERAL GEORGE S. PATTON** is born, or born again, since he was a firm believer in reincarnation. And bad news, fat guy reading this who collects guns and memorabilia and stores them in his parents' basement—you're not him!

PATTON LEATHER.

NOVEMBER 11, 1918 The war to end all wars, World War I, ends, without ending war. Subsequent failure celebrated as Armistice Day, which was later changed to Veterans' Day so that Americans could more easily pronounce what they annually ignored.

NOVEMBER 11, 1921 President Warren G. Harding presides over the dedication of the **TOMB OF THE UNKNOWNS** at Arlington National ← Cemetery. Sadly, like everyone whose name he didn't know, Harding refers to the corpse as "Buddy" and "Mac" throughout the ceremony.

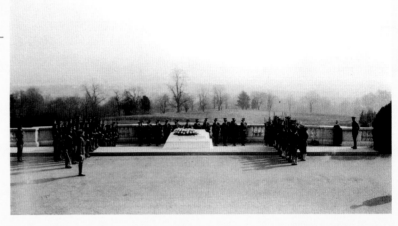

NOVEMBER 11, 1940 Britain clashes with Italian forces by launching the Battle of Taranto, the first-ever aircraft carrier attack. The Italian fleet was cut in half, and since half a boat doesn't float, by 1941 Mussolini's navy could effectively fuggedaboutit.

INTRODUCE US TO YOUR FRIEND?

NOVEMBER 11, 1942 With World War II in full swing, the United States lowers the draft age from twenty-one to eighteen. African-Americans of any age are still not allowed to serve, which is why elderly African-Americans roll their eyes whenever that "greatest generation" business comes up.

NOVEMBER 12, 1927
Holland Tunnel, Not in Holland, Opens!

THE HOLLAND TUNNEL, which links lower Manhattan with Jersey City, opened to traffic on this day in history in 1927 (and since we have decided to profile an event as dazzling as a tunnel opening, you can be sure this day in history has traditionally been a pretty slow news day).

The Tunnel was originally known as the Hudson River Vehicular Tunnel or the Canal Street Tunnel, but was eventually named after its first chief engineer, Clifford Milburn Holland. His soot-covered bust sits near the tunnel entrance on the Manhattan side, awaiting the saliva of all who are hopelessly jammed in traffic.

The tunnel consists of two tubes beneath the Hudson River carrying two lanes of traffic each. In the 1990s, the tubes were wired for both cell phone and radio reception, so that even ninety-three feet below the Hudson River, you won't have to miss a second of New York radio's dazzling variety of shouting hip-hop DJs or 24/7 Bad Company classic rock formats.

The tunnel was added to the National Register of Historic Places in 1993, meaning it is an object worthy of preservation, although try telling that to al-Qaeda or Homeland Security Secretary Michael Chertoff.

JERSEY CITY FUN FACT:
IT'S ESCAPABLE VIA THE HOLLAND TUNNEL!

Everything Comes Up Roses for Rosa.

THE SUPREME COURT UPHELD *BROWDER V. GALE* on this day in 1956, and drove a stake through the heart of *Plessy v. Ferguson*. Of course you know what those cases were, right? No? Well, let's continue on, Mr./Ms. Racist, or Mr./Ms. Slept Through Most of Eleventh-Grade American History!

Essentially, the court ruled that Alabama's laws regarding racial segregation onboard its buses were unconstitutional, and now blacks could sit wherever they wanted while taking an extremely slow, fume-filled trip onboard public transportation.

This ruling ended the 380-day long Montgomery Bus Boycott, which was started when a forty-two-year-old seamstress named Rosa Parks refused to give up her seat for a white passenger, even though she was sitting in the colored section. (The white passenger in question was a very early form of wannabe Whigga, none of whom have ever gone over particularly well with members of the African-American community.)

Parks was found guilty of disorderly conduct and fined. Community activists, including Dr. Martin Luther King Jr., called for the bus boycott days later. It was very effective, and the city of Montgomery took a severe financial hit (with the abolition of free labor, our Southern neighbors have always had trouble with the concept of rainy-day savings).

CALL ME HERMAN MELVILLE.

Melville's "Dick" Disappoints.

ON THIS DAY IN HISTORY, Herman Melville's *Moby Dick* was published in America, and the critics declared "Thar she blows!"

Not only did the lengthy tome get generally cruddy reviews, but it didn't sell (the opposite of what happens in today's publishing world). It sold under 3,000 copies, and only earned its publisher, Harper & Brothers, a few hundred dollars. And no, none of this should make you feel better about your unpublished manuscript/graphic novel from 1994 entitled *Thunder Between Us: A Grunge NecRomance*. That will never be rediscovered and recognized as an allegorical work of genius, even if your girlfriend at the time (with all the connections in the publishing industry) blurbed it as such.

Melville then went on the lecture circuit, published more novels and poems that didn't find an audience, and by 1867 he had taken a job as a customs officer in New York City, where the only thing he had to declare was "This is what I do—it's not who I am."

After he died in 1891 at his home at 26th and Park (incidentally, there's a coffee shop named after a *Moby Dick* character nearby), the *New York Times* obituary called him "Henry Melville." That's pretty rotten, especially when you consider how often that paper lazily relies on "Typee" for the Sunday crossword puzzle.

[crossword grid with handwritten "SUCK IT" at 91 across, and handwritten note: "91 ACROSS 'AUTHOR MELVILLE'S RESPONSE TO THIS NEWSPAPER.'"]

NOVEMBER 15, 1887
Georgia O'Keeffe Born!

AFTER BEING BORN, the baby looks up at where she came from, and gets her first—and last—idea for a painting.

NOVEMBER 16, 1906
The Grope Caruso.

ON THIS DAY IN HISTORY, famed Italian tenor Enrico Caruso allegedly tried to elicit a few high notes from a young lady in the Monkey House at the Bronx Zoo and was arrested for indecency.

The opera star, while touring the exhibit, supposedly pinched a woman on the bottom, which at one time was the universal sign for "Hello, I am an Italian Man!"

The mysterious woman who leveled the charges wound up giving a false name and address to the arresting officer and never showed up to trial. This is because after touring the Monkey House, she realized that most primates have the potential to push "indecent" way beyond a little grabass, and she counted her blessings.

Eventually, despite some shaky evidence presented by the prosecution, Caruso was found guilty and fined $10. This will never happen to modern-day Italian singing sensation Andrea Bocelli, who just chalks up all his indecent gropings to unfortunate Braille mishaps.

PERFORMING "THE TACKY FURRIER OF SEVILLE."

HISTO-POURRI: Transportation Edition.

TODAY IS A DAY WHEN THINGS GET MOVING, on the moon, in the water, in the air, and at the wheel of a drab yet efficient Honda Accord.

Maybe Some of This Water Could Be Used for Plants?

NOVEMBER 17, 1869 The 101-mile-long **SUEZ CANAL** opens, linking the Mediterranean with the Red Sea—meaning European ships no longer had to circumnavigate already-exploited Africa to get to not-exploited-enough Asia. The French began construction of the canal, and the British eventually took over, while both nations politely ignored the "aheming" of the Egyptians, in whose country the trench was dug.

NOVEMBER 17, 1906 Son of a blacksmith (not a derogatory term) Soichiro Honda is born in Japan. Honda's motorcycle company started churning out cars in the 1960s and cracked the American market during the energy crisis of the 1970s. *People* magazine called him the Henry Ford of Japan in their 1980 *50 Most Beautifully Cruel Statements Ever Hurled at the Hearts of Detroit's Unemployed* issue.

NOVEMBER 17, 1962 John Fitzgerald Kennedy dedicates Dulles International Airport in Washington, D.C., the first airport specifically designed for jet aircraft. It was a busy day for the president, who had to leave the dedication mid-sentence to oversee the inauguration of a nearby D.C. 10 Mile High Club.

NOVEMBER 17, 1970 The moon saw its first wheeled vehicle traversing its craters on this day (if you don't count the wooden wheels of the ancient astronaut "Chariots of the Gods." Although if you believe that, you probably doubt the moon landing). The craft was the Soviet *Lunokhod 1*, and it explored the Mare Imbrium region of the Sea of Rains, took soil samples, and sent back television images. It was considered a triumph of space exploration, until word got out that the Soviets were just scouting an amenable location to put their Jews, dissidents, and/or Chechens.

A Good Day to Die.

IF YOU DIE TODAY, look on the bright side. You share a date of death with plenty of people more famous than you.

NOVEMBER 18, 1886 Shortly after leaving office, President Chester Alan Arthur died in New York City, from complications of Bright's disease, hypertension, and chronic chin exposure (the last ailment plagued him most of his adult life).

NOVEMBER 18, 1922 The bad news? Writer Marcel Proust becomes a thing of the past. The good news? He finally has an excuse to leave his bedroom.

NOVEMBER 18, 1969 Shady Kennedy family patriarch Joseph P. Kennedy Sr. dies at an extremely advanced age for a Kennedy. Among his many credits were bootlegger, insider trader, anti-Semite, election rigger, and Hollywood executive (the latter was an attempt to finally do something "technically honest").

NOVEMBER 18, 1978 Plenty of bunk space opens up in Jonestown on this day as followers of the Reverend Jim Jones partake in a mass suicide with poisoned Kool-Aid. Large anthropomorphic Kool-Aid pitcher hears name, runs through jungle brush happily shouting, "Oh yeeeah!" and is then repulsed by what he sees and shamed by his inappropriate enthusiasm.

NOVEMBER 18, 1982 Korean boxer Duck Koo Kim dies after being pummeled in the ring for fourteen rounds by boxer Ray "Boom Boom" Mancini. Horrified, the boxing commission enacts stringent new rules shortening fights to twelve rounds, and forces surviving boxer to change his name to a slightly less threatening Ray "Lovetap Lovetap" Mancini.

NOVEMBER 19, 1863

Seven Score and Five Years Ago Lincoln Drops "Four Score and Seven Years Ago."

THE GETTYSBURG ADDRESS. Abraham Lincoln gave perhaps this most famous and significant speech in the history of American democracy on this day in 1863. (BTW, Fox News ranks this address number two on the "Famous and Significant Speeches in the History of American Democracy" list, right after the Mission Accomplished Aircraft Carrier Pep Talk.)

Lincoln gave his 272-word address at the site of the bloody battle, during the dedication of the cemetery, so he wisely didn't open with a joke, although the "proposition that all men are created equal" to this day gets an eye roll and snicker from the harder of heart.

STAGE DIVE!!!

Lincoln intoned that "from these honored dead we take increased devotion . . . that we here highly resolve that these dead shall not have died in vain—that this nation, under God, shall have a new birth of freedom—and that government of the people, by the people, for the people, shall not perish from the earth." The crowd of Pennsylvanians did not know when to applaud, because the president forgot to end his address with "Go Steelers!"

NOVEMBER 20, 1955
Bo Knows . . . Pissing Off Ed Sullivan.

ON THIS DAY IN HISTORY, Bo Diddley (born Ellas McDaniel, a name the performer soon realized was not very fun to use in the third person in every other song) became the first African-American to ever appear on *The Ed Sullivan Show*. He also became the first African-American to ever be banned from *The Ed Sullivan Show*, a dual achievement rarely noted whenever Black History Month rolls around.

The Ed Sullivan Show, immensely popular in the days of three channels, had booked the singer to perform a cover of Tennessee Ernie Ford's "Sixteen Tons," a song about how sucky it is to be a coal miner. Not at all appropriate to the performer's style, especially when he was told it was to be a duet with puppet mouse Topo Gigio.

Diddley, without informing anyone, instead ripped into his number-one R&B hit "Bo Diddley." ("Ellas McDaniel" had stalled at number seventy-nine. See?) Sullivan forever banned the star from the show, and Diddley later said, "Ed Sullivan said that I was one of the first colored boys to ever double-cross him." (For later colored-boy double crosses, see *Mass Historia*: April 4, 1965, Nipsey Russell Refuses Sullivan Request for Amusing On-Air Series of Couplets.)

The only other stars to ever be banned by Ed Sullivan were the Doors and Jackie Mason. (Unfortunately, they were performing a number they wrote together, and "L.A. Goyim" fared more miserably on the charts than even "Ellas McDaniel.")

BO DIDDLEY

NOVEMBER 21, 1980
Americans Find Out Who Shot JR on *Dallas*!

IT WAS KRISTIN SHEPARD, who was JR's sister-in-law and former mistress.

See tomorrow, November 22, for a less-than-perfect resolution to a Texas murder mystery.

Americans Find Out Who Shot JFK in Dallas!

IT SEEMS TO HAVE BEEN ONE LEE HARVEY OSWALD, who was firing from the Texas School Book Depository as the president's motorcade passed through Dealey Plaza.

But if you don't believe that, feel free to blame it on Kristen Shepard, who was JR's sister-in-law and former mistress on the TV show *Dallas*. This theory is as valid as most offered by conspiracy theorists.

About to Be Messed with in Texas.

Franklin Pierce Born!

TODAY MARKS THE BIRTHDAY OF FRANKLIN PIERCE, one of history's most handsome presidents, especially if you find sobriety to be unappealing. Let's look at some fun facts about this rather unpopular one-term president.

Even in This Engraving, You Can Smell His Breath!

- He was born in a log cabin in the state of New Hampshire. Although nowadays, living in a log cabin in New Hampshire usually means you don't recognize the federal government or any "president."

- A colonel in the Mexican-American War, he badly injured his leg in battle and kept fighting, but later passed out from the pain. It would mark the first and only time that Pierce passed out and didn't wind up in his clothing, facedown on the bed.

- He was good friends with Nathaniel Hawthorne, who wrote a biography of Pierce in 1852. Of course you haven't read it. You still haven't finished *The Scarlet Letter*.

- He was known as a Doughface, a Northerner with Southern sympathies, a name he preferred to his usual nickname, "Totally Faced."

- Pierce is one of only three presidents who chose to affirm rather than swear the oath of office, the others being Herbert Hoover and John Tyler, who was already too deeply in debt to the official White House Swear Jar.

- Thanks to a disastrous four years, he became one of two presidents to be refused renomination by his party. When asked what his plans were upon leaving office, Pierce replied, "There's nothing left to do but get drunk," which at least then earned him his party's nomination for King of the Kegger.

NOVEMBER 24
A Boom in Boomer Milestones.

TODAY IS AN IMPORTANT DAY FOR OUR NATION'S BABY BOOMERS, who are the most important people on Earth. (Just ask them, their self-absorbed answer will be groovy!)

NOVEMBER 24, 1963 Strip-joint owner and small-time mobster Jack Ruby guns down Kennedy assassin Lee Harvey Oswald on national television. It is the only time a strip-club worker has ever been involved in a presidential assassination, if you don't count **JOHN WILKES BOOTH**'s struggling actor/go-go boy period.

NOVEMBER 24, 1969 The U.S. Army announces that Lieutenant William Calley will be court-martialed for the premeditated murder of 109 Vietnamese civilians during what came to be known as the My Lai Massacre. Calley winds up serving three-and-a-half years under house arrest for his horrible actions, which were later awarded "Three Thumbs Up" on the Official Lynndie England Scale of Inappropriate Military Behavior.

NOVEMBER 24, 1971 A hijacker who gives his name as D. B. Cooper parachutes out of a plane with $200,000 in a briefcase and is never seen again, although 1970s budget airline People's Express does see a cost-effective method of getting people off planes more quickly.

NOVEMBER 24, 1976 Hippie favorites The Band give their last performance, which is later released as the Martin Scorsese documentary *The Last Waltz*. It was the only film for which Scorsese failed to shoehorn the Rolling Stones' "Gimme Shelter" onto the soundtrack.

NOVEMBER 25, 1952
A Better *Mousetrap*!

ON THIS DAY IN HISTORY, Agatha Christie's whodunit *The Mousetrap* opened in London's West End, and for nearly sixty years now, generations have been flocking to the thriller and gasping at the revelation of Sergeant Trotter's true identity as the murderer.

What?

FDR Loses Turkey Vote.

ON THIS DAY, PRESIDENT FRANKLIN DELANO ROOSEVELT signed a bill establishing the fourth Thursday of every November as Thanksgiving Day, once again showing that he was another politician hopelessly in the pocket of Big Giblet.

Roosevelt had changed the date in 1939 to the next-to-last Thursday of the month, in order to lengthen the Christmas shopping season during the Depression. (Lengthening the holiday season seemed like a good idea before the invention of the songs "I Saw Mommy Kissing Santa Claus" and "Jingle Bell Rock.")

Twenty-two states refused to follow this new edict, and dismissed Roosevelt's new holiday as "Franksgiving," a name traditionally given to the day by poor college students who bypassed turkey for hot dogs (bunless and mustardless, for the additional savings).

The U.S. Congress in 1941 split the difference and established that Thanksgiving would occur on the fourth Thursday of November, which was sometimes the last Thursday and sometimes the next-to-last. And then two weeks later the Japanese attacked us and we stopped worrying about stupid crap like this.

Why They Hate Us: Reason Number One.

"I, or rather the Lord, beseech you as Christ's heralds to publish this everywhere and to persuade all people of whatever rank, foot-soldiers and knights, poor and rich, to carry aid promptly to those Christians and to destroy that vile race from the lands of our friends. I say this to those who are present, it meant also for those who are absent. Moreover, Christ commands it."

THUS POPE URBAN II kicked off the First Crusade after making this speech at the Council of Claremont. For some time, the Muslim Seljuk Turks had controlled Jerusalem, and had forbidden Christian pilgrims from visiting (thanks to Islam's strict No Fanny Packs Rule), and now they seemed poised to take Constantinople, and change it into something more Istanbul-ey.

Byzantine Emperor Alexius I asked Urban for help, and since he was Byzantine, his appeal was no doubt tangled and overcomplicated, so the pope issued the edict probably just to shut the man up.

By making this proclamation, Pope Urban hoped to unite all Christians in an effort to take back the Holy Lands from the "Infidels" and promised absolution for any sins that might be committed in the process. He also demanded a few souvenirs, and once again invoked the whole "Christ Commands It" bit so as not to be stuck with some cheapo ashtray crap that a Crusader obviously picked up on his last day of Crusading.

Jerusalem fell to the Crusaders four years later, but sadly, Pope Urban II died before he got the news. That's OK. It was a very minor event that has had very little impact on the world since.

NOVEMBER 28, 1987
Tawana Tells the Un-truth.

ON THIS DAY IN 1987, fifteen-year-old Tawana Brawley was found lying conscious but unresponsive in a garbage bag, her clothing torn, her body smeared with feces, and with racial slurs written on her body in charcoal. Upon learning she would not be awarded an NEA grant, she then offered up a tale of being sexually assaulted by six police officers from Wappingers Falls, New York.

During her interview with the police, Brawley refused to express herself verbally, only uttering the word "Neon." (Keep in mind this was the 1980s.) A rape kit wound up not showing any indication of an assault, and friends claimed she had been seen at several parties during the time of her supposed abduction. (The trash bag having been a lazy attempt to crash a Toga Party.)

Before long she had legal representation, in the form of attorneys Alton H. Maddox and C. Vernon Mason, and the fiery Reverend Al Sharpton, who was once the subject of actress Marlo Thomas's false claims that he had stolen her haircut.

A Grand Jury eventually determined that there was not enough evidence to bring the case to trial. Tawana never testified and both Maddox and Mason were disbarred. The Reverend Sharpton was forced to . . . run for president, speak at the Democratic National Convention in 2004, and serve as a frequent lovable guest on many a late-night talk show.

Like the pretend rapists he once pursued, Al Sharpton continues to go unpunished.

NOVEMBER 29, 1963
Warren Commission Gets (Back and to the)Right to Work.

ONE WEEK AFTER PRESIDENT JOHN F. KENNEDY was fatally shot by Lee Harvey Oswald, Fidel Castro, Sam Giancana, and a variety of Woody Harrelson's dads, President Lyndon Johnson announced the establishment of the Warren Commission, headed up by Supreme Court Chief Justice Earl Warren.

It is a moment that narcissistic grief-junkies often try to immortalize with the uninspiring declaration, "I'll never forget where I was when I first heard that Kennedy was shot . . . and an investigative commission was established to half-ass it."

After ten months of examining evidence and grilling witnesses, the Warren Commission concluded there was no conspiracy and that Lee Harvey Oswald acted alone. They did this mostly just to watch conspiracy nut Mort Sahl's head explode even more violently than the fallen president's.

They also concluded that Oswald was actually aiming at Nellie Connelly, wife of Governor John Connelly, because he felt her "Mr. President, you certainly cannot say that Dallas doesn't love you" statement was "incredibly suckass."

The report relied heavily on snuff perv Abraham Zapruder's film, which is slightly easier to watch than Oliver Stone's *JFK*, mostly because Zapruder's camera didn't capture any Joe Pesci gold body paint nipple-tweaking action.

NOVEMBER 30, 1835
When Life Gives You Clemens . . .

SAMUEL CLEMENS was born on this day in 1835 in Florida, Missouri, which makes sense since that area is known as Mark Twain Country. Although Elmira, New York, also claims to be Mark Twain Country, since the noted author used to summer there (nice try, Elmira). For twenty years he also lived and raised his family in Hartford, Connecticut, which would call itself Mark Twain Country but wouldn't want to out-dazzle its other nickname, the Insurance Capital of the World. Either way, the chambers of commerce in all these areas are probably glad that Twain did not stick with his other early penname "Thomas Jefferson Snodgrass."

The name "Mark Twain" was actually a cry one would hear on the Mississippi River. "Mark Twain" meant that the mark on the sounding line measured a safe depth of two fathoms ("Twain" being an antiquated word for "two.") This is not to be confused with the meaning behind the name Shania Twain, which is a call that means "Nothing deep here, just go ahead and stare at my two friends."

STUDY OF FOGEY WITH STOGIE.

December

The Last President/
Presidential Son to
Read a Book.

Son of Former President Loses Popular Vote, Still Becomes President.

YEP, but it's not the one you're thinking of.

On this day in 1824, the House of Representatives selected John Quincy Adams to become the sixth president of the United States, even though he had almost 50,000 fewer popular votes and fifteen fewer electoral votes than his rival Andrew Jackson. At that point, Jackson challenged the Electoral College to a duel but sadly only winged it.

ADAMS, SON OF JOHN ADAMS, WOUND UP BEING A ONE-TERMER, AND WAS FAIRLY INEFFECTUAL, BUT HE DOES HAVE HIS FUN FACTS:

- He was the first president to wear long pants to his inauguration, making good on a promise to free the presidency from the powers of Big Knicker.

- He was the first president to have a flush toilet installed in the White House. It remained until 1912, when it was destroyed an hour after President William Howard Taft installed the first-ever White House Burrito Bar.

- In 1826, the Marquis de Lafayette gave John Quincy Adams an alligator. The alligator lived in the White House for several months. It helped draft the Tariff Act of 1828.

- Would take nude, early morning swims in the Potomac, which saw his presidency fall under the influence of Big Shrinkage.

- In 1843, he became the first president to have his photograph taken. A year later, he became the first president to be photographed doing "The Shocker."

- He was the first president to serve as a congressman after leaving office. And he died in the House of Representatives after suffering a stroke on the floor. (See Congressman Jerrold Nadler, any day now. Seriously, stay away from the White House Burrito Bar!)

He Also Freed His Shaving Cream.

John Brown's Body Is A-Hanging Off a Tree.

DEPENDING ON YOUR POINT OF VIEW, today marks the hanging death of the radical abolitionist (or the radical, evil abolitionist) John Brown, who was executed for leading the raid on Harpers Ferry in Virginia.

Brown and his small army of freemen and slaves raided the town and took sixty prominent citizens hostage, hoping their slaves would join the rebellion. None did, but their response to Brown's call to violence did see the invention of the now-common phrase, "He be buggin', yo!"

Public opinion has traditionally been so split on Brown that actor Raymond Massey played the zealot in two movies in the 1940s, one in which Brown was a hero, and another in which he was a villain. In a third movie, entitled *Panty Raid on Harpers Fairy*, he portrayed Brown as a sympathetic nerd trying to lose his virginity. This seems to have been everyone's favorite.

Dread and Methyl.

ON THIS DAY IN 1984, the multinational chemical company Union Carbide hit a bump on Wall Street, as their Bhopal, India, pesticide plant leaked a toxic cloud of methyl isocynate into the air for a full hour before anyone noticed. Well, actually, about 2,000 people noticed, but they were too dead to appreciate the fact that they were no longer being bothered by flies or mosquitoes.

Another 600,000 people were injured, and some say up to 20,000 have died since the accident in the city of over a million people. Statistically, one might think that's not too bad, if one is on the board of directors of Union Carbide.

Local health officials had no emergency procedures in place in the event of a leak, and officials say that many lives would have been saved had victims only covered their mouths and nostrils with a wet towel. Although in India, this might leave one open to a variety of waterborne diseases that'll make methyl isocynate poisoning seem like a walk in the park.

Eventually, Union Carbide settled for nearly $500 million, which meant that most victims received about $550, which they could take in cash, or in an opportunity to live in a cubicle while telemarketing for Union Carbide for five to seven years.

There's Something About the *Mary Celeste*.

ON THIS DAY IN 1872, a discovery was made that would go on to become one of the most astounding and enduring mysteries in nautical history, if you don't count the popular appeal of Patrick O'Brian novels.

The *Mary Celeste*, a 103-foot brigantine under the command of Captain Benjamin Briggs, was discovered drifting near the Azores Islands. The crew of seven, along with the captain, his wife, and two-year-old daughter, were missing.

Once boarded, investigators noticed the ship's sextant and chronometer were gone, along with a lifeboat. There were bloodstains along three railings, and another railing was covered with scratches. The cargo had been 1,700 barrels of alcohol, and nine barrels were later discovered to be empty and . . . oh!

Nevermind, the mystery of the *Mary Celeste* has been solved!

Actually, the alcohol, like the entire family of Coors products, was unfit for human consumption. Mutiny or pirates were possible explanations, but the most popular theory is that some leaking barrels led to a buildup of fumes in the hold, which when opened would have led to a violent rush of escaping gas or a sudden, quick-burning fireball that would not have left scorch marks.

Believing the ship was about to blow up (this was years before tableside Bananas Foster preparations onboard cruise ships made fireballs commonplace), Captain Briggs probably forced everyone into the lifeboat, their towline broke, and they drifted out to sea.

And if that doesn't cut it for you, *In Search of* fan, then they were picked up by aliens and/or devoured by Champ, the Lake Champlain monster.

THAR SHE ANAL-PROBES!

Martin van Buren Born!

MARTIN VAN BUREN, our eighth president, and one of the eight one-term presidents who served between Jackson and Lincoln, was born on this day in Kinderhook, New York. Let's celebrate with some fun facts, or "facts you didn't know about a president you don't care about."

• He was one of the founders of the Democratic Party, and was known for his political cunning and win-at-all-costs attitude. He was also the last Democrat to display any of these qualities.

• Van Buren was our first "real" American president, since he was the first one born after the signing of the Declaration of Independence and was never a British subject. And he was the last Democrat to not have his "Real American" credential called into question by the Far Right.

FORSOOK
THE COMB-OVER
FOR THE
COMB-OUTER.

• His wife and mother to his four children died at age thirty-five, years before he became president. In his autobiography, he does not mention her once, placing him right behind Bill Clinton in the ranking of President Most Indifferent to Existence of Spouse.

• He was the only president for whom English was a second language, having grown up in a Dutch-speaking household. So one also assumes that he was our most "420-friendly" president (right behind Clinton).

• After losing a second term, he later ran for president on the anti-slavery Free Soil ticket, a party that was later absorbed by the Republican Party.

• Because of his mishandling of the financial panic of 1837, his Whig opponents referred to him as "Martin Van Ruin." The Whigs dull sense of humor was later absorbed by the Republican Party.

DECEMBER 6, 1884

Washington Monument Completed.

ON THIS DAY IN HISTORY, the Washington Monument was finally finished, nearly thirty-six years after its cornerstone was laid.

And by the end of the day, a college student named Leland Fenwick became the first person to lie down on the mall, and have a buddy take a picture so that the monument looked like a giant penis sticking out of Fenwick's pants.

Washington would have approved.

A MONUMENTAL GAG!

DECEMBER 7, 1941

Suck On It, Lindbergh

YEP, today was a bad day for famous aviators who felt the United States needed to stay out of World War II, as Japanese bombers attacked the American Naval Base at Pearl Harbor at 7:55 a.m.

Despite valiant efforts on the ground to repel the attack, the United States Pacific Fleet was all but decimated. Two hundred aircraft were destroyed, and 2,400 Americans were killed. So now you know why Grandpa feels that even Christmas morning is an appropriate time to wax poetic about Tojo.

Many believe that the attacks on the World Trade Center were "our" Pearl Harbor, except that five years after Pearl Harbor, the war was over, the proper countries had been occupied, the villains behind the attack were brought to justice, and weapons of mass destruction had been unveiled in two key Japanese cities.

Note: This event is not to be confused with an evening of greater carnage a few years later at New York's Stork Club, when one-too-many Rob Roys had been given to a singer with the Count Basie Band, leading to the Bombing of Pearl Bailey.

WHATEVER HAPPENED TO . . . JAPAN?
They now make great electronics, cute robots, and have very niche sexual proclivities. These three goals have oddly been left off the table in the current plans to rebuild Iraq. Write your congressman.

Labor Pains.

THIS IS A DAY that marks both an important stride and a setback for the American Labor Movement.

DECEMBER 8, 1886 The American Federation of Labor, or AFL, was born on this day in Columbus, Ohio, under the leadership of Adolph Strasser and Samuel Gompers—back in the days before every labor union leader was named "Tony," "Big Mike," or "Hey, Kiss My Ass, *That's* My Name." The organization acted as an umbrella union over a variety of smaller craft unions, and urged the Local Reds for the Manufacture of Cherry Bombs and Marxist Propaganda to tone it down a bit.

DECEMBER 8, 1993 The North American Free Trade Agreement, or **NAFTA**, is signed into law by President Bill Clinton. Ross Perot said that it would lead to a "giant sucking sound" of jobs being drawn to Mexico (this was in the days before one could make a "giant sucking sound" attack on the president without following it up with a Lewinsky joke). On a side note, we would like to say hi to Jorge G., who has spent today binding over 1,000 copies of this book, and warn him to get back to work before "Big Miguel" comes over and yells at him.

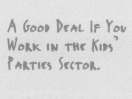

A Good Deal If You Work in the Kids' Parties Sector.

DECEMBER 9, 1872
First Black Governor (Not Elected).

THIS MAN (pictured below) is **PINCKNEY BENTON STEWART PINCHBACK**, or P. B. S. Pinchback (his name was later given to the process of cutting budgets for Public Television stations) and on this day in 1872, he became the first African-American governor of a U.S. state. Seriously, don't let the picture fool you, he was African-American.

Pinchback was born in 1837 in Georgia to a slave, Eliza Stewart, and a white planter named William Pinchback (you just said, "Oh, OK, that explains it!").

During the Civil War, Pinchback traveled to Louisiana and became the only African-American captain in the Union's First Louisiana Native Guards, where he was famous for his battle cry "Seriously, I'm black!"

After the war, he became active in Louisiana's Republican Party and in 1868, he became acting lieutenant governor upon the death of Oscar Dunn, who had been the first elected African-American lieutenant governor of a U.S. state. (In all fairness, after the Civil War, it was pretty easy to become the First African-American Anything.)

After then-Governor Henry Clay Warmoth was impeached for political corruption (which used to be illegal in Louisiana), Pinchback then became governor and served for five weeks, twice as long as an African-American senator from Illinois has to hold an office nowadays before he is considered a serious presidential contender.

While Pinchback's term was brief, he did pave the way for America's second African-American governor, Virginia's Douglas Wilder, who was elected 118 years later. As you can see, even now, becoming the First African-American Anything is not as hard as it might be.

BLACK.

DECEMBER 10, 1965
Dead Come to Life.

ON THIS DAY IN "HIGH"-STORY, the hippie rock outfit known as the Grateful Dead, or "the band that made your sister run away and get an ankle tattoo," performed their first-ever show at San Francisco's Fillmore Auditorium.

The concert lasted two hours, in which time they played one song and lost four keyboardists to drug overdoses.

MASS HISTORIA **FUN FACT:**
THE GRATEFUL DEAD'S ORIGINAL NAME WAS MOTHER MCCREE'S UPTOWN JUG CHAMPIONS, WHICH IS TOO HARD TO SAY WHEN YOU'RE HIGH.

Indiana Shoots—and Scores—
Its Way Into the Union.

THAT IS A BASKETBALL REFERENCE, a sport Indiana is known for. Let's try and squeeze more fun out of this great state, which excitedly muttered "two points" at the prospect of joining the U.S. on this day in 1816.

- Indiana means "Land of the Indians," an ethnic group that has yet to have their turn dominating the NBA.

- No one quite knows the origin of the word "Hoosier." Anyone suggesting that it stems from the licentious query "Who's yer daddy" is quickly shushed by an Indianan and told to "speak simply!"

- The first professional basketball game was played in Fort Wayne in 1871. (Sorry, that's more basketball.)

- High school basketball was first played in Indiana. (Well, it's true!)

- Parke County is the Covered Bridge Capital of the World, with thirty-two covered bridges. A cherished place, although it is pretty hard to throw an alley-oop pass inside a covered bridge.

- At one time, the state was over 80 percent forest, and now it is only 17 percent, after locals chopped the trees down for being too showy.

- Many Mennonite and Amish live in northeastern Indiana, although occasionally the locals try to chop them down for being too showy.

- Indiana's famous Indianapolis 500 race on Memorial Day weekend is just like a NASCAR race, except the attendees at Indy have at least once in their lives felt the icy grip of a shirt with sleeves.

- Famous people from Indiana are Larry Bird (basketball player), Glen "Big Dog" Robinson (basketball player), Oscar Robertson (basketball player), Brad Miller (basketball player), and Alfred Kinsey (sex researcher, probably thought of basketball to prolong his research).

THE OFFICIAL FLOWER OF INDIANA.

DECEMBER 12, 1098
Cru-Sadism.

IT SEEMS THAT EVERY TIME an American uses the word "Crusade," those grumpy Middle Eastern folks blow a gasket, even at the mention of "Crüesade," a St. Paul, Minnesota, Mötley Crüe cover band. (Several Muslim clerics declared their cover of *Generation Swine* unclean.) One reason for this hostility occurred on this day in 1098 during the assault on the town of Ma'arrat al-Numan in Syria.

An army travels on its stomach, and sometimes does terrible things because of it, and the Crusaders that breeched the town's walls were no different. After massacring 20,000 of Ma'arrat al-Numan's residents, the starving army of crusaders began resorting to cannibalism.

One of the commanders of the siege wrote to Pope Urban II, "A terrible famine racked the army in Ma'arra, and placed it in the cruel necessity of feeding itself upon the bodies of the Saracens." Unfortunately, since Urban II had never sent any children to camp or college, he did not recognize that the letter was a blatant request for a "care package."

Radulph of Caen, a chronicler of the event, wrote, "In Ma'arra our troops boiled pagan adults alive in cooking-pots; they impaled children on spits and devoured them grilled." Later, the Arab world would employ a similar punishment toward any teenage girl who dared to walk down the street with any male who was not at least her second cousin.

DECEMBER 13, 1978
Handsome Susan B. Anthony Dollar Debuts.

ON THIS DAY IN 1978, the Susan B. Anthony dollar coin went into circulation. And by "circulation," we mean into the hands of people who worked in the post office, who were too eager to hand them over to customers, who then in turn ran out and tried to use them at newsstands where the clerks didn't know enough English to complain about being given a Susan B. Anthony dollar.

The dollar proved unpopular, because it was smaller than the previous Eisenhower coin and often mistaken for a quarter, despite the U.S. Mint's catchy slogan, "Carry Three for Susan B," which was eventually replaced with "B a Pal—Take These Goddamned Things Off Our Hands."

AVAILABLE FOR
50 CENTS AT THE
DOLLAR STORE.

DECEMBER 14, 1911

Norwegian Amundsen Tells Scott to Sjuck It!

WORLD'S BOTTOM DWELLERS.

ON THIS DAY IN 1913, Roald Amundsen becomes the first man to reach the South Pole, beating Englishman Robert Scott by a month. Even worse—on December 12, Scott had "discovered" what he thought was his coolest nickname ever, "Scott of the Antarctic." And by December 13, he'd already had T-shirts and mugs made with the name on it. So needless to say, this was a pretty crappy day for Scott of the Antarctic.

The Norwegian team was on four different sleds pulled by fifty-two dogs, and Amundsen later became the first man to scrape his boot on the South Pole after stepping in something left on the ground by "King." The daily rations for his men were 20 ounces of biscuits, one ounce of chocolate, and 12 ounces of something called pemmican—a high-calorie, durable food consisting of dried meat, dried berries, and rendered fat, which was slightly less appetizing than 12 ounces of whatever King was dropping on the ground.

Amundsen later became the first person to fly a dirigible over the North Pole in 1926, a fact which, oddly enough, was reported to the world by a radio reporter who started bawling like a wussy on-air. Even if it involved good news, dirigibles always had that effect on radio reporters.

DECEMBER 15, 37 AD

Nero Piddles.

ROMAN EMPEROR NERO was born on this day in Anzio, Italy, to his mother Agrippina, who he would later sleep with and then have brutally murdered.

ALSO ON THIS DAY:

DECEMBER 15, 37 AD The baby Nero, only a couple of hours old, is forced into an immediate and almost gladiatorial session of toilet training by his mother. It apparently leaves a few scars.

First Time Bostonians Sing Along to "Dirty Water."

ON THIS DAY IN HISTORY, colonial patriots staged an act of rebellion against the British Crown that came to be known as the Boston Tea Party. And it was the last time that a tea party was ever held in Boston without its participants being deemed "a wicked buncha queehahs" by local toughs.

The Stamp Act of 1765 and the Townsend Acts of 1767 were the catalysts, as colonists found themselves taxed by, yet not represented in, the British Parliament, leading to cries of "No Taxation without Representation." (The last-ever remotely eloquent cry used by American antitax nuts.)

Eventually, John Hancock organized a boycott of Chinese tea sold in the colonies by the British East India Company. British ships were turned away from most American port cities, but the Crown-appointed governor of Massachusetts (he always obnoxiously peppered his conversation with words like "flat" and "lorry") allowed vessels into Boston Harbor, and three ships loaded with tea were waiting to be unloaded on the evening of December 16.

The ships were boarded by the Sons of Liberty, a group of Boston citizens organized by Samuel Adams. (Note: Since Adams has been associated with both the Boston Tea Party and a popular microbrew beer, historians have called him the most "Beveragey" of the Founding Fathers.)

The Sons, bravely dressed as Indian braves to avoid punishment, boarded the ship and proceeded to dump nearly four hundred crates of tea into Boston Harbor. At that point, some elderly Bostonians then tried to add some tea-appropriate fruit wedges to the harbor, which kicked off something called the Boston Lemon Party. (For more info, do a Web search for "Lemon Party." It should be quite educational.)

ANCIENT FORM OF TEABAGGING.

The Wright Stuff.

ON THIS DAY IN 1903, two bicycle repairmen named Orville and Wilbur Wright made their first-ever trip in a plane. And like most people on their first trip in a plane, they brought way too much baggage on board and took too many pictures.

The two brothers from Ohio were the first (unless you are some rabble-rouser who insists some South American guy did it earlier) to pilot a self-propelled, heavier-than-air craft on this day during an experimental tryout in Kitty Hawk, North Carolina. They chose that spot for its heavy ocean winds and soft sands, in case of a crash. (Also, the two bachelors were desperate to get an aerial view of a nearby all-girls' beach volleyball game.)

(Note: Since this was achieved in North Carolina by Ohio natives, both states' quarters claim some sort of ownership over the event, with North Carolina claiming "First Flight," and Ohio declaring itself the "Birthplace of Aviation Pioneers." The conflict is unfortunate, but both mottoes are preferable to North Carolina's original boast, "Not as Rednecky as South Carolina," and Ohio's "We Rigged the 2004 Election!")

Their first attempt lasted twelve seconds and they traveled 120 feet. Before the day was done, Wilbur had taken the craft for an 850-foot ride that lasted fifty-nine seconds, or slightly more time than it now takes for a passenger in Business Class to take a dump on the bar cart after he is refused his ninth Brandy Alexander.

Oddly enough, few Americans knew about this achievement because the Wrights kept quiet about it in order to protect their patents. It wasn't until 1908 that the brothers made a public flight in France, where the citizens were so impressed they immediately began drafting plans to make Charles de Gaulle Airport as confusing and unpleasant as possible, so the act of actually boarding a plane will always seem like a glorious event.

WRIGHT WINGS NUT

MASS HISTORIA FUN FACT:
ORVILLE WRIGHT TOOK HIS LAST FLIGHT IN A LOCKHEED CONSTELLATION FLOWN BY HOWARD HUGHES IN 1944. ALTHOUGH THE PLANE ALMOST DIDN'T MAKE IT OFF THE GROUND DUE TO THE WEIGHT OF HUGHES'S COLLECTION OF "DUTY-FREE" URINE BOTTLES ON BOARD.

DECEMBER 18, 1620
Pilgrims Come to (and All Over) America.

THE OPPRESSIVE, FUNDAMENTALIST RELIGIOUS NUTJOBS who helped found this great nation arrived here on this day in 1620. One imagines that they were barely able to muster up the strength to put on their buckled hats and shoes to walk down the gangplank after all the rampant sex onboard, which was then continued on the lusty, carnal sandbar known as Plymouth Rock. How else can one explain the millions of Americans who claim to be descended from this mob of 102 supposed "Puritans," fifty of whom were dead two months later?

You read it here first—the Pilgrims were pervs!

WEAR DID THOU PLACE THE CAR KEY BOWL?

DECEMBER 19
A Publishing Clearinghouse of Publishing Firsts.

MANY FAMOUS READS were first published on this day in history. Feel free to bring up these factoids to impress the other folks at your book club tonight. (Although to be fair, if they are the kind of people who join book clubs, they are impressed by even the tiniest attempt at human interaction.)

DECEMBER 19, 1732 Founding Horndog Benjamin Franklin first publishes *Poor Richard's Almanack*, showing that while Franklin invented many useful items, he never got around to perfecting a working spell-check program.

DECEMBER 19, 1776 Thomas Paine publishes his first "American Crisis" essay to prepare and steel Americans for the coming Revolution, writing, "These are the times that try men's souls. The summer soldier and the sunshine patriot will, in this crisis, shrink from the service of their country; but he that stands it now, deserves the love and thanks of man and woman. Tyranny, like hell, is not easily conquered; yet we have this consolation with us, that the harder the conflict, the more glorious the triumph." It was no "Let's roll," but it worked at the time.

DECEMBER 19, 1843 **CHARLES DICKENS**'s classic Yuletide tale, *A Christmas Carol* (War on Christmas, indeed!), first appeared in England on this day. If you belong to a book club, chances are you framed the *Playbill* you received when you saw Patrick Stewart do his *A Christmas Carol* one-man show on Broadway. ←

A DICKENS OF A DICKENS PORTRAIT.

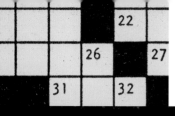

OLD-TIMEY
TIMES SQUARE.

Broadway Gets Turned On (Not in the Way It Did During the 1970s and 1980s).

ON THIS DAY IN HISTORY, all of Broadway in New York City was illuminated by electric lights for the first time.

As a result, the famed thoroughfare was called the Great White Way, a name that has stuck throughout generations, and one that provides some comfort to out-of-towners until they realize that black people are indeed allowed to walk the street (except for a few years during the Giuliani administration).

Charles Francis Brush and his Brush Electric Light Company installed the carbon arc lights from 14th Street to 34th Street. Area perverts stood by waiting for the lights to burn out, so the stretch could go back to being called "The Great Grope 'n' Run Away."

F rst Cros word uzzle Pub ishe .

ON THIS DAY IN HISTORY IN 1913, there was a new way to tell which newspaper readers were smarter than the dimwits who did the word jumbles, as British journalist Arthur Wynne first published his "word-cross puzzle" in the *New York World*. Many consider it the first crossword puzzle ever.

News of this invention soon traveled across the Atlantic to Paris, where young designer Erté was informed that his name would forever be co-opted by lazy crossword-puzzle editors, a fate that would later befall smoldering Latino hunk Esai Morales and the moldering British public school Eton.

THIS DAY IS ALSO IMPORTANT TO MANY PEOPLE WHOSE NAMES ARE OF SOME IMPORTANCE TO CROSSWORD FANS:

DECEMBER 21, 1942 President of the People's Republic of China Hu Jintao is born. Crossword fans say "Thank Hu."

DECEMBER 21, 1952 Major-league baseball pitcher Joaquín Andújar born in the Dominican Republic. The "qui" and "duj" letter clusters are consistent performers in the world of crosswords, more consistent than his abilities on the mound.

DECEMBER 21, 1965 American comedian Andy Dick born; provides convenient four-letter word in puzzles with "no pornography" rules.

DECEMBER 21, 2001 American sports writer Dick Schaap dies. He was on the A-list of recurring double-A cluster clues.

DECEMBER 22, 1956
A 3.75-Pound Gorilla in the Room.

IT'S RARE THAT GOOD NEWS comes from the realm of famous gorillas, but this day—a slow news day, obviously—was a merry exception as Columbus, Ohio, became the site of the first gorilla born in captivity. The baby was named Colo, after the city and state of her birth, which was a nicer name than "Dirty and Too-Small Enclosure," after the exact location of her birth. She weighed only three-and-three-quarter pounds and was fifteen inches long, which led many to assume, correctly, that her mother Millie had been drinking during the pregnancy.

Colo is still alive and still lives at the Columbus Zoo, where she became a grandmother to the first gorilla twins born in captivity, and later a great-grandmother to the first gorilla born via artificial insemination. (Although, like most multiple births these days, everyone assumed the twins were probably the result of artificial insemination, especially since their mother, Bongo, was so career-oriented.)

Colo's birth was an important step in the preservation of the lowland gorilla, since there are only an estimated 100,000 left in the wild. Over thirty have been born at the Columbus Zoo, all of whom, if locked in a room with typewriters, could come up with a better local nickname for Columbus than the "Arch City" in a matter of moments.

BABY GOT
SILVER BACK.

DECEMBER 23, 1888
Van Gogh's EARly Work.

IT WAS ON THIS DAY IN 1888 that Postimpressionist Vincent van Gogh made a bad impressionist on a prostitute named Rachel when he sliced off most of his left ear and presented it to her in an envelope. As with most offerings to a prostitute, she assumed it was cash, tucked it away in her cleavage with a wink, and then later tried to roll up the ear to "blow a rail" in the ladies' room.

While living in his "Yellow House" in Arles, van Gogh had gotten into a terrible screaming match with his good friend Paul Gauguin, which the artist later immortalized in his painting *Scary, Scary Fight*. He was jealous that Rachel apparently preferred Gauguin to him, being one of those girls who only cares about a guy's money, looks, and ability to pull off not one but two hoop earrings.

HINT: IT'S NOT A CD!

Van Gogh spent the next two weeks in the hospital, and when he was released, painted various self-portraits of himself with a bandage around his mutilated ear, before killing himself with a gunshot to the chest, having only sold one painting in his lifetime. This is sad, because nowadays, most artists of his success level can usually just turn their rage outward at whatever customer didn't speak loudly enough while placing his order at Starbucks.

DECEMBER 24, 1865
America Develops Klan-Do Attitude.

THIS IS PROBABLY THE WORST DAY ON EARTH for a department store to inadvertently hold a White Sale, because today is the anniversary of the founding of the Ku Klux Klan.

The group of Confederate soldiers (surprise) who kicked off the festivities in Pulaski, Tennessee (a town sadly named after some pope-lover) got their name from the Greek word *kyklos*, for "circle." "Klan" was a variation on the Scottish "Clan," with a "K" added for alliteration, which made the Klan the most heavy metal of all domestic hate groups.

The group was originally founded in reaction to restrictive Reconstruction policies, and to combat the actions of Carpetbaggers and Scalawags (who later became much scarier once they changed their name to Skalawags. Seriously—Ks are scary!).

The first Grand Wizard of the organization was Confederate General Nathan Bedford Forrest, despite the fact that he was most well-known for a victory at the battle of the effeminately named Fort Pillow. Under Forrest, membership swelled to 500,000 members. (It was an easy recruitment because most Americans were of a rather slim build in those days, and, unlike modern racists, the whiteness of the robes didn't accentuate their roundness in an unflattering manner.) He later left the organization, having grown unhappy with its increasingly violent behavior, and he tried to dismantle it, which is why the scores of Southern parks, monuments, and high schools named after this former Grand Wizard of the KKK don't seem so problematic. Maybe.

This first incarnation of the Klan (not one of the countless cash-in nostalgia revivals) was over by the 1880s, thanks in part to President Grant's declaration of martial law in nine South Carolina counties to suppress the organization's activities, which saw devastating economic effects on that state's Wooden Cross and Mustard-Based Barbecue Sauce Sectors (both have rebounded).

DECEMBER 25
Famous Happy Birthdays!

NO ONE KNOWS what date Jesus was born. If anything, this day was selected as Jesus's birthday to put an end to pagan solstice celebrations, and to destroy the "BC" desk calendar industry.

DECEMBER 25, 1821 Founder of the Red Cross **CLARA BARTON** born. The Lord Jesus offered his blood more freely than you and your coworkers do when her organization holds a drive at the office.

DECEMBER 25, 1887 Hotelier Conrad Hilton emerges from a womb, the same kind of organ that when later attached to his great-granddaughter, would see more traffic than one of his hotels.

DECEMBER 25, 1907 Famed entertainer Cab Calloway born, later becomes known for his signature tune "Minnie the Moocher" with its chorus "Hi De Ho," which is also an acceptable greeting to Conrad Hilton's great-granddaughter.

DECEMBER 25, 1924 Writer and television personality Rod Serling born, promptly sees signpost ahead reading "You're born on the same day as Christmas. You are about to enter the no presents zone."

DECEMBER 25, 1946 Musician and leader of Parrotheads Jimmy Buffett born. Struggles of the savior Jesus Christ akin to crucifying torments of a lost shaker of salt.

DECEMBER 25, 1950 Political strategist Karl Rove born. To overcome anger at not getting both birthday and Christmas presents, he vows to exploit Jesus for the rest of his career.

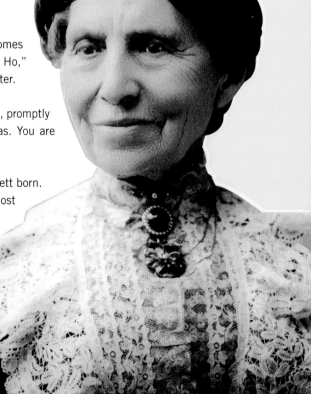

THIS NICE LADY JUST WANTS YOUR BLOOD!

FM DOB.

ON THIS DAY IN 1933, FM radio was patented, meaning it is now over seventy-five years old, or as long as the keyboard solo in beloved 1960s FM staple "In-A-Gadda-Da-Vida."

Darwin Launches Voyage Around the World— Wisely Avoids Kansas.

TWENTY-TWO-YEAR-OLD NATURALIST CHARLES DARWIN set off on his five-year voyage on the HMS *Beagle* on this day in 1831. And unlike most people his age who go on a trip around the world, he didn't stop in Amsterdam and get stoned for six weeks, forcing him to skip his stops in Germany and Poland.

It was on this voyage that Darwin began his study of both fossils and living organisms, which launched his theory of evolution and the transmutation of species, which usually gets an "opposable digit down" from Evangelical Christians.

His studies made him a superstar in the scientific world at the time, and he went on to publish such works as *On the Origin of Species by Means of Natural Selection or the Preservation of Favored Races in the Struggle for Life* (1859) and *The Descent of Man, and Selection in Relation to Sex* (1871), both of which display Darwin's own failure to evolve into a writer with a gift for punchy titles.

Carrie Nation Invents the Buzzkill.

ASIX-FOOT-TALL, 175-POUND WICHITA, KANSAS WOMAN named **CARRIE NATION**, whom one imagines could have carried just about anything, attacked her first saloon on this day in 1900, using a hatchet to smash the bar up, doing the kind of damage to a tavern that wouldn't be seen again until the 1989 invention of the Jagermeister-Dwarf-Tossing Morning Zoo Radio Promotion.

SADLY, BEER GOGGLES MIGHT HAVE BEEN APPRECIATED.

Nation hated alcohol, and was convinced it destroyed families (nut!), and was out to stop its usage entirely after her first marriage was destroyed by her husband's drinking. He had taken up alcohol when learning that the old adage, "the Taller the Tree, the Sweeter the Fruit," wasn't enough to get him through an evening with the missus.

Alcohol was illegal in Kansas, but prohibition was rarely enforced because the emergence of bootleggers would lead to excitement. Nation took it upon herself to right that wrong, and would enter saloons, calling tavern-keepers "Destroyers of Men's Souls" and singing hymns to patrons while she played a hand organ. Sadly, since the jukebox had not been invented, no one was able to drown her out with the slightly less pleasant aural experience of "Paradise by the Dashboard Light."

Nation's "Hatchetations," as she called them, got her arrested over thirty times between 1900 and 1910, but she was always able to pay her legal fees with help from the sales of souvenir hatchets, a far more eye-catching piece of swag than the souvenir plastic fetuses sold to raise money for incarcerated Operation Rescuers.

DECEMBER 29, 1845
Texas Messes with American Flag.

O N THIS DAY IN 1845, the great state of Texas was welcomed into our great nation. Let's take a look at some ten-gallon facts about our second-biggest state.

- Texas was once its own nation. To find out more, talk to someone from Texas for over a minute.

- It is known as the Lone Star State, as an homage to the Republic of Texas flag, not as an homage to the average rating of the state's fine-dining establishments.

- Texas is the only state to have had the flags of six different nations fly over it: Spain, France, Mexico, the Republic of Texas, the Confederate States, and the United States. Most residents are far more ashamed of the French Period than the Confederate one.

- The state capital, Austin, is considered the live music capital of the world. It is also the Record Company Executives Shouting Over Live Music So As to Be Heard by the Local Gal They Are Trying to Pick Up Capital of the World.

- In 1885, Dr. Pepper was invented in Waco, where there is a Dr. Pepper Museum. That's certainly interesting, but not enough to erase the memory of the Branch Davidians. Nice try.

- The president of the Republic of Texas was **SAM HOUSTON**, the namesake of ← the city of Houston. The city of Dallas, of course, was just named after a stripper.

HOUSTON, WE
HAVE A PORTRAIT.

Rasputin Dies After Long Struggle . . .

. . . with poison, a few bullets, some knives, a couple of clubs, and finally with the icy water of the Neva River in Russia. He was approximately forty-seven years old, which was ascertained by counting the rings on his notoriously large penis.

Grigori Rasputin, the Mad Monk, Russian mystic, and Tstud to Tsarina Alexandra, succumbed after a group of Russian noblemen acted in a decidedly unnoble manner to his person. Fearing he was becoming too popular with the Russian royal family, who were about a year away from being on the losing end of their own popularity contest, Prince Felix Yusopov invited Rasputin to his country estate.

There, he was allegedly fed cakes and wine laced with cyanide, which didn't seem to do anything, although the abundance of crumbs left in his beard proved fatal to everyone else's appetite.

Yusopov then shot his guest in the back, and even though the bullet pierced the monk's abundant shoulder pelt, Rasputin did not die, and instead hurled the prince across the room, while hissing "you bad boy" at him. Realizing those would be terrible "last words," Rasputin struggled for life and ran out of the house.

The conspirators chased after him, and wound up firing another three shots into his body. He was still struggling, so they then began to club and stab him. (Normally, when something that hairy is clubbed, it is saved by PETA activists.)

While he was still breathing, they then tied him up and dumped him in a hole in the icy river. Legend has it that he only died of drowning, although it was most likely the physical shock of being washed.

News Year's Eve, Made Rockin'.

A GRAND NEW YEAR'S EVE TRADITION began on this day in 1904, when people gathered in Longacre Square—later known as Times Square, then known as "Hell-on-Earth Square," before reverting back to Times Square in the mid-1990s to watch the ball drop.

A thirty-five-year-old Dick Clark was on hand to celebrate the festivities.

BEFORE THE HARD ROCK CAFÉ CLASSED THE PLACE UP.

The End

ROLL CREDITS

ACKNOWLEDGMENTS

Mass Historia started out in 2006 as a Web site called (impulsively) *This Day in Mythstory*, until I realized that no one without a lisp could pronounce the name properly. Either way, I must thank the loyal fans of that Web site (all six of them) and the people who helped send them my way: Bill Wadman, Jane Borden, Bob Powers, Adam Felber, Todd Levin, and everyone who ever generously provided a link.

About a day or two into the site's existence, I began to wonder if there was any way to make the endeavor less profitable, so I decided to turn it into a book. That would not have happened without the help of Daniel Greenberg, Monika Verma, and everyone at Levine Greenberg Literary Agency; Lynn Fimberg and Sarah Self at the Gersh Agency; the immensely gifted people at Quirk Packaging; illustrator Kathryn Rathke; and my enormously helpful and supportive editor Chris Schillig, John Carroll, and everyone at Andrews McMeel. The people I have worked with and met in the book publishing world have made me question my decision to associate with the bastards in TV for as long as I have.

Among the bastards are the men and women I wrote with at *The Daily Show with Jon Stewart*, who kept me on my toes for seven years. Thanks for putting up with my belief that the best jokes were crafted around obscure facts and/or personalities.

Finally, I must thank my family, my friends in the Lindsay Milligan Society, and my wife Susannah Keagle, who scoured the Library of Congress for many of the images in this book, patiently explained to me what "public domain" and "copyright" meant, and who kept me sane and loved during the long writing process. The day she first appeared on Earth was a great day indeed. Also, it was the day when the Diet of Worms ended in 1521, and it's the birthday of nineteenth-century baseball player Lip Pike. But we already know that.

Don't we?

All photographs courtesy of the Library of Congress, Washington, D.C., and the National Archives, College Park, Maryland, except page 24, "Buzz" Aldrin, courtesy of the Granger Collection, New York; page 35, President Bush and Vice President Quayle, courtesy of the George Bush Presidential Library; page 86, Mel Gibson mug shot, July 28, 2006, courtesy of the Los Angeles County Sheriff's Department; and page 90, Adolf Hitler, courtesy of the Granger Collection, New York.

This book was typeset in Claredon, Trade Gothic, and FF Erikrighthand on a 2 x 2.66 GHz Dual-Core Intel Xeon Mac. The designer takes no responsibility for the graffiti that some unnamed (but very clever) artist added to many of the images throughout this book.

Mass Historia